SPECTRUM MULTIVIEW BOOKS

ORIGINAL SIN
AND THE FALL

FIVE VIEWS

EDITED BY J. B. STUMP
and CHAD MEISTER

ivp
Academic
An imprint of InterVarsity Press
Downers Grove, Illinois

InterVarsity Press
P.O. Box 1400, Downers Grove, IL 60515-1426
Ivpress.com
email@ivpress.com

InterVarsity Press® is the book-publishing division of InterVarsity Christian Fellowship/USA®, a movement of students and faculty active on campus at hundreds of universities, colleges, and schools of nursing in the United States of America, and a member movement of the International Fellowship of Evangelical Students. For information about local and regional activities, visit intervarsity.org.

Cover design and image composite: David Fassett
Interior design: Jeanna Wiggins
Images: apple: © Mike Kemp/Getty Images
      tree: © Isarapic/iStock/Getty Images Plus

ISBN 978-0-8308-5287-1 (print)
ISBN 978-0-8308-5393-9 (digital)

Printed in the United States of America ∞

InterVarsity Press is committed to ecological stewardship and to the conservation of natural resources in all our operations. This book was printed using sustainably sourced paper.

Library of Congress Cataloging-in-Publication Data

A catalog record for this book is available from the Library of Congress.

P	25	24	23	22	21	20	19	18	17	16	15	14	13	12	11	10	9	8	7	6	5	4	3	2	1
Y	38	37	36	35	34	33	32	31	30	29	28	27	26	25	24	23		22		21		20			

"With some of the presentations I identified closely; with others I disagreed strongly. But this is the way a multiview book is supposed to be. *Original Sin and the Fall* provides a wide spectrum of positions, ranging from Reformed to Eastern Orthodox and beyond, and each of the five authors provides a strong, well-written chapter. This book serves as an excellent survey of the current debate about the doctrine of original sin."

Kenneth Keathley, senior professor of theology and director of the L. Russ Bush Center for Faith and Culture, Southeastern Baptist Theological Seminary

"I found this discussion fascinating as the writers probed and illuminated the mysteries of original sin and the fall from different angles. I came away with a sense that the interlocutors were talking to one another, not just saying their own piece and walking away. This is exactly how a multiview volume should work, modeling charitable yet critical discussion and moving the reader to offer a personal response."

Matt Jenson, associate professor of theology, Torrey Honors Institute of Biola University

"Usually multiple-views books help us to sort out better and worse articulations of our approaches to especially difficult theological ideas or dogmatic formulations. Every so often, however, what we find is that one truth has many viable explanations and accents that derive from and reflect the catholicity of the church's dynamic theological traditions. Our five contributors here remind us of the rich resources available within the church for understanding the human condition of sinfulness, frailty, and finitude and for empowering theological exploration and inquiry in the third millennium."

Amos Yong, professor of theology and mission, and dean of the School of Theology and the School of Intercultural Studies, Fuller Seminary

"Why do nice people do terrible things? Sherlock Holmes was on to something when he assured Watson that 'the lowest and vilest alleys of London do not present a more dreadful record of sin than does the smiling and beautiful countryside.' Here are five theological explanations of humanity's perennial predicament, five ways of reading the story of Adam's fall and its consequences. The responses each of the authors gives to the four others are especially helpful in identifying the key talking points as well as respective strengths and weaknesses."

Kevin J. Vanhoozer, research professor of systematic theology at Trinity Evangelical Divinity School

"Original sin and original guilt—and along with them the conviction by many in the history of the church that everyone is born destined for damnation—these interconnected ideas (and others that follow) have created a hornet's nest of complexities, exegetical conclusions, and theological musings for this generation. That's all to the good; this is a topic worthy of serious thinking by as many diverse thinkers as we can get in the conference room. Stump and Meister have done us all a wonderful service by their careful selection of representative views, and the level of discussion will pave the way for civil conversations for a long time. This will be a great classroom discussion book, but don't expect to end the class on time!"

Scot McKnight, professor of New Testament at Northern Seminary

"We all believe in the doctrine of original sin, but nobody really knows what it means. As originally developed, it is something of a theological relic; as currently used in popular preaching, it is a placeholder for vague notions of evil. Nobody seems to know what it means, but everybody says it is the only Christian doctrine that is empirically verifiable. It is time to blow the whistle on this ridiculous state of affairs. This volume of essays gives us exactly what we need in these circumstances. We have a clean-cut set of proposals that clear the air and provide a splendid resource for serious engagement with the doctrine of sin in the future. Written with irenic poise, we have here a set of specific, competing options that cry out for extended reflection."

William J. Abraham, Outler Professor of Wesley Studies, University Distinguished Teaching Professor, Southern Methodist University, Dallas

Contents

Introduction

J. B. STUMP AND CHAD MEISTER

Theologians throughout most of Christian history have almost universally agreed that God created the world for a good and loving purpose, which included a community of morally good human beings. It has also been almost universally agreed on that this divine plan was impeded in some significant way and that restoration was required. The commonly used term to denote this impediment is *the fall*, and a term often used to indicate its source is *original sin*. But beyond these basic claims of agreement regarding the divine plan for humanity, there has been much debate both in times past and in the present. This book examines these two important notions of original sin and the fall and explores different interpretations of them in Christian theology today. Before presenting these interpretations, some background material may be beneficial.

BACKGROUND OF THE DOCTRINES

The traditional *doctrine* of the fall in Western Christian history can be traced in its developed form to Augustine in the fifth century. It is rooted in the idea that God created Adam de novo, from the dust, and Eve from Adam's rib. They were created sinless and in the image of God, and sometime after the creation they disobeyed God in a garden created for them, the Garden of Eden. Because of this act of disobedience, they "fell" from a state of per-fection and brought sin and evil into a good and perfect world. This act of disobedience (the eating of the forbidden fruit), the first act of human sin—the original sin—brought about the fall: tragic physical, social, and spiritual consequences for the entire human race. This sin and the curse it incurred by God account for the origin of pain, suffering, and death (physical and spiritual) and explain how all this evil could occur in a world that a good, loving, and all-powerful God created.

The terms *original sin* and *fall* had been used by theologians before Augustine, but he took those early, inchoate ideas and developed them into full-fledged doctrines. They are based on several key passages in the Bible, most notably very early in the book of Genesis.

In chapter three of the Genesis account of creation, the Lord God asks Adam if he had eaten from the forbidden tree. Adam acknowledges as much and places blame on Eve for enticing him, and in turn Eve blames the tempting serpent for her capitulation. In response, God curses Adam, Eve, and the serpent:

> Because you have listened to the voice of your wife,
>   and have eaten of the tree
> about which I commanded you,
>   "You shall not eat of it,"
> cursed is the ground because of you;
>   in toil you shall eat of it all the days of your life;
> thorns and thistles it shall bring forth for you;
>   and you shall eat the plants of the field.
> By the sweat of your face
>   you shall eat bread
> until you return to the ground,
>   for out of it you were taken;
> you are dust,
>   and to dust you shall return. (Gen 3:17-19)

The text then adds the following proclamation:

> Then the LORD God said, "See, the man has become like one of us, knowing good and evil; and now, he might reach out his hand and take also from the tree of life, and eat, and live forever"—therefore the LORD God sent him forth from the garden of Eden, to till the ground from which he was taken. He drove out the man; and at the east of the garden of Eden he placed the cherubim, and a sword flaming and turning to guard the way to the tree of life. (Gen 3:22-24)

Perhaps surprisingly, the word *fall* is nowhere to be found in this text. Neither is *original sin*. Nor are these terms found anywhere in the Bible. As with a number of important Christian doctrines, such as the doctrine of the Trinity, while the terms that were later utilized to denote the doctrines of original sin and fall are not found explicitly in the Bible, those who affirm them argue that the biblical text nevertheless points to them.

These two doctrines have endured the test of time for a number of reasons. One is their apparent interpretive perspicuity. They just seem to fit the story. Adam and Eve were created good, even very good. But they disobeyed the Lord. Thus, they were cast out of the garden and told that suffering would follow, as would death. If one connects this narrative with some of Paul's statements in the New Testament—"sin came into the world through one man" and "one man's trespass led to condemnation for all" (Rom 5:12, 18); "as all die in Adam, so all will be made alive in Christ" (1 Cor 15:22); and "the creation was subjected to futility" (Rom 8:20)—it is not much of a leap to get to the traditional doctrines of original sin and fall.

Another reason for the longevity of these doctrines is the apparent explanation for the origin and universality of evil that is derived from them. They seem, at first glance at least, to provide an explanation for how there could exist a world that God created, which is filled with pain and suffering, and a mechanism for explaining how the sin of one or two human beings could permeate the entire cosmos. These doctrines are powerful indeed.

While these doctrines have received widespread acceptance in Western Christian thought throughout the centuries, concerns have also been raised about them. For example, Augustine, in his developed views on the matter, maintained that original sin was transmitted from one generation to the next through sexual intercourse. The manner in which this occurred, in his view, is due to concupiscence—a theological term referring to sinful physical desire, especially sexual lust. Augustine believed that after the fall all sexual acts, even in marriage, entail concupiscence. It is through this sinful event, when a child is produced, that original sin gets passed along to the offspring from father to child. Augustine also held that original sin transmits both humanity's sinful nature and its guilt. In his account, infants are born both sinful and guilty before God. Unless they are baptized and thus regenerated through the sacrament of baptism, they will not enter heaven. Most modern theologians, both Catholic and Protestant, deny that babies are born guilty (and thus punishable) before God. So some aspects of the traditional view of original sin and the fall have passed into the annals of history.

While the fall and original sin are not scientific theories, they do not stand in isolation from what we have learned about the world through science. Christians themselves are divided on just what science can tell us about the origins of humanity, original population sizes, the existence of death and evil in prehuman history, and other related issues. These scientific claims pose challenges to the traditional view of the theological doctrines that cannot just be ignored.

There are also interpretive challenges with the Bible itself. How are we to interpret the creation account? What are the options? It is tempting to think there are only two: (1) a literal interpretation in which the events actually happened in time and space (an actual talking snake, seven literal twenty-four-hour days of creation, etc.) and (2) a mythological interpretation in which the account is a fairy tale and did not really happen in history at all. While it is sometimes presented in this twofold manner, the literature contains much more nuance than this oversimplified dichotomy would indicate. And the hermeneutical principles used in interpreting the creation narrative will certainly influence the doctrines derived from them.

Furthermore, while these traditional doctrines of original sin and fall have been influential in Western Christianity, they have not been so in Eastern Christianity. Augustine was a Western, Latin theologian, and his works were not translated into the Greek that was used in the East until the fourteenth century. So Augustine's works and ideas were not widely disseminated among Eastern Christians until many centuries after his death, and even then they have not been very theologically formative. In fact, his influence has never been significant in Eastern Orthodox Christianity.

All told, while the doctrines of original sin and the fall have been influential throughout Christian history, many factors push sincere interpreters in different directions, and many Christian lay persons, pastors, church leaders, and even scholars are unaware of the divergent viewpoints on these important doctrines. In an attempt to rectify this situation, we, the editors of this book, chose five leading Christian thinkers to explain and defend their views of original sin and the fall.

SUMMARY OF VIEWS

The general format of these multiple "views" books will be familiar to many readers. Specifically for this volume, contributors were first asked to submit original essays presenting their views. Then, once those had been finalized, they were distributed to all, and each wrote an essay responding to the others' original essays. We think this has allowed for fair representations of these positions and then honest critiques. We offer here brief summaries of the positions presented in the volume.

The first essay, written by Hans Madueme, associate professor of theological studies at Covenant College, presents an Augustinian-Reformed view. This is closest to the traditional view of original sin and the fall, including a literal understanding of the Garden of Eden story and the claim that there was no animal death before the first human sin. Madueme claims that we should understand Adam as the head of the entire human race in a biological (not just representational) sense, and his first sin condemns all subsequent people to be born in a state of moral corruption and guilt before God.

Madueme is not unaware of the scientific findings that challenge this story. He claims, though, that the science is always provisional and its current findings on the subject of human origins are not secure enough to give sufficient reason to abandon or reformulate this traditional view. For he believes that only this view does the gospel and our understanding of the human condition make sense. Furthermore, he argues that the plausibility and rationality of our hope for a future eschaton free from sin and suffering hinges on there being such a period in the past to which we can be returned.

The second view comes from Oliver Crisp, professor of analytic theology at the University of St. Andrews. He approaches the doctrines from a distinctively Reformed perspective but calls his a "moderate Reformed" doctrine of original sin, claiming that he is consistent with the Reformed tradition but acknowledging the need to depart from the more traditional interpretation. Specifically, while original sin and original guilt are often seen as a package deal, Crisp notes that they have been—and should be—separated. He accepts the claim that we inherit original sin as fallen human beings, which leads to death and separation from God. But he denies the claim that we inherit original guilt. We are guilty only for the actual sins we commit (which we inevitably will). Crisp believes this nuance can be defended as a minority view within the tradition and that it has the possibility of a more ecumenical rapprochement with other strands of Christian theology.

Crisp is looking for a minimalist doctrine of original sin and the fall, one that does not depend on any particular view of Adam and Eve, nor on monogenism (the view that all humanity descended from an original couple), thus eliminating any conflict with what science says about human origins. Whether there was an actual first couple or whether "Adam and Eve" are just placeholders according to which we are sons and daughters of Adam and Eve, it is still the case that the choices of our ancestors affect and constrain us in ways without thereby making us responsible or culpable for what they have done.

Our third contributor is Joel Green, professor of New Testament interpretation and associate dean for the Center for Advanced Theological Studies at Fuller Theological Seminary, who presents and defends a Wesleyan view of original sin and the fall. This is attributed, of course, first to John Wesley himself, for whom the doctrine of original sin was integral to his understanding of Scripture and the gospel. Wesley affirmed the depravity and corruption of all people, but also free will, as God's prevenient grace is already at work in everyone. Wesley understood Genesis 3 as a fall narrative, but in his view subsequent humans were not guilty because of what Adam and Eve did. Rather, for Wesley, sin is a disease that all acquire by their involvement in Adam's sin. God is less a judge of the guilty than a doctor for the diseased.

Green goes on to show the diversity of thought about Genesis 3 from early commentators. He also deals specifically with the relevant New Testament passages, especially from James and Paul. In these he finds the traditional doctrine of original sin to be less than obvious. In Romans 5, for example, Paul's concern was not to show the origin of sin but rather that Jews and Gentiles are on common ground because all sin. Paul takes Adam to be a kind of pattern that all people follow rather than the source of sin that is passed on to all people. Green follows the spirit of Wesley with respect to recent discoveries of science, allowing for some rethinking of traditional interpretations rather than simply dismissing the testimony of

Scripture. Green finds a doctrine of original sin that is consistent with the evolutionary story and that testifies to sin's universal character.

In the fourth essay, Andrew Louth, professor emeritus of patristic and Byzantine studies in the Department of Theology and Religion at Durham University, represents the Eastern Orthodox view. Louth first notes that the concept of original sin sits awkwardly with Orthodox thought, as it was a theological development in the Latin West. Eastern Orthodox thinkers generally do affirm a notion of the fall, but this is separated from original sin. Instead of the fall-redemption theological arc that is taken as basic for people in the Western tradition, more typical of the Orthodox understanding is the creation-deification arc. That shift leads to seeing the consequences of the fall not as guilt, which is more typical in the traditional Western theologies, but as death.

The notion of ancestral sin is still affirmed by Orthodox theologians as the fount of disordering that the world has experienced. This disordered world means there is more at stake in setting things right than just a guilty standing before God. It is the cosmos itself that has been affected and needs fixing, and humanity's role in the cosmos needs to be restored, which culminates in *theosis* or deification as we "become participants of the divine nature" (2 Pet 1:4).

In the final essay, Tatha Wiley, who taught theology and New Testament at the University of St. Thomas and the College of St. Catherine, argues that the doctrine of original sin retains relevance for us today but needs to be reconceptualized in light of modern science. The traditional doctrine is a human explanation, not handed down from heaven fully formed, and therefore it is limited and bound by the cognitive context in which it was formed. When that context changes, as it certainly has for us today because of our scientific discoveries, then our explanations need to change. Wiley shows that the Bible itself contains a wide range of concepts of sin, which were reflections of the changing contexts in which its authors wrote, and that it contains no fully developed doctrine of original sin. She also traces the changing conception of original sin through major theological traditions, showing that it has not been a static concept. Seen in this light, the biblical creation accounts and the scientific explanation of evolution are not competing accounts but rather truths on different planes.

Drawing on the thought of Bernard Lonergan, Wiley argues that a contemporary account of original sin needs to understand sin as the failure to love properly. This sinful condition is inauthentic living, which God remedies through intellectual, moral, and religious conversion. These conversions are not just individual developments but are collective for humankind. We as a species become more authentically human as we embody the kingdom of God that Jesus preached.

As is typical in these multiple views books, the contributors do not persuade each other of their own positions. But the dialogue between them does show strengths and weaknesses of each and persuades us of the importance of grappling with these doctrines. Whatever your own position on original sin and the fall, we hope you find these five contributors to be helpful conversation partners. We certainly do.

PART ONE

PERSPECTIVES ON ORIGINAL SIN AND THE FALL

1

An Augustinian-Reformed View

HANS MADUEME

Once upon a time, the doctrine of the fall enjoyed virtual canonical status. This Augustinian doctrine played a vital role in the development of modern culture and thought. Seventeenth-century natural philosophers, for example, widely believed that the first disobedience left humanity not only morally depraved but *cognitively impaired*. Those theological assumptions inspired doubt in the ability of human minds to fathom the inner workings of nature, which led them to explore God's creation directly, thus giving rise to empirical science.[1] In early modern medicine, the healing ministrations of physicians were thought to relieve suffering caused by the fall.[2] So too with pioneers of technology who saw themselves as restoring the glory lost by humanity after Adam's trespass.[3] This script replayed itself in other areas of Western thought.[4]

But in many Christian academic settings today, Augustine's hamartiology has fallen out of favor.[5] In an ironic twist, natural science disowned its

---

[1]Peter Harrison, *The Fall of Man and the Foundations of Science* (Cambridge: Cambridge University Press, 2007).

[2]See, e.g., John Wesley's preface to his *Primitive Physik* (London: William Pine, 1765).

[3]See Clarence Glacken, *Traces on the Rhodian Shore: Nature and Culture in Western Thought from Ancient Times to the End of the Eighteenth Century* (Berkeley: University of California Press, 1976).

[4]The "creation-fall-redemption" motif—with Adam's fall as fulcrum—was vital to Abraham Kuyper's neo-Calvinism and became integral to many schools affiliated with the Council for Christian Colleges and Universities (CCCU). See Cornelius Plantinga, *Engaging God's World: A Christian Vision of Faith, Learning, and Living* (Grand Rapids, MI: Eerdmans, 2002).

[5]Irenaeus has become the patron saint of many evolutionary creationists. As one scholar puts it, "It is a tragedy that in the Western Churches the Irenaean understanding of Genesis 2-3 has been

erstwhile parents when it jettisoned the fall. Even prior to Darwin and the more recent scientific challenges, people were already asking questions about Genesis 3. How could Adam and Eve, created holy, ever choose to sin? How was sin even possible in the blissful presence of God? And how did one peccadillo trigger such devastating consequences? Skeptics who asked such questions had lost faith in the received tradition.

Similar burdens bedevil the doctrine of original sin. In Roman Catholic tradition, during the Pelagian controversy, the Augustinian doctrine of original sin became official church dogma at the Councils of Carthage (411–418) and Orange (529); subsequent developments of the doctrine were only variations on Augustine. That tradition was equally dominant among the Reformers and was enshrined in later confessional statements. By the following century, however, people questioned the viability of original sin, some decrying the rationality of "inherited" guilt, others convinced that original sin undermines divine justice. Thinkers like Jean-Jacques Rousseau (1712–1778), Immanuel Kant (1724–1804), and Friedrich Schleiermacher (1768–1834) reinterpreted original sin in light of modernity. Over the same period on the American scene, original sin faced similar pressures.[6] Soon after, Darwin drove the nail in the coffin.

In the present chapter, I argue that these radical moves away from the Augustinian tradition are premature and in fact wrong-headed. I make a case for the doctrine of the fall and a Reformed understanding of original sin, with an eye to recent scientific challenges.[7] Although these doctrines are often maligned as intellectually obsolete, I believe they are indispensable for a right understanding of the gospel and the human condition.

THE ORIGIN OF SIN

James Barr famously claimed that Genesis 3 "had a different style and purport altogether, and the 'origin of sin' was only marginal to it."[8] According

---

eclipsed by the Augustinian doctrine of the Fall." John Bimson, "Doctrines of the Fall and Sin After Darwin," in *Theology After Darwin*, ed. Michael Northcott and R. J. Berry (Milton Keynes, UK: Paternoster, 2009), 120.

[6]See H. Shelton Smith, *Changing Conceptions of Original Sin: A Study in American Theology Since 1750* (New York: Charles Scribner's Sons, 1955).

[7]While I recognize the theological diversity within the Reformed tradition, this chapter draws out one of those strands as worthy of serious consideration.

[8]James Barr, *Biblical Faith and Natural Theology* (Oxford: Clarendon, 1993), 59.

to Barr, Paul invented the fall by drawing on noncanonical Jewish tradition rather than the Hebrew Bible.[9] W. Sibley Towner argued similarly that "there is no Fall in scripture. . . . There is no account of the origin of evil and no primeval encounter with Satan."[10] In Towner's view, "the rise of historical-critical biblical studies accounts for much of the relief from the heavy hand of dogma about the Fall."[11] Such assumptions are familiar in academic circles, but similar conclusions are increasingly common among evangelicals and their allies.[12]

The fall of Adam and Eve. These shifts reflect a modern tendency to doubt the historical reliability of Genesis 1–11, as if "real" history in the Bible begins with Abraham in Genesis 12. However, later passages in the Old Testament assume the historicity of the Eden narratives (e.g., Ezek 28:11-19; Hos 6:7; Eccles 7:29; 1 Chr 1:1; Lk 3:38; Jude 14).[13] The New Testament apostolic witness is unambiguous; consider Paul's claims about women in the church (1 Cor 11:3-12; 1 Tim 2:13-14), his polemic against false apostles (2 Cor 11:1-3), and his Adam-Christ typology (Rom 5:12-21; 1 Cor 15:21-22)—at *every* point he draws historically on very particular details in Genesis 1–3 (along similar lines, see also Mt 19:4; Jn 8:44; Acts 17:26; Rev 12:9; 20:2).[14] Skeptical claims about Genesis 1–11 are subverted by the apostolic sense of those passages.[15]

Genesis 1 and 2 are the backdrop to the events in Genesis 3:1-6. God created everything, including the land, sea, plants, animals, and humanity;

---

[9]Barr, *Biblical Faith and Natural Theology*, 58-63.

[10]W. Sibley Towner, "Interpretations and Reinterpretations of the Fall," in *Modern Biblical Scholarship: Its Impact on Theology and Proclamation*, ed. Francis Eigo (Villanova, PA: Villanova University Press, 1984), 81.

[11]Towner, "Interpretations and Reinterpretations," 58.

[12]See, e.g., Dennis Venema and Scot McKnight, *Adam and the Genome: Reading Scripture After Genetic Science* (Grand Rapids, MI: Brazos Press, 2017).

[13]For further canonical allusions to Adam and Eve, see C. John Collins, *Did Adam and Eve Really Exist? Who They Were and Why You Should Care* (Wheaton, IL: Crossway, 2011), 51-92.

[14]The same historical assumptions pervade Second Temple Jewish literature (e.g., Sir 25:24; 2 Bar 18:2; 23:4; 48:42-43; 54:15; 2 Esd 7:118-126). For my defense of monogenism against polygenic scenarios, see "Adam Revisited: First Man or One of Many?" published at Books at a Glance, May 2, 2016, http://www.booksataglance.com/blog/adam-revisited-first-man-one-many/.

[15]The stale debate pitting figurative (or poetic) language against historicity is a red herring. Scripture often describes historical events using figurative language—e.g., Psalm 78, 105–106 (the history of Israel), Isaiah 5:1-2 (Yahweh's love for his people), and Romans 11:17-24 (God's relationship with Jews and Gentiles in salvation history). The presence of figurative language hardly precludes the fact that Genesis 1–11 imparts historical knowledge. See Ardel Caneday, "The Language of God and Adam's Genesis and Historicity in Paul's Gospel," *Southern Baptist Journal of Theology* 15 (2011): 26-59, esp. 37-41.

in doing so he repeatedly calls each ingredient "good" (Gen 1:10, 12, 18, 21, 25), even "very good" (Gen 1:31). By implication the original created order was free from sin. Sometimes it is suggested that *good* (*tov*) in Genesis 1 is merely aesthetic, not moral.[16] In my view, original creation is both aesthetically *and* morally good, especially in light of God's revealed character as the thrice Holy One (Is 6:1-7).

God's only stipulation to Adam and Eve was not to eat from the Tree of the Knowledge of Good and Evil (Gen 2:17). Alas, they disobeyed (Gen 3:1-6). The text never mentions "the fall" explicitly, but the unfolding story chronicles the spread of sin in the wake of their rebellion, culminating in the global flood. Even after the flood, sin permeates the life of Israel and the Gentiles, moving the Lord to extend grace through the call of Abraham; Israel's election; the era of the judges, priests, kings, and prophets; and climaxing in the incarnation (Jn 1:14). The movement of the story itself presses the question, Why do all sin and die? Guided by Romans 5:12-21 and 1 Corinthians 15:21-22, we rightly identify Genesis 3 as the origin of sin in the human experience.

But sin has an even deeper origin. Tradition interpreted Lucifer as a holy archangel cast out of heaven after revolting against Yahweh (e.g., Is 14:12-15; Ezek 28:12-19; 2 Pet 2:4; Jude 6).[17] The classic proof texts are not decisive, but the tempter's malice and the prophecy in Genesis 3:15 taken up by later biblical testimony identify the serpent as a surrogate for the devil (e.g., Jn 8:44; Rom 16:20; Rev 12:1-17; 13:1-3; 16:13; 20:2). Since the devil is not a second deity or a manifestation of God, the only option left is that he is one of God's creatures, a holy angel who corrupted himself irredeemably. The *ultimate* origin of sin, then, is Satan's fall, its proximate origin the fall of Adam.

Does this picture make any sense? If our first parents were created sinless, unimaginably happy, enjoying the very presence of God, what could possibly motivate them to disobey? This question of intelligibility intensifies

---

[16]See, e.g., Walter Moberly, *Theology of the Book of Genesis* (Cambridge: Cambridge University Press, 2009), 43n4, where he argues that *good* involves aesthetics rather than "the sinless nature of creation prior to the Fall or the moral dimensions integral to creation."

[17]Early Jewish tradition interpreted Genesis 6:1-8 as a fall story in which the "Watchers"—fallen angels—introduced wickedness on earth. N. P. Williams, *The Ideas of the Fall and of Original Sin* (London: Longman, Green & Co., 1927), 20-29.

with Satan, who was tempted by no one. It seems inexplicable that any of them chose to sin.[18] Even if we were to find a causal explanation within the internal constitution of Adam or Lucifer, we would succeed only in rationalizing sin's origin by blaming some element within creation, thus implicating the Creator.[19] We should not apologize here for invoking mystery, for some things are beyond our ken (Deut 29:29). We can confess what we do know: "Adam was created sinless but not impeccable, uncorrupted but not incorruptible."[20]

Physical death resulted from the fall, although it was delayed (Gen 2:17; 3:19); at any rate, it was symptomatic of a deeper and far more serious spiritual death (see Eph 2:1; Col 2:13), a harbinger of hell, the "second" death (Rev 20:6, 14; 21:8). The promise of a Redeemer was the only hope (Gen 3:15). Some have buckled under pressure from the sciences, reinterpreting Paul as saying that Adam's sin introduced spiritual, *not* physical, death.[21] However, such rescue moves crash against the pillars of Romans 5:12 and 1 Corinthians 15:21, in which Paul confirms the sin-death nexus; as one theologian explains, "The primary point is the death of the body, since its antithesis is the resurrection of the body."[22] Spiritual and physical death are therefore both in view.

The fall is midwife to the gospel. The original goodness of creation is a truth brimming with hope, for it means that sin began in time; it is contingent, not intrinsic to creation. Creation's original goodness not only safeguards God's holiness but also renders sin an accidental, not essential, feature of human nature. If redemption from sin is a real possibility, then

---

[18]Michael Murray dubs this problem the "Paradisaical Motivation Argument" in *Nature Red in Tooth and Claw: Theism and the Problem of Animal Suffering* (New York: Oxford University Press, 2008), 83-87.

[19]Robert Brown, "The First Evil Will Must Be Incomprehensible: A Critique of Augustine," *Journal of the American Academy of Religion* 46, no. 3 (1978): 315-29; and G. C. Berkouwer, *Sin* (Grand Rapids, MI: Eerdmans, 1971), 11-26.

[20]James Anderson, "Calvinism and the First Sin," in *Calvinism and the Problem of Evil*, ed. David Alexander and Daniel Johnson (Eugene, OR: Pickwick, 2016), 218.

[21]See, e.g., R. J. Berry: "When the bible—and particularly Paul—speak of 'death' they are concerned essentially with spiritual death." "This Cursed Earth: Is 'the Fall' Credible?" *Science & Christian Belief* 11 (1999): 34.

[22]Henri Blocher, *In the Beginning: The Opening Chapters of Genesis* (Downers Grove, IL: InterVarsity Press, 1984), 184. John Murray reminds us that "the separation of the body and spirit and the return to dust of the former had far more significance [for Paul] as the epitome of the wages of sin than we are disposed to attach to it." *The Epistle to the Romans* (Grand Rapids, MI: Eerdmans, 1959), 1:181.

the gospel is *truly* good news: "Human beings can again become sinless without ceasing to be human."[23] Without the fall, all of that is threatened; even eschatology becomes baseless, wishful thinking. The Christian conviction that suffering, sin, and death will disappear at the eschaton hinges on the same divine revelation that affirms the goodness of prelapsarian creation. If we deny the latter, on what grounds can we hope for the former? As Michael Lloyd notes, "We cannot look forward to any golden age in the future, because we cannot now look back to any golden age in the past."[24] Just so. Adam's fall is integral to the very shape of Christian doctrine.[25]

The cosmic fall. The divine curse targeted the serpent, Eve, and Adam, and was followed by expulsion from Eden (Gen 3:14-24). In particular, the third curse sentenced Adam to toilsome labor and subjected "the ground" (v. 17)— by synecdoche, *the entire cosmos*—to futility and decay. This doctrine of a cosmic fall is scorned by many as the benighted mantra of fringe creationists. It was the norm in premodern theology, but by the eighteenth century geologists were defending earth's antiquity; they inferred animal predation and death eons before the dawn of humanity. Evolution revolutionized biology a century later.

As the doctrine of a cosmic fall was being eclipsed, there were attempts to refurbish it for the strange new world. Some, like C. I. Scofield and C. S. Lewis, speculated that an angelic fall ruined an earlier creation, triggering millions of years of pre-Adamic animal suffering and death (the "gap" between Gen 1:1 and 1:2).[26] Others resurrected Origen's ghost by imagining a pretemporal fall in which each of us preexisted as disembodied souls who

---

[23]Anthony Hoekema, *Created in God's Image* (Grand Rapids, MI: Eerdmans, 1986), 117.

[24]Michael Lloyd, "The Humanity of Fallenness," in *Grace and Truth in the Secular Age*, ed. Timothy Bradshaw (Grand Rapids, MI: Eerdmans, 1998), 72n18.

[25]For a thoughtful attempt to preserve key theological commitments of the fall doctrine *within* an evolutionary context, see James K. A. Smith, "What Stands on the Fall? A Philosophical Explora-tion," in *Evolution and the Fall*, ed. William Cavanaugh and James K. A. Smith (Grand Rapids, MI: Eerdmans, 2017), 48-64.

[26]Scofield's 1910 study Bible popularized this "ruin-reconstruction" view. See Bernard Ramm, *The Christian View of Science and Scripture* (Grand Rapids, MI: Eerdmans, 1954), 195-210; C. S. Lewis, *The Problem of Pain* (New York: HarperCollins, 1996), 132-47; and Michael Lloyd, "Are Animals Fallen?" in *Animals on the Agenda: Questions About Animals for Theology and Ethics*, ed. Andrew Linzey and Dorothy Yamamoto (London: SCM Press, 1998), 147-60. For a related argument for "modified dualism," in which evolutionary evil is the mysterious handiwork of Satan and the elusive powers and principalities, see Nicola Hoggard Creegan, *Animal Suffering and the Problem of Evil* (New York: Oxford University Press, 2013).

sinned against God and were then sentenced to embodiment in this earthly life.[27] A third proposal hypothesized that pre-Adamic predation and death *were* caused by Adam's fall but only *retroactively*, much like Christ's atonement was "retroactively" effective for Old Testament believers.[28] Each of these speculative moves falls short, however, by erasing the causal nexus between Adam's sin and death, or their redemptive-historical, temporal ordering.

In any event the new consensus among theologians rejects a cosmic fall entirely. Evolutionary creationists instead reimagine suffering and death not as a lapsarian affliction but as the *necessary* cost of the freedom God gave creation to be itself; or, as some put it, this vale of tears was *the only way* for God to secure the beauty, complexity, and diversity of nature.[29] The new theodicy attempts to justify God in the face of untold animal death and suffering in evolutionary history.[30] Such evolutionary hamartiologies render natural evil (and possibly moral evil) *intrinsic* to divine creation, or alternatively, evil becomes a dualistic reality existing alongside God and intruding itself into his creation. I do not doubt that God brings good out of evil, as Scripture attests repeatedly (e.g., Gen 50:20; Acts 2:23-24), but the notion that the Creator originates evil to bring about good violates his holy self-revelation in Scripture.

Perhaps, then, the cosmic fall should be reenlisted, especially given its robust exegetical warrant (assertions to the contrary are misleading).[31] Paul's allusion to Genesis 3:17-19 (and 5:29) in Romans 8:19-22 confirms that the cosmic fall was God's curse on the ground. God subjected creation "to futility," in "bondage to decay" (Rom 8:20, 21). Creation (*ktisis*) is the entirety of "sub-human nature both animate and inanimate"—that is, the whole

---

[27] Williams, *Ideas of the Fall*. Kant and the German theologian Julius Müller made similar claims.

[28] William Dembski, *The End of Christianity: Finding a Good God in an Evil World* (Downers Grove, IL: InterVarsity Press, 2009). The idea already appeared in Horace Bushnell, *Nature and the Supernatural* (New York: Charles Scribner, 1858), 194-219.

[29] On the first, see Arthur Peacocke, *Creation and the World of Science: The Reshaping of Belief* (Oxford: Oxford University Press, 1979), 50-111; on the second, see Christopher Southgate, *The Groaning of Creation: God, Evolution, and the Problem of Evil* (Louisville: Westminster John Knox, 2008).

[30] See also Creegan, *Animal Suffering*; and Gijsbert van den Brink, "God and the Suffering of Animals," in *Playing with Leviathan: Interpretation and Reception of Monsters from the Biblical World*, ed. Koert van Bekkum, Jaap Dekker, Henk van de Kamp, and Eric Peels (Leiden: Brill, 2017), 179-200.

[31] "No mention is made in Genesis of any ill effects of the Fall directly to creation itself." Keith Miller, "'And God Saw That It Was Good': Death and Pain in the Created Order," *Perspectives on Science and Christian Faith* 63, no. 2 (2011): 87.

cosmos minus angels and humans.[32] God held creation "in bondage to corruption, decay, and death . . . a state of futility with hope."[33] Isaiah's picture of the new heaven and new earth (Is 11:6-9; 65:17, 25), when the cosmic fall will be annulled, arguably includes the absence of animal predation—for example, "the lion shall eat straw like the ox" (Is 65:25). In light of biblical eschatology (e.g., 2 Pet 3:13; Rev 21:1-2), I take these passages to imply the absence of animal predation and death in the prefallen world (admittedly, my argument is inferential since Scripture is not explicit).[34]

For those who reject the cosmic fall, their position is saddled with eschatological instability. Many proponents of this view believe that humans *and* animals will not experience pain or death in the new heaven and new earth.[35] But this hope sits awkwardly with the denial of a cosmic fall. Scriptural eschatology points to a future reality of finitude *without* mortality, which suggests that mortality is not a creaturely given.[36] The notion that creation's God-given "freedom to be itself" is an intrinsic good leaves open the possibility that tornadoes, earthquakes, diseases, and the like will be present in the eschaton.

Some evolutionary and old-earth creationists split the difference by positing that only human—not animal—death results from the fall. This is a well-meant but misbegotten compromise. The problem is that prelapsarian Adam was in a state of "original righteousness." Since he had not yet sinned, his physical constitution was free from death. Such a sinless state, however,

---

[32]This conclusion is amply defended in C. E. B. Cranfield, *Romans 1–8* (New York: Doubleday, 1993), 411-12. See also Richard Longenecker, *The Epistle to the Romans* (Grand Rapids, MI: Eerdmans, 2016), 719-21.

[33]Joseph Fitzmyer, *Romans* (New York: Doubleday, 1993), 505.

[34]But this conclusion is consistent with the exclusively vegetarian diet in Eden (e.g., see Gen 1:29-30; 3:18-19). Although Augustine and Aquinas were notable exceptions, it was the dominant view of the tradition. See, e.g., Peter Almond, *Adam and Eve in Seventeenth-Century Thought* (New York: Cambridge University Press, 1999), 118-26; and Ryan McLaughlin, *Preservation and Protest: Theological Foundations for an Eco-Eschatological Ethics* (Minneapolis: Fortress, 2014), 30-32. Iain Provan, representing most Old Testament commentators today, critiques original vegetarianism in his *Discovering Genesis: Content, Interpretation, Reception* (Grand Rapids, MI: Eerdmans, 2016), 120-24.

[35]For example, Southgate speaks of "heaven for pelicans" (*Groaning of Creation*, 78-91); Creegan envisions an eschatological future of "peace between humans and animals and between all levels and types of life" (*Animal Suffering*, 172).

[36]Wolfhart Pannenberg recognizes this point in his *Systematic Theology* (Grand Rapids, MI: Eerdmans, 1991), 2:271-72, although he does not think it is decisive. Admittedly, an alternative interpretation might take future immortality as indicative of God bringing about something eschatologically *new* rather than merely a return to a prelapsarian creational norm.

is impossible on any account of evolutionary creationism because physical death is part of the warp and woof of evolution itself.[37] Adam inherits a liability to death from his evolutionary ancestors (the mortality of earlier species is the same mortality genetically inherited by *Homo sapiens*). Prelapsarian Adam is *already dying*; ergo, human death precedes the fall after all. To dodge this conclusion, one may posit that God supernaturally *removed* that liability to death in Adam and Eve; however, that move undermines the biblical witness to the sheer goodness of original creation (given that it assumes a fatal defect in original humanity). In short, striving to run with the hare and hunt with the hounds, the argument that only human death results from the fall ends up incoherent.[38]

Evangelical biblical scholars increasingly deny *any* causal relationship between Adam's fall and mortality—the fall enabled physical death, not mortality as such. According to this view, Adam was created mortal and had to eat regularly from the Tree of Life in order to fend off death (only the Tree of the Knowledge of Good and Evil was out of bounds). Once expelled from Eden and without access to the Tree of Life, he succumbed to his innate mortality and died (Gen 5:5).[39]

Others have also questioned the traditional interpretation of relevant biblical texts.[40] For example, many commentators for apologetic reasons have ignored, rationalized, or mythologized the Isaiah 11 and 65 texts because they strain credulity.[41] Laurie Braaten argues that the groaning of

---

[37]According to current evolutionary thinking, however, natural selection is driven by differential reproductive success rather than organismal mortality; even if we grant that point, biological death on this view has always been part of evolutionary history.

[38]For a similar critique, see Nigel Cameron, *Evolution and the Authority of the Bible* (Exeter, UK: Paternoster, 1983), 64-67. One possible exception is an evolutionary setting with a de novo creation of Adam.

[39]For example, John Walton takes this line in *The Lost World of Adam and Eve: Genesis 2–3 and the Human Origins Debate* (Downers Grove, IL: InterVarsity Press, 2015), 73-74.

[40]See, for example, Van den Brink, "God and the Suffering of Animals," 188-90; and Ronald Osborn, *Death Before the Fall: Biblical Literalism and the Problem of Animal Suffering* (Downers Grove, IL: InterVarsity Press, 2014).

[41]Modern commentators in this camp include John Goldingay, Walter Brueggemann, John Oswalt, Hans Wildberger, and many others. Citing passages like Psalm 104; 147; and Job 38–41, C. John Collins and Henri Blocher allege that animal death and predation are never depicted in Scripture as evil. See, e.g., Henri Blocher, "The Theology of the Fall and the Origins of Evil," in *Darwin, Creation and the Fall: Theological Challenges*, ed. R. J. Berry and T. A. Noble (Nottingham, UK: Apollos, 2009), 165-68; C. John Collins, *Genesis 1–4: A Linguistic, Literary, and Theological Commentary* (Phillipsburg: P & R, 2006), 162-66.

creation in Romans 8 alludes not to the divine curse of Genesis 3 but to the Hebrew prophetic tradition of creation that mourns ongoing human sin.[42]

Conflicting pre-exegetical intuitions are at play. These attempts at reinterpreting the tradition derive most of their plausibility from their ability to accommodate the dramatic shifts in scientific understanding.[43] But the normalization of death stands in stark contrast to the biblical presentation. Death is frequently meted out as punishment for law breaking (e.g., Ex 21:12, 14-17; 22; Lev 20:2, 9-13, 15-16, 27; Deut 22:21, 24). The wickedness of the Canaanites (Deut 9:5; 18:9, 12) and the people of Sodom and Gomorrah (2 Pet 2:6; Jude 7) justifies their death. Isaiah the prophet anticipates that death will be swallowed forever when Christ returns (Is 25:8). Scripture is adamant that the wages of sin is death (Rom 6:23). Death is the last enemy (1 Cor 15:26), a symptom of the fall. Christ's resurrection abolished its reign and took away its sting (v. 55). Every tear from our eyes will one day be wiped away forever (Rev 21:4). This logic of salvation faces difficulties if death is included in God's original creation.

And what about the Tree of Life?[44] The tree's significance is a puzzling question. It was a literal tree symbolizing divine fellowship and eternal life with God (e.g., Ps 36:9). Many noble interpreters think Adam and Eve were protected from death by eating regularly from it. While I agree the tree pointed sacramentally to eternal life, I suspect that Adam and Eve had *not yet eaten* from the tree despite having access (hence Gen 3:22—"he might reach out his hand and take also from the tree of life, and eat, and live forever"). They were conditionally immortal and conditionally sinless.[45]

---

[42]Laurie Braaten, "All Creation Groans: Romans 8:22 in Light of the Biblical Sources," *Horizons in Biblical Theology* 28 (2006): 131-59. Richard Bauckham endorses Braaten's thesis in *Bible and Ecology: Rediscovering the Community of Creation* (Waco, TX: Baylor University Press, 2010), 92-101.

[43]"The greatest single problem of a 'cosmic fall' on the basis of humanity's sin is the state of creation during the long period of earth and the solar system prior to the creation of humankind." Anthony Thiselton, *Discovering Romans: Content, Interpretation, Reception* (Grand Rapids, MI: Eerdmans, 2016), 176.

[44]On how to interpret the two trees, commentaries are the Wild West. See, e.g., Brevard Childs, "Tree of Knowledge, Tree of Life," in *Interpreter's Dictionary of the Bible* (New York: Abingdon, 1962), 4:695-97. I was instructed by Paul Watson, "The Tree of Life," *Restoration Quarterly* 23, no. 4 (1980): 233-38.

[45]The precise nature of Adam's original state was debated in the early church, but the catholic position held that mortality resulted from his sin. For example, against Pelagianism, the first canon of the Council of Carthage (AD 418) states, "If any one says that Adam, the first man, was created mortal, so that, whether he sinned or not, he would have died from natural causes, and not as the

Adam and Eve became mortal after eating from the Tree of the Knowledge of Good and Evil. Banished from Eden as a result (Gen 3:24), Adam's descendants yearn for eternal life; we will do anything to have it (e.g., see the Tower of Babel in Gen 11:1-9 and, more recently, transhumanist efforts). But the only way back is *through* Christ, the "bread" and the "water" of eternal life (Jn 6:35; 4:14; 1:4) who takes us from Eden to the New Jerusalem, where we will eat freely from the Tree of Life (Rev 22:2, 14).

In light of Romans 8:19-22 and other passages, I have argued that the moral integrity of Adam and of the created order are mutually implicated. Adam's sin brought about the cosmic fall. That conclusion invites a weighty objection:

> In order for moral wrongdoing to leave such catastrophic consequences in its wake it must be the case that God created things so that the integrity of the natural order was, in some important sense, initially *dependent upon* the integrity of the moral order. And this fact itself stands in need of some sort of explanation. If God were omniscient, he would surely know that the natural order was fragile in this way. Unless there is some reason why the fragility of nature is necessary, or why making it fragile in this way makes possible certain outweighing goods, the fragility of nature itself seems to be a puzzling defect in creation.[46]

There was, in fact, no "fragility" in God's original creation. Adam's sin on its own lacked any power to change the structure of nature. God's judicial response to the broken commandment—the divine curse of Genesis 3:17—was the power that unleashed the cosmic fall. The fallen order of creation is continuous with the original creation and yet at key points utterly different (e.g., the presence of physical death and its implications). Creation was thus "subjected to futility" (Rom 8:20 ESV). The cosmic fall, then, far from signaling a "defect" or "fragility" in God's original creation, points to the terrifying gravity of sin and prompts a longing for the Last Adam, the head of a new humanity, who in conquering sin and death will restore—indeed surpass!—Eden.

---

wages of sin, let him be anathema." Henry Bettenson, ed., *Documents of the Christian Church*, 2nd ed. (Oxford: Oxford University Press, 1963), 59.

[46]Murray, *Nature Red in Tooth and Claw*, 83. See also John Schneider, "The Fall of 'Augustinian Adam': Original Fragility and Supralapsarian Purpose," *Zygon* 47, no. 4 (2012): 949-69.

THE ORIGIN OF SINFULNESS

The doctrine of original sin has also fallen on hard times. As one historian remarked, "Modern science has killed original sin."[47] Augustine is routinely blamed for burdening Western theology with an indefensible concept of inherited guilt. I concede that the North African bishop was by no means faultless, but regarding original sin he is a man more sinned against than sinning.[48]

The human predicament. Examining ourselves and those around us, we see flawed, morally deficient people and lives tainted by sin—often subtle, sometimes flagrant, but ever present. No one shines with unblemished holiness. Sin is universal; save Christ, there are no exceptions. After the events in Eden, Cain's murder of Abel signals the new reality (Gen 4:8; Lamech's sin in v. 23). God wipes out the prediluvian generation with a flood because "the wickedness of humankind was great in the earth," and "every inclination of the thoughts of their hearts was only evil continually" (Gen 6:5; see also 8:21). Even "righteous" Noah and his family were not sinless (Gen 9:18-29).

Scripture routinely portrays humanity in a negative light—"perverse; there is no one who does good, no, not one" (Ps 14:3). Sinful from birth (Ps 51:5; 58:3), unclean (Is 64:6; Prov 20:9), full of evil and with madness in our hearts (Eccles 9:3). The New Testament yields the same bleak picture. Death reigns in our hearts (Mk 7:21-22; Mt 12:33-34; 15:19). As Paul writes, we are dead in our transgressions (Eph 2:1). Many similar passages sing the same dirge (e.g., Ps 130:3; Jer 17:9; Gal 3:22), and they are not isolated proof texts. Quite the opposite; Scripture's explicit statements support this diagnosis:

- "There is no one who does not sin" (1 Kings 8:46).
- "No one living is righteous before you" (Ps 143:2; Eccles 7:20).
- "All, both Jews and Greeks, are under the power of sin" (Rom 3:9).
- "All have sinned and fall short of the glory of God" (Rom 3:23).

---

[47]Julius Gross, *Entwicklungsgeschichte des Erbsündendogmas seit der Reformation* (Munich: Reinhardt, 1963), 352, cited in Christof Gestrich, *The Return of Splendor in the World: The Christian Doctrine of Sin and Forgiveness* (Grand Rapids, MI: Eerdmans, 1997), 228.

[48]Original sin is often defined as the fall of Adam and Eve ("originating sin") *and* the inborn moral corruption of their descendants ("originated sin"). In this chapter, however, I am using *original sin* as a synonym for *originated sin*.

- "If we say that we have no sin, we deceive ourselves, and the truth is not in us" (1 Jn 1:8; see also v. 10).

The Old Testament sacrificial system presupposes the universality of sin. Each family offered sacrifices year after year, implying that no one was free from sin (Heb 10:11)—even Job, "blameless and upright," offered regular sacrifices (Job 1:1, 5). Jesus gives the same verdict: unless we are born again (Jn 3:3, 5), no one will see the kingdom of God, which implies that *all of us* are sinners.

But to be human does not *entail* being sinful. Consider that Adam and Eve were without sin before the fall, Jesus was sinless throughout his incarnational ministry, and glorified saints will be sinless in the new heaven and new earth. The point is that humans *after the fall*—and before the eschaton—inevitably sin. From childhood, sin pervades our souls (Gen 6:5; 8:21); indeed, we are sinful at birth (Ps 51:5).[49] Human existence dominated by the flesh (*sarx*) opposes God (see Rom 7:5; 8:3, 9). Sin is innate to postlapsarian humanity, so we all die. The sin-death nexus also applies to infants, the mentally disabled, and others who cannot commit any actual sins, for sin is a reality that conditions us, antecedent to any thought, word, or deed (Rom 5:15, 17; 1 Cor 15:21).

The idea that sin is innate to humanity, a state we are born into, seems to threaten moral responsibility. I have no control over my natural condition. It was not a choice I made for which I can be held responsible. But then why use the language of sin at all? After all, the very idea of sin entails culpability, guilt before God (Ps 51:4). The inevitability of human sinning thus needs an explanation: Why are all men and women sinners by necessity?

The doctrine of original sin. The fall's impact on humanity was widely affirmed in the Catholic tradition,[50] but opinions varied on *how* that first sin impacted Adam's descendants. According to Augustine the whole human race was "that one man who fell into sin." At the root of our sinful condition, "there already existed the seminal nature [of Adam] from which we were to

---

[49]The meaning of Psalm 51:5 is admittedly contested, with some disavowing any relation to the doctrine of original sin; see, e.g., Tremper Longman, *Psalms* (Downers Grove, IL: InterVarsity Press, 2014), 220. But I agree with Marvin Tate, *Psalm 51–100* (Dallas: Word, 1990), 19: "The emphasis is on the sin of the speaker, who admits that sin . . . goes back to the roots of personal existence."

[50]Recent attempts to deny the doctrine of the fall in the Eastern tradition—pitting "Augustinian" West against "Irenaean" East—are tendentious. See, e.g., the convincing critique in Andrew McCoy, "Becoming Who We Are Supposed to Be: An Evaluation of Schneider's Use of Christian Theology in Conversation with Recent Genetic Science," *Calvin Theological Journal* 49 (2014): 63-84, esp. 66-74.

be begotten."[51] In this *realist* account of original sin, the whole human nature was seminally present in Adam's very act of sinning.[52] As Augustine writes, "By the evil will of that one man all sinned in him, since all were that one man, from whom, therefore, they individually derived original sin."[53] God can therefore justly punish Adam's descendants for the first sin since they *were* really there. Augustine mistranslated the last clause of Romans 5:12, but his doctrine of original sin did not hinge on it as he drew on other biblical passages and the wider logic of Christology and soteriology.

Infant baptism for Augustine implied our inability to justify ourselves before God, that babies were sinners before they committed any actual sins. God would be unjust to allow infant mortality *unless* they were sinners (Rom 6:23). If everyone needs salvation in Christ, Augustine reasoned, then obviously we all suffer from original sin. The Pelagian (and semi-Pelagian) emphasis on free will denied the truth embodied in infant baptism, the common practice of the church. Pelagianism jeopardized God's mercy and grace. Hence Augustine's reply to his Pelagian nemesis Julian of Eclanum: "It is not I who made up original sin! The catholic faith has believed it from its beginnings. But you who deny it are undoubtedly a new heretic."[54]

The exegetical facts belied Pelagius's argument. According to Paul in Romans 5:12, all people die because they sinned individually. He goes on to appeal to solidarity with Adam to explain why *all* are sinners and *all* die without exception: the many died by the trespass of one man (v. 15), Adam's sin brought judgment and condemnation to all (v. 16), his disobedience brought universal death and condemnation (vv. 17-18). In short, "by the one man's disobedience the many were made sinners" (v. 19). These verses lead to the conclusion that the sin of "all" (v. 12) somehow corresponds to the sin of Adam, a point reiterated in 1 Corinthians 15:21-22 ("all die in Adam"). But how should we reconcile Adamic and individual responsibility?[55]

---

[51]Augustine, *City of God*, trans. Henry Bettenson (New York: Penguin Classics, 2003), 501.

[52]Augustinian realism has modern defenders, such as William Shedd, Augustus Strong, Philip Hughes, and (arguably) Jonathan Edwards.

[53]Augustine, *On Marriage and Concupiscence* 2.15.

[54]Augustine, *Marriage and Desire*, in *Answer to the Pelagians II*, trans. Roland Teske (Hyde Park, New York: New City, 1998), 68.

[55]Douglas Moo, *The Epistle to the Romans* (Grand Rapids, MI: Eerdmans, 1996), 322-25.

Augustinian realists believe that Adam's fall condemns all people to be born in a state of guilt and moral corruption. I agree with Augustine on both counts, but his realistic framework falls short as an account of original guilt. The federal (or representative) account of original sin makes better exegetical sense of the parallelism in Romans 5:12-21.[56] This parallelism contrasts Adam as head of the human race, *biologically* and covenantally, to Christ as head of the redeemed human race, *spiritually* and covenantally.[57] Adam is the federal head of all humanity, while Christ is the federal head of those reborn by the Spirit (Jn 1:13; 3:3-8; 1 Jn 2:29; 3:9; 4:7; 5:1, 4, 18; Jas 1:18; 1 Pet 1:3, 23). Adam's disobedience, imputed to the human race, brought sin, condemnation, and death; Christ's righteousness, imputed to those united to him, brought grace, justification, righteousness, and eternal life.

Many find imputed guilt a pill too bitter to swallow. They are struck by passages affirming that God holds us guilty for our own sins and *not* those of our parents (e.g., Deut 24:16; 2 Kings 14:6; Jer 31:29-30; Ezek 18:20). But the federal account of original sin happily embraces such texts. God counts us guilty for Adam's first sin, not the sins of our parents or other ancestors. Adam and Christ had unique roles in redemptive history (Rom 5:12-21; 1 Cor 15:21-22). "Only two persons have existed," Bavinck remarks, "whose life and works extended to the boundaries of humanity itself, whose influence and dominion had effects to the ends of the earth and into eternity."[58] Adam is the head of the old humanity, and Christ is the head of the new humanity.

The nub is divine justice: Why am I blamed for an act that I could not possibly have committed? I never consented to Adam as my covenantal representative; thus, original guilt seems monumentally unfair.[59] However, the critique cuts both ways—for the righteousness that comes from God

---

[56]Hence this view is rightly called an "Augustinian-Reformed" view. As Bavinck says, "Federalism certainly does not rule out the truth contained in [Augustinian] realism; on the contrary, it fully accepts it. It proceeds from it but does not confine itself to it. It recognizes a unity of nature on which the federal unity depends." *Reformed Dogmatics*, ed. John Bolt, trans. John Vriend (Grand Rapids, MI: Baker Academic, 2006), 3:104.

[57]The Adam-Christ analogy should not be pressed too far, but—minimally—Paul assumes a direct parallel between the nature of our connection with Adam, on the one hand, and the nature of our connection with Christ, on the other (*pace* Moo, *Romans*, 327n58).

[58]Bavinck, *Reformed Dogmatics*, 3:105.

[59]A point argued emphatically by William Shedd and Oliver Crisp, among others.

apart from the law is not of our own doing (Phil 3:9; 2 Cor 5:21). If original guilt is unjust, the same must be said for Christ's imputed righteousness. We can either accept—or reject—both.[60] In any case, the operative concept of "fairness" seems to be that we are responsible only for actions or states that are within our control. By that logic, if it is unjust to be reckoned guilty merely because of our federal union with Adam, then it is also unjust to be born morally corrupt merely because of natural descent from Adam.

One way to save original guilt and intuitions about fairness is to appeal to divine omniscience. God knows—via his middle knowledge—that every human being would have fallen had he or she been in Adam's place. Based on that knowledge, God *justly* imputes Adam's disobedience to all his descendants. Friedrich Schleiermacher takes this line when he writes, "We certainly admit a universal imputation of the first sin, an imputation resting upon the belief that to whatever human individual had fallen the lot of being the first, he, too, would have committed the sin."[61] But this seems implausible. If the first human being is genuinely able not to sin, why is the first sin *inevitable*? Furthermore, for libertarians, there is no basis on which one could even know what each of us would have done "counterfactually" in the Garden of Eden; the very idea of middle knowledge is incoherent.[62]

In seventeenth-century France, Josua Placaeus (1596–1655) was likewise troubled by the alleged injustice of original guilt. He proposed, controversially, that we are guilty of Adam's sin because of hereditary corruption; Adam's sin is imputed to every human being *on account of* our corrupt nature (mediate rather than immediate imputation).[63] On this view, guilt does not cause corruption; rather, a *prior* moral corruption causes guilt. However, since I am not morally responsible for inheriting corruption from Adam, it is not clear why I should be guilty of Adam's sin.

---

[60]Some concede the point and reject both original guilt and a penal account of atonement. See, e.g., Richard Swinburne, *Responsibility and Atonement* (New York: Oxford University Press, 1989).

[61]Friedrich Schleiermacher, *The Christian Faith* (London: T&T Clark, 1999), 304.

[62]See, e.g., Steven Cowan, "The Grounding Objection to Middle Knowledge Revisited," *Religious Studies* 39 (2003): 93-102.

[63]For a more detailed account, see John Murray, *The Imputation of Adam's Sin* (Grand Rapids, MI: Eerdmans, 1959), 42-47.

Why not restrict original sin to inherited moral corruption only? Our innate moral condition is divine penalty for Adam's sin, *without* original guilt. We become liable only for sins we personally commit. This account is common among New Testament scholars today and was defended by Huldrych Zwingli (1484–1531) and, more tentatively, by Jacob Arminius (1560–1609).[64] The position raises questions for incompatibilist (or libertarian) accounts of freedom. If we are guilty for sinful acts that inevitably result from our moral corruption, then we must be guilty of the moral corruption itself—alternatively, if we are not guilty for innate moral corruption, then we cannot be guilty for sinful acts that arise necessarily from it. Inherited-moral-corruption-only is not really intelligible on incompatibilist premises. Compatibilists are free to defend the view; however, they do so in violation of Ephesians 2:3, in which Paul informs us that our very nature (*physis*), *our innate condition*, deserves the full wrath of God. Moral corruption, then, is the penal consequence of God's judgment in response to our original guilt in Adam (Rom 5:12-21).[65]

Inherited moral corruption without guilt was also defended by the early Greek fathers. They eschewed Augustinian notions of inherited guilt, placing the emphasis on mortality, corruption, and sickness, a tradition taken up by the Eastern Orthodox Church.[66] It is tempting to ask whether Augustine corrupted this earlier, "purer" practice. At least three observations are germane: First, the Greek emphasis on free will and personal responsibility was understandable given the prevalence of deterministic Gnostic heresies. Second, the Greek tradition carried the seed if not the full flower of original sin. As one theologian remarked, "There was here the outline of a real theory of original sin. The fathers might well have filled it in and given it greater sharpness of definition had the subject been directly canvassed in their day."[67]

---

[64]On Arminius, see Keith Stanglin and Thomas McCall, *Jacob Arminius: Theologian of Grace* (New York: Oxford University Press, 2012), 149-50. Recent advocates include Charles Cranfield, James Dunn, and Oliver Crisp. See, e.g., Crisp's "Retrieving Zwingli's Doctrine of Original Sin," *Journal of Reformed Theology* 10 (2016): 340-60.

[65]See David Turner, "Ephesians 2:3c and *Peccatum Originale*," *Grace Theological Journal* 1 (1980): 195-219; and Andrew Lincoln, *Ephesians* (Nashville: Thomas Nelson, 1990), 99.

[66]See, e.g., John Meyendorff, *Byzantine Theology*, rev. ed. (New York: Fordham University Press, 1983), 143-46; and Constantine Tsirpanlis, *Introduction to Eastern Patristic Thought and Orthodox Theology* (Collegeville, MN: Liturgical Press, 1991), 49-53.

[67]J. N. D. Kelly, *Early Christian Doctrines*, 4th ed. (London: Adam and Charles Black, 1968), 351.

Lastly, the argument of this chapter implies that the Augustinian doctrine of original sin was more true to the apostolic tradition than what came to dominate the Eastern Orthodox tradition.[68]

The source of human sinfulness. In a post-Darwinian intellectual climate, in which naturalistic science enjoys epistemic privilege, the doctrines of the fall and original sin seem like premodern relics. Scientific fields like sociobiology, evolutionary psychology, neuroscience, and behavioral genetics depict persons as victims of biological forces that predispose them to sin. These scientific disciplines, and especially the way they are often popularized, offer alternative narratives of the human predicament that have subtle looping effects on how people—even Christians—perceive themselves.[69] The looping effects deepen the tensions and widen the distance between the doctrine of original sin and the medicalized image of the human condition.

There have been heroic efforts to bridge this gap. One proposal, for example, describes original sin as the selfishness that humans inherited from their evolutionary ancestors: "Our inclination to sin, in short, arose out of our animal nature itself."[70] God made the universe with a built-in freedom for novelty, genetic mutations, and natural selection, and this freedom necessarily generates natural evil. Evolution itself is driven by a biological selfishness that becomes "sinful" in human beings when they self-consciously harm each other—"moral evil evolves out of physical 'evil.'"[71] In a less radical account, original sin is redefined as the symbiosis of genes and environment, the interplay of nature and nurture: "Neither the genotype nor the cultural systems are perfect in their ability to guide and sustain human behavior."[72] Even the atheist philosopher Michael Ruse weighs in, describing original

---

[68]In fact, Augustinian or proto-Augustinian motifs were never absent from the East but prevailed as a minority report (Kelly, *Early Christian Doctrines*, 350-51). For a persuasive argument that Irenaeus actually paved the way for Augustine's doctrine of original sin, see Manfred Hauke, *Heilsverlust in Adam: Stationen griechischer Erbsündenlehre: Irenäus-Origenes-Kappadozier* (Paderborn, Germany: Bonifatius, 1993).

[69]On looping effects, see Ian Hacking, "Degeneracy, Criminal Behavior, and Looping," in *Genetics and Criminal Behavior*, ed. David Wasserman and Robert Wachbroit (New York: Cambridge University Press, 2001), 141-67.

[70]Daryl Domning and Monika Hellwig, *Original Selfishness: Original Sin and Evil in Light of Evolution* (Burlington, VT: Ashgate, 2006), 108.

[71]Domning and Hellwig, *Original Selfishness*, 184, original emphasis removed.

[72]Philip Hefner, *The Human Factor: Evolution, Culture, and Religion* (Minneapolis: Fortress, 1993), 135.

sin as the self-interested Darwinian struggle for existence with adaptations for success: "Original sin is part of the biological package. It comes with being human."[73]

Such evolutionary hamartiologies are growing in frequency and sophistication—collectively, however, they face insuperable theological burdens. Setting aside concerns in biblical exegesis, there appears to be a fundamental misunderstanding as to what exactly sin *is* and whence it originates. Reducing human sinfulness to either nature or nurture (or both) is a category mistake. As Bavinck rightly says, "Sin is not a physical but an ethical phenomenon."[74] The source of our sinfulness is original sin, a deeper, more pernicious problem.

In Scripture, moral agency is always attributed to the individual before God. "Against you, you alone, have I sinned" (Ps 51:4). It is *I* who am guilty. Scripture never hints at a more basic cause than the person.[75] Jesus said that evil thoughts, murder, adultery, and other such sins flow "out of the heart" (Mt 15:19). Our sins arise from "out of the abundance of the heart" (Mt 12:34)—the "heart" is what most fully discloses *me* (e.g., Gen 6:5; Ps 14; 58:3; Mk 7:21; Rom 3:9-20). Persons are therefore culpable for actions for which they are "deeply responsible," actions that truly *disclose* their hearts. Sin is not authored by our genes; rather, sin is an act or a state of the soul.[76]

In recent decades Christians across a wide range of disciplines have tried to reinterpret human nature along physical or material lines. Human persons are constituted by physical things only, we are told, in lockstep with the naturalistic belief that no other ontological entities exist in the world (e.g., souls). Such Christian materialists adopt nonreductive strategies to create space for moral, spiritual, and transcendent human experience without invoking the

---

[73]Michael Ruse, *Can a Darwinian Be a Christian? The Relationship Between Science and Religion* (Cambridge: Cambridge University Press, 2001), 210.

[74]Bavinck, *Reformed Dogmatics*, 3:137.

[75]Among libertarian philosophers, something like this view is often called agent causation (defined indeterministically). But it seems to me that agent causation as such is an underdetermined concept—libertarians and compatibilists can offer their respective accounts of agent causation.

[76]In this paragraph, I am indebted to Jesse Couenhoven, "What Sin Is: A Differential Analysis," *Modern Theology* 25 (2009): 563-87. Soul-body dualism, as I defend it, assumes a compatibilist rather than a libertarian account of freedom. Deep responsibility is a compatibilist (self-disclosure) notion, not a libertarian (self-making) one. We are deeply responsible for those things that truly disclose our hearts, even if God has ordained them.

soul.[77] It is difficult, however, to see how physicalist anthropologies can account for genuine moral accountability, without which the very idea of sin falls to pieces.[78] Philosophers have debated these matters extensively, but I wish to register an Augustinian concern: if sin is causally or ontologically reducible to biology or physics, then human sin *must* arise from matter, and we are not far from the Manichaean heresy that God's original creation was evil.[79]

Early Christian tradition also struggled to understand sin in light of biology. Even as church fathers polemicized anti-Christian movements like Gnosticism and Manichaeism, they were influenced by Platonic and Neoplatonic thought. The human body was sometimes seen as the source of moral evil. This ambiguity emerged in the debate over the transmission of original sin. Traducianism says that original sin is transmitted from parental souls to the souls of offspring; creationism holds instead that God creates each fresh soul that then contracts sin when implanted in the body at conception.

Throughout his life Augustine vacillated between these two options and set the terms of the debate for later Catholic and Protestant traditions. Traducianism offers a plausible mechanism for the transmission of original sin but raises worries about materialism (especially Tertullian's version). Conversely, creationism implies that God is responsible for souls being born sinful or that souls become sinful by coming into contact with the body— either God is responsible for original sin or the body causes original sin.[80] I agree with Augustine that the soul, not the body, is the source of sin, but the federal account of original sin circumvents deciding between creationism versus traducianism on the transmission of sin. Adam's sin was imputed to

---

[77]For a range of perspectives, see R. Keith Loftin and Joshua Farris, eds., *Christian Physicalism? Philosophical Theological Criticisms* (Lanham, MD: Lexington Books, 2017); Joel Green, ed., *What About the Soul? Neuroscience and Christian Anthropology* (Nashville: Abingdon, 2004); and Nancey Murphy, *Bodies and Souls, or Spirited Bodies?* (Cambridge: Cambridge University Press, 2006).

[78]See, e.g., one attempt in Nancey Murphy and Warren Brown, *Did My Neurons Make Me Do It? Philosophical and Neurobiological Perspectives on Moral Responsibility and Free Will* (New York: Oxford University Press, 2007). Key proposals have also been offered by Philip Clayton, Malcolm Jeeves, Donald MacKay, Joel Green, and others.

[79]Christopher Brunner, "The Ontological Relation Between Evil and Existents in Manichaean Texts and in Augustine's Interpretation of Manichaeism," in *Philosophies of Existence: Ancient and Medieval*, ed. Parviz Morewedge (New York: Fordham University Press, 1982), 78-95.

[80]See, e.g., Augustine's *The Nature and Origin of the Soul*.

all his physical descendants except Christ; because of this original guilt, we come into existence with fallen bodies and sinful souls.

Evolutionary doctrines of sin also raise difficult christological and soteriological questions. If human beings inevitably sin because of underlying biological forces, then Jesus Christ either was not completely free from sin (i.e., deny his impeccability) or did not fully participate in bodily human nature (i.e., deny his humanity). This unhappy dilemma exists because biologized doctrines of original sin collapse the distinction between "natural" and "moral" evil. As Ted Peters notes, "By removing primary agency from the decisions of allegedly free human persons, what we previously thought was moral perversion becomes an expression of a more basic biological nature."[81] Sin ceases to be a disclosure of my heart and instead becomes a complex interplay of nature and nurture.

A biologized hamartiology conflates the doctrine of creation and the doctrine of sin. Sanctification reduces to the process of overcoming genetic (and environmental) constraints.[82] But creation is fallen, *not* sinful. Our bodies are fallen and prone to suffering and death, but they are not sources of sin. Original sin itself tracks far deeper than biology and genetics. In the biblical mindset, sin is always portrayed as sourced in the immaterial part of humanity, "the heart"—a nonphysical reality best conceptualized by the doctrine of the soul.[83]

Having said that, original sin is always conditioned by embodiment. Sin reigns in our mortal bodies (Rom 6:12). Scripture assumes close ties between the frailty of our bodies and our sinful condition.[84] Indwelling sin expresses its dominion over us *through* our bodies; it uses the body as an instrument of wickedness (Rom 6:13). The glory of humanity is that we are embodied souls, higher than animals but a little lower than angels (Ps 8:4-6). Embodiment gives a "bodily" character to our sins that distinguishes us

---

[81]Ted Peters, "The Evolution of Evil," in *The Evolution of Evil*, ed. Gaymon Bennett, Ted Peters, Martinez Hewlett, and Robert Russell (Göttingen: Vandenhoeck & Ruprecht, 2008), 21.

[82]Matthew Nelson Hill defends this approach in *Evolution and Holiness: Sociobiology, Altruism and the Quest for Wesleyan Perfection* (Downers Grove, IL: IVP Academic, 2016).

[83]Space only allows me to assert—without defending!—this controversial claim. For elaboration, see my "From Sin to the Soul: A Dogmatic Argument for Dualism," in *The Christian Doctrine of Humanity: Explorations in Constructive Dogmatics*, ed. Oliver Crisp and Fred Sanders (Grand Rapids, MI: Zondervan, 2018), 70-90.

[84]Bavinck, *Reformed Dogmatics*, 3:55.

from fallen angels. As Bavinck says, "While the sensual nature of humans is not itself sin, nor the source or principle of sin, *it is its dwelling place.*"[85] The embodied nature of existence is not divorced from the principle of sin; sin may not be physical, but it operates in and through the physical members of the body (Rom 7:23): "Corporeal flesh is weak because of its physical needs and desires, and therefore easy prey for sin."[86] We serve our bodily appetites instead of the Lord Jesus (Rom 16:18): our minds are distracted by earthly things, and our stomach becomes our god (Phil 3:19). Creaturely desires are a gift from God but are also expressed by "deeds of the body" (Rom 8:13).

We sin because we are sinners; actual sins spring from original sin. Our fallen bodies are the occasion for the expression of actual sins. Our beliefs, desires, and actions are sinful so long as they disclose my soul's moral condition. We are morally responsible for desires and beliefs—and actions or inactions motivated by them—if they are produced in us in a "properly functioning" way that *reliably* discloses the heart.[87] Psychiatric or medical conditions such as Tourette Syndrome, bipolar disorder, and orbitofrontal lobe tumors can sometimes appear (misleadingly) as sinful beliefs, desires, and/or actions; however, attributing actual sin should be moderated to the degree that they are a skewed reflection of the heart. In such exceptional cases, persons no longer function properly and their actions do not reliably disclose the contents of the heart. Moral culpability is mitigated. Making such clinical judgments is not easy, but the One whose judgment ultimately counts sees the heart, not merely the outward appearance (1 Sam 16:7).

CONCLUSION

As we have seen, the quest for a viable doctrine of original sin faces formidable challenges. That was true in Augustine's day; the stakes are even higher today. Significant proposals span the theological spectrum; some enjoy much, others less, harmony with science. Two forces pull in opposite directions. On the one hand, the desire for greater resonance with scientific

---

[85]Bavinck, *Reformed Dogmatics*, emphasis mine.
[86]Robert Gundry, *Sōma in Biblical Theology* (Cambridge: Cambridge University Press, 1976), 137.
[87]For this application of "proper function," see Jesse Couenhoven, *Stricken by Sin, Cured by Christ: Agency, Necessity, and Culpability in Augustinian Theology* (New York: Oxford University Press, 2013), 126-61.

conclusions is commendable in itself because God's Word, rightly understood, *cannot* conflict with what is true in nature. On the other hand, given the reality of human finitude and the noetic effects of sin, chasing that holy grail may also betray the ephemerality of the theological syntheses, for scientific consensus is a moving target.

This chapter is obviously at odds with accepted scientific perspectives. That is no small thing, yet we should recall that biblical faith is not fundamentally *scientific*—although Christians should care about how it relates to science since God is Creator, we bear his image, his revelation addresses areas of scientific import, and he shines in all that's fair. Nor is faith fundamentally *historical*, by which I mean that the epistemic warrant for faith is not historical inquiry—although historical events *are* the lifeblood of orthodoxy. Rather, Christian faith is fundamentally *revelatory*— although we should reject ill-conceived strategies that try to shield faith from any possible contact with science and history. The doctrines of the fall and original sin are warranted for me *dogmatically*—that is, on the basis of divine revelation, not history or science. If I am convinced by exegetical and theological evidence, scientific counterclaims will strike me as implausible.[88]

Original sin and the fall of Adam and Eve are essential to how God has chosen to reveal himself in Holy Scripture. These revelational truths are not random items that can be discarded indiscriminately or creatively refashioned along modern yet sub-biblical modes of thinking. They are threads in a garment, so that pulling them loose threatens to unravel the entire biblical story. A doctrine of sin that is no longer revelatory inevitably breaks faith with the premodern tradition, the catholic creeds, and the confessional statements of the Protestant tradition. That is not accidental; they all share the same epistemology of revelation.

The fall and original sin may be marginal to current plausibility structures, unflattering to the human psyche, and gloomy in their diagnosis, but to embrace them fully allows the light of the gospel to shine much more

---

[88]I do not deny that science can sometimes legitimately overturn a biblically warranted interpretation, but the threshold should be very high for doctrines that lie more central to Scripture and the tradition. See, e.g., my "'A Rock of Offense': The Problem of Scripture in Science and Theology," *Ex Auditu* 32 (2016): 169-92.

brightly and Christ the Savior to be cherished much more deeply. Those great things of the gospel prepare the people of God for our final destination, the Holy City, the New Jerusalem, coming down out of heaven from God, where we will eat, drink, and be merry—singing alleluias and amens in the presence of the Lord—and to live happily ever after.[89]

---

[89]My thanks to Robert Erle Barham, Bill Davis, Tim Morris, Keith Plummer, Michael Radmacher, Brian Tabb, Paul Wells, John Wingard, and Todd Wood for helpful comments on an earlier draft.

2

A Moderate Reformed View

OLIVER D. CRISP

In this chapter I shall defend what I call the moderate Reformed doctrine of original sin. This comprises the following theological claims:

1. All human beings barring Christ possess original sin.

2. Original sin is an inherited corruption of nature, a condition that every fallen human being possesses from the first moment of generation.

3. Fallen humans are not culpable for being generated with this morally vitiated condition.

4. Fallen humans are not culpable for a first, or primal, sin either. That is, they do not bear original guilt (i.e., the guilt of the sin of some putative first human pair or human community being imputed to them along with original sin).

5. This morally vitiated condition normally inevitably yields actual sin. That is, a person born with this defect will normally inevitably commit actual sin on at least one occasion provided that person lives long enough to be able to commit such sin. (The caveat *normally* indicates limit cases that are exceptions to this claim, such as infants that die before maturity and the severely mentally impaired.)

6. Fallen human beings are culpable for their actual sins and condemned for them, in the absence of atonement.

7. Possession of original sin leads to death and separation from God irrespective of actual sin.

It seems to me that, taken together, these claims represent a moderate, and therefore defensible, version of the doctrine of original sin that is consistent with one strand of the Reformed tradition. Because it is a moderate account, it may also be more promising as the basis for ecumenical rapprochement with other strands of the Christian tradition than some versions of the doctrine found within Reformed theology. To begin, I offer some explanatory gloss on each of the claims of the moderate Reformed doctrine of original sin just given, so as to flesh out its dogmatic claims. In doing so I also compare this moderate doctrine with relevant voices in the Reformed tradition to show that it is, indeed, a legitimate expression of Reformed theology even if some will think it represents a minority report in that tradition. In a second section, I defend this moderate Reformed view against several criticisms. A short concluding section offers some reflections on the scope of this moderate Reformed doctrine of sin.

THE MODERATE REFORMED DOCTRINE
OF ORIGINAL SIN EXPOUNDED

Let us treat the numbered sentences of this moderate doctrine as dogmatic claims, considering and expounding each in turn.

According to the first claim of the moderate Reformed doctrine, *all human beings barring Christ possess original sin.* Historically, most Christians have held that there was some primal sin by means of which original sin was introduced into the human race. By *primal sin* I mean that first act of sin supposedly committed by our first parents, Adam and Eve, which led to all subsequent human beings being generated in a morally vitiated condition—the condition of original sin. The notion that human beings, after the sin of our first parents, possess original sin is relatively uncontroversial in the Christian tradition. Only those who, like Pelagius, deny the doctrine of original sin (and are therefore outside the bounds of theological orthodoxy) would be troubled by it. However, the notion that this affects *all* human beings is more controversial because many Roman Catholic Christians maintain that Mary *Theotokos* (that is, Mary the God-bearer, and mother of Christ) was born without original sin by means of an immaculate conception. Those Christians who want to include Mary Theotokos along with Christ as being without original sin may make the relevant mental reservation in what follows. Whatever we make of the moral state of Mary Theotokos, the notion that Christ is an exception to the humanity-wide condition of original sin is not theologically contro-versial in the Christian tradition. It is an assumption of all Christians that Christ is without sin, although some theologians have believed Christ was in some sense "fallen" in his human nature yet never committed sin. There is not space to enter into that debate here, but suffice it to say a person with a fallen human nature would already be in a morally precarious state, one that would seem to disbar that person from being in the presence of God, whose eyes are too pure to look on evil (Hab 1:13). For what is it to be fallen, apart from being in a morally vitiated state that inevitably gives rise to actual sin? If Christ is God incarnate and God is incapable of sinning, then it is only a short, though crucial, step to saying that his human nature is without sin—in which case, it is difficult to see what to make of the claim that his human nature is fallen but not sinful. This seems like a distinction without a difference.[1]

So, the first claim of the moderate Reformed doctrine—that original sin is a condition all human beings barring Christ possess—seems fairly theologically secure. Few Christians would deny it. However, the fact that this first dogmatic claim makes no reference to a primal sin, or an aboriginal pair, is much more controversial. For belief in some putative aboriginal pair from which all humanity is descended, and whose primal sin is (somehow) transmitted to all subsequent humans barring Christ, is a constituent of almost all historic Christian attempts to make sense of original sin. The moderate Reformed doctrine of sin does not require an original pair, nor does it require monogenism (the notion that we are descended from an original pair). However, it does not deny that there was an original pair from which we are descended either. Instead it is a doctrine that makes *no* judgment about this matter. In other words, it prescinds from making a judgment about this dogmatic question. This, as we shall see, is an important consideration that marks what might be called a dogmatic minimalism that is part and parcel of the moderate Reformed view. By *dogmatic minimalism* I mean an approach to a par-ticular doctrine that attempts to affirm as "thin" an account as is doc-trinally possible yet consistent with wider theological and confessional

---

[1]I have discussed this in more detail in *Divinity and Humanity: The Incarnation Reconsidered* (Cam-bridge: Cambridge University Press, 2007), ch. 4.

commitments.[2] On the question of the etiology of original sin, the moderate Reformed doctrine is dogmatically minimalist.

This brings us to the second dogmatic claim, which is that *original sin is an inherited corruption of nature, a condition that every fallen human being possesses from the first moment of generation.* As is well known, the Reformed have a rather dim view of fallen human beings. The *T* of TULIP, the popular acrostic summarizing the five points of Calvinism derived from the teaching of the Synod of Dort, stands for "total depravity." The idea is not that fallen human beings are as depraved as they could be but rather that they are in bondage to sin, which affects every area of human life. We could put it like this: Reformed theologians have traditionally taught that fallen human beings are morally corrupt and that original sin itself is a moral corruption that we are generated with which affects us profoundly. There is also a distinction to be made between original sin (the morally vitiated condition we are generated with) and actual sin. Actual sin connotes the sins we commit as moral agents. I sin because I am a sinner, born with original sin. But the sins I commit as a sinner are actual sins for which I am morally responsible.

Some Reformed theologians have argued that God immediately and directly imputes original sin from our first parents to all subsequent generations of humanity, and that on this basis we are reckoned to be guilty of original sin. But this seems a very strange arrangement, one in which the moral consequences of someone else's sin are transferred directly to me by divine fiat, yielding guilt in me for something I did not do. For one thing, that seems monumentally unjust, for then a sinful condition that I did not choose is immediately transferred to me, rather like having someone else's debt immediately electronically transferred to my bank account so that money is debited from my account as a result. For another, it implies a strange doctrine of guilt in which culpability can be transferred from one person (Adam) to another (me).

Other theologians reverse these claims so that Adam's original guilt is said to be communicated to me by God because I am generated with the

---

[2]I have written about dogmatic minimalism elsewhere. See Oliver D. Crisp, "Desiderata for Models of the Hypostatic Union," in Oliver D. Crisp and Fred Sanders, eds. *Christology, Ancient and Modern: Explorations in Constructive Dogmatics* (Grand Rapids, MI: Zondervan Academic, 2013), 19-41.

corrupt nature that is mediated to me by my forebears. So, either God imputes Adam's sin and guilt to me prior to my existence or he ensures a corrupt nature is transmitted to me by natural generation and, as a consequence, imputes guilt to me. These traditional Reformed ways of thinking about the transmission of original sin and guilt are convoluted and not terribly intuitive.

By contrast, the notion that original sin is an inherited moral condition, rather like humans inheriting physical conditions from their parents, seems plausible and is not necessarily unjust. Suppose a mother is a drug addict. She passes on her addiction to her unborn child because they share the same blood supply. The child inherits the addiction through no fault of her own. Similarly, if an ancestor sells himself into slavery, then his heirs are born in that state through no fault of their own. Yet they inherit the moral burden their forebear has placed on them. We do not condone the mother or the ancestor who sells himself and his heirs. Nevertheless, such arrangements are familiar and seem plausible though reprehensible. Similarly, suppose that through some (collective) transgression a first human community is estranged from God. That estrangement, and any consequent moral disruption it causes, may be passed down the generations to later members of that community through no fault of their own. Whether we like it or not, our sinful choices often have effects on others around us. In cases like the addict mother or the ancestor slave, these choices have consequences that are inherited by the children born to such individuals. To commit some action that leads inexorably to one's own moral torpor is a terrible thing. To commit an act that adversely affects generations yet to come is much worse. Yet such actions are not unusual, as our two examples suggest. Of course, if original sin is inherited like this, rather than being transmitted immediately and directly, then presumably it is transferred from one generation to another mediately, as certain congenital conditions are passed down from two parents to a child. It is not a condition that is picked up by imitation, as the Pelagians averred. It must be transferred—in this way of thinking, by inheritance rather than by immediate divine imputation.

We come to our third claim, that *fallen humans are not culpable for being generated with this morally vitiated condition.* With this in mind, let us return to our earlier examples of the addict mother and the ancestor slave. It is clear that the child born to an addict is not morally responsible for being born in that condition. Similarly, the child born into a family of slaves is not responsible for being born a slave. In neither case is the child concerned culpable for the plight into which they were born. In a similar fashion, the child born with the condition of original sin cannot be culpable for being generated with that condition. How could she be? Culpability presumes some sort of action on the part of the agent to whom it is ascribed, and the child born with original sin cannot have acted in a way that ascribes culpability.

This brings us to the fourth claim, which goes to the heart of the moderate Reformed view: *Fallen humans are not culpable for a first, or primal, sin either. That is, they do not bear original guilt (i.e., the guilt of the sin of some putative first human pair or human community being imputed to them along with original sin).* One of the characteristics of much, though by no means all, historic Reformed theology has been the emphasis placed on the doctrine of original guilt alongside a doctrine of original sin. Often the two notions are bundled together so that all human beings after Adam and Eve are said to bear the moral corruption *and* guilt introduced to the race through the first sin of our aboriginal parents.

The idea seems to be something like this. Adam and Eve commit the first, or primal, sin. This brings about alienation from God and leaves humans with a morally disordered nature, one that lacks the moral structure and integrity with which humanity was originally created. This condition is then transmitted to subsequent human beings. But how are subsequent generations of humanity guilty of Adam and Eve's primal sin? Historic Reformed theology has two broad answers to this question. According to the first, we are guilty of Adam's sin because he acted as our representative; when he sinned it had consequences for the rest of humanity. There are many human analogs to this sort of arrangement, such as diplomatic representatives acting on behalf of a nation, binding that nation to certain international agreements. Similarly, our elected representatives in Parliament or on Capitol Hill represent our views and make political decisions on our behalf that bind us in certain ways—if, say, the decision becomes law. So the idea that Adam may represent us and that we may be bound by his action is a familiar one in other, mundane contexts. However, in the case of the diplomat and the politician, their roles as representatives depend on having a political mandate granted by the nation, or the voters, that they represent. There is no such arrangement with respect to Adam. We did not authorize our first parents, or some putative early human community, to act in this capacity. If someone represents us without authorization, we would normally think this unjust.[3] Perhaps it might be claimed that in the case of Adam, God authorizes his role as representative. Some may suppose this gives us reason to think that the arrangement is authorized. Nevertheless, it still seems unjust, for it is not a decision to which we were party or to which we could assent as moral agents. Surely God would not act unjustly.

The main alternative to representationalism is often called Augustinian realism because it is supposed to have originated with St. Augustine of Hippo (though this ascription is moot). Whether Augustine was an Augustinian realist or not, the idea is that I may be guilty of Adam's sin because I am somehow united with Adam in one metaphysical whole of which we are parts (hence, *realism*: we are really united to Adam as parts of one metaphysical whole object scattered across space and time).

Consider an analogy with an oak tree. Suppose we introduce a contagion into an acorn and plant it. What springs up is a sapling, then a young tree, and finally, after many years, a full-grown oak. However, as it grows and matures the oak is misshapen and deformed because of the contagion introduced at the acorn stage of its life. Consequently, all the later stages of the oak as it grows and develops across time are marred by the contagion it bears. Now, the realist says that humanity is like the oak. Through his own deliberate fault Adam introduces a contagion to humanity that is original sin. This contagion affects all later stages of humanity so that they are morally deformed. Just as the later life stages of the oak may be said to share in the one life that began when the acorn was planted, so human beings living after Adam's first sin share in his life and therefore partake of his sin. If we are parts of one metaphysical whole that is "fallen humanity," then perhaps the sin and guilt for Adam's transgression can be transferred to all the later stages of humanity.

---

[3]Is it unjust if Christ represents us without authorization? That is an interesting question. My view is that Christ is authorized by God, whereas Adam was not authorized to sin. So there is a relevant difference here.

It seems to me that there is something to be said for the notion that Adam and his progeny are metaphysically united in the way that Augustinian realism presumes. However, it is not clear to me that this provides a good reason for endorsing original guilt as well as original sin. Consider Romans 5:12-19, which is arguably the most important biblical text for the doctrine of original sin as well as being the putative basis for a doctrine of original guilt. This passage tells us that "sin came into the world through one man, and death came through sin, and so death spread to all because all have sinned." It also says that "death exercised dominion from Adam to Moses, even over those whose sins were not like the transgression of Adam, who is a type of the one who was to come [i.e., Christ]." What is more, "many died through the one man's trespass"; indeed, "judgment following one trespass brought condemnation." For it is "because of the one man's trespass" that "death exercised dominion through that one." The passage concludes, "Just as one man's trespass led to condemnation for all, so one man's act of righteousness leads to justification and life for all. For just as by the one man's disobedience the many were made sinners, so by the one man's obedience the many will be made righteous."

Now, it is not at all clear to me that this passage implies original guilt. It may be consistent with something like the Augustinian realist picture of how sin is transmitted. It does seem commensurate with something like the inheritance of a morally vitiated condition. But it is difficult to see how it yields the notion that all human beings (barring Christ, and perhaps Mary Theotokos) are *guilty* of Adam's primal sin. The condemnation spoken of in the passage is surely most naturally coupled with the penalty of sin, which is death. In which case, the judgment following the trespass yields the penalty of death and condemnation, and nothing here implies that culpability is included in the judgment made, or in the condemnation that is passed in consequence, or in the penalty that is applied to human beings as the upshot.

Happily, the notion of original guilt can be separated from the doctrine of original sin. One could be born with a condition of moral corruption inherited from some first ancestors and yet not be guilty of the sin of that ancestor—on analogy with being born with some genetic condition that is attributable to some distant ancestor, for which we bear no blame either. Nevertheless, some may worry that if this is to be a truly Reformed doctrine of original sin some account must be given of the fact that original guilt is embedded in a number of the confessions of the Reformed churches.

For instance, in the Westminster Confession we read this: "They [our first parents] being the root of all mankind, the guilt of this sin was imputed; and the same death in sin, and corrupted nature, conveyed to all their posterity descending from them by ordinary generation" (6.3). But there is no unanimous voice in the Reformed confessional tradition on this point. Earlier confessions such as the Scots Confession (1560), the Belgic Confession (1561), and the Thirty-Nine Articles of Religion (1563) all elaborate a doctrine of original sin without original guilt. Nor is the doctrine of original guilt to be found in the writings of all the fountainheads of Reformed thought. Neither Huldrych Zwingli nor John Calvin endorse it. In fact, Zwingli denies that human beings are born guilty of sin, which he seems to regard as something like a disease passed from one generation to the next.[4] Calvin writes about original sin as a contagion and corruption of human nature. He defines it thus:

> Original sin, therefore, seems to be a hereditary depravity and corruption of our nature, diffused into all parts of the soul, which first makes us liable to God's wrath, then also brings forth in us those works which Scripture calls "works of the flesh" [Gal 5:19-20]. And that is properly what Paul often calls sin.[5]

Earlier in the same passage he writes,

> Adam, by sinning, not only took upon himself misfortune and ruin but also plunged our nature into like destruction. This was not due to the guilt of himself alone, which would not pertain to us all, but was because he infected all his posterity with that corruption into which he had fallen. . . . Adam so corrupted himself that infection spread from him to all his descendants.[6]

---

[4]See, e.g., Huldrych Zwingli, *Declaration of Huldreich Zwingli Regarding Original Sin, Addressed to Urbanus Rhesus, August 15, 1526*, an English translation of which can be found in *On Providence and Other Essays*, ed. Samuel Macauley Jackson (Durham, NC: Labyrinth, 1983). I discuss Zwingli's view in more detail in Oliver D. Crisp, "On Original Sin," *International Journal of Systematic Theology* 17, no. 3 (2015): 252-66; and Oliver D. Crisp, "Sin," in *Christian Dogmatics: Reformed Theology for the Church Catholic*, ed. Michael Allen and Scott R. Swain (Grand Rapids, MI: Baker Academic, 2016), 194-215.
[5]John Calvin, *Institutes of the Christian Religion*, ed. John T. McNeil, trans. Ford Lewis Battles (1559; repr., Philadelphia: Westminster Press, 1960), 2.1.8.
[6]Calvin, *Institutes*, 2.1.6. Regarding the claim that fallen humans are subject to divine judgment through Adam's sin, he adds, "We are to understand it not as if we, guiltless and undeserving, bore

To sum up, original guilt does not rest on a strong biblical foundation. The main text used to defend the doctrine, Romans 5:12-19, does not appear to teach anything like a doctrine of original guilt. It is not a doctrine universally affirmed in Reformed theology—in fact, the two Continental fountainheads of Reformed theology deny it. And whether original sin is transmitted by imputation or via some realist doctrine (the two main alternatives in historic Reformed thought), original guilt need not be included in this arrangement. Thus, the rejection of original guilt seems consistent with at least one strand of early Reformed theology.

A good philosophical reason for setting it aside, independent of these theological and traditional considerations, which has already been intimated in the foregoing, is that guilt is nontransferable. A person's guilt cannot become the guilt of her son or daughter, or their sons and daughters, and so on. Even if that person is punished for her sin so that she is no longer culpable for it, she, and only she, is the one guilty of having sinned. Guilt is the inalienable property of the person who has sinned.[7] This is due in large measure to the fact that guilt is intimately connected to a person's moral agency. We say that it was because Jones committed a particular moral action that she is the appropriate referent of this ascription of blame. Blame is ascribed to her because it was her action, and hers alone, and because she committed the act as a moral agent (not under the influence of a drug, or under duress, or because she was forced to do so, or whatever). Because she is blameworthy, she bears culpability.

If she does it together with some other person (as Adam did with Eve), then culpability, and thus guilt, may be shared. But that is because *both* moral agents participate in the same action. But clearly Jones's great-grandson who is removed by a great distance in time from Jones's sinful action cannot be said to be guilty of the sin committed by Jones, because her great-grandson was not present when Jones committed the sin and did

---

the guilt of his offense but in the sense that, since we through his transgression have become entangled in the curse, he is said to have made us guilty." *Institutes* 2.1.8. Yet given his previous admission that we are not guilty of Adam's sin, and the qualification "*he is said* to have made us guilty," I think the ascription of guilt here is best understood in a metaphorical sense, just as the child of a murderer may be said to be tinged with her father's guilt. We are not *literally* guilty of Adam's sin.
[7]What about Christ taking our guilt? In my view, he takes on himself the penal consequences of our sin but not our guilt, strictly speaking. I have discussed this elsewhere in *The Word Enfleshed: Exploring the Person and Work of Christ* (Grand Rapids, MI: Baker Academic, 2016).

not approve it or participate in it. Consequently, Jones's great-grandson cannot be held accountable for her sins. But this is just what the doctrine of original guilt stipulates: we are guilty of Adam's primal sin although we were not present when he committed the sin and did not sanction it or participate in it. Yet this appears to be monumentally unjust. Since God cannot perform unjust actions, this gives us a strong independent reason (that is, reason independent of appeals to theological authority or tradition) for thinking there is something seriously amiss with the doctrine of original guilt.

With this made tolerably clear we can move on to the fifth theological claim of the moderate Reformed doctrine, according to which *this morally vitiated condition normally inevitably yields actual sin. That is, a person born with this defect will normally inevitably commit actual sin on at least one occasion provided that person lives long enough to be able to commit such sin. (The caveat* normally *indicates limit cases that are exceptions to this claim, such as infants that die before maturity and the severely mentally impaired.)*

Thus far we have seen that, according to the moderate Reformed doctrine of original sin, all human beings barring Christ are born with a corrupted nature. This means we inherit a state of moral corruption. But we are not culpable for bearing this condition any more than the child of the addict is culpable for being born an addict, or the child of the slave is culpable for being born a slave. Now, on this account all those born with original sin will normally inevitably commit actual sin for which they do bear responsibility. However, this is not true of all human beings. At least two sorts of limit cases are salient to this aspect of the doctrine. The first encompasses those fallen human beings that do not live to an age at which they are capable of making the moral decisions that yield actual sin. The second includes those who are never in a position to commit actual sin because they never become fully developed moral agents, owing to some severe mental impairment.

Here I side with a minority report in the Reformed tradition. The nineteenth-century American Presbyterian theologian William G. T. Shedd argued that some fallen human beings are incapable of exercising faith, so they cannot be held responsible for failing to have faith in Christ.[8] He

---

[8]W. G. T. Shedd, *Dogmatic Theology*, 3rd ed., ed. Alan W. Gomes (1888; repr., Phillipsburg, NJ: P&R Publishing, 2003). See also Oliver D. Crisp, *An American Augustinian: Sin and Salvation in the*

included in this category infants before the age of moral responsibility and the severely mentally impaired. In his way of thinking, such people are elected en masse and without the requirement of faith in Christ. I suggest that something similar be said of those who are born in a state of sin and never reach a point at which they can commit actual sins—that is, actions of a moral nature that are sinful and for which they are morally responsible. Since children in utero and infants before the age of maturity are not fully formed moral agents and are incapable of making moral choices, they cannot be the subjects of moral responsibility. Similarly, those who are severely mentally impaired are incapable of making moral choices owing to developmental deficiencies and cannot be the subjects of moral responsibility either. They still possess original sin as a "congenital" moral condition. But they are not responsible for committing actual sins for which they bear guilt. In fact, it would seem that these two classes of individual are not moral subjects, or cannot be counted as moral subjects, for the purposes of ascribing culpability for actual sin.

This does not necessarily mean that infants who perish before the age of discernment and the severely mentally impaired are elected as a class, as Shedd reasoned. Rather, the claim is only that such entities are not the proper subjects of moral responsibility because they are incapable of actual sin and not culpable for bearing original sin. However, it may be that God does elect these two sorts of individual (the infant before the age of reason and the severely mentally impaired) as a class, without the requirement of faith. In fact, that is a view to which I am sympathetic. It is not part of the doctrine set forth here because it belongs to another topic—namely, the doctrine of election.

Our sixth claim is that *fallen human beings are culpable for their actual sins and condemned for them, in the absence of atonement.* Earlier, in discussing the second dogmatic claim of the moderate Reformed doctrine of sin, we distinguished between original and actual sin. Original sin is the condition we inherit from our forebears; actual sins are those we commit as sinners. That is, being in a state of original sin, we commit actual sins—those misdeeds that are our own rather than simply the moral state in which we are generated. Now, when a person is a moral agent and commits an actual sin, that

---

Dogmatic Theology of William G. T. Shedd (Milton Keynes, UK: Paternoster Press; Eugene, OR: Wipf and Stock, 2007), ch. 7.

person is normally culpable for that sin (provided she did it freely, without compulsion, was in her right mind, and so on). He or she is blameworthy for that sin, and guilt may be ascribed to the person as a consequence. Some Reformed theologians have argued that fallen human beings possess a double guilt: the guilt of Adam's original sin (that is, original guilt) and the additional guilt accruing as a consequence of the actual sins that a person goes on to perform as a moral agent. But since I have already given reasons for thinking we do not have original guilt (in discussing the fourth dogmatic claim), it seems the only sorts of actions for which a person can be held accountable are actions they themselves perform or to which they are party. It makes sense to think that such actions are ones for which we are blameworthy, just as it makes sense to think that virtuous actions are ones for which we are praiseworthy. And it is theologically uncontroversial among Christians committed to what Thomas Oden calls "consensus Christianity" to maintain that, in the absence of atonement, these actual sins incur guilt, the upshot of which is condemnation.[9]

The seventh and final dogmatic claim of the moderate Reformed view of sin is that *possession of original sin leads to death and separation from God irrespective of actual sin.* Here the idea is that possession of original sin alone, without taking into account the guilt of actual sins, disbars a person from entering the presence of God without the application of the benefits of Christ's reconciling work. Imagine a leprous man granted an audience with his king. He is born with the condition through no fault of his own. Nevertheless, once it is discovered that the man has leprosy, he will be disbarred from the presence of the king. His leprous condition prevents him from being ushered into the presence of his potentate. Similarly, in the moderate Reformed view of sin, fallen human beings are in a morally corrupted state irrespective of actual sin. Although they have inherited this corruption through no fault of their own, the presence of such corruption renders them unfit for the presence of God.

A similar view can be found in the work of Zwingli. He writes,

> Original sin, as it is in the children of Adam, is not properly sin . . . for it is not a misdeed contrary to law. It is, therefore, properly a disease and

---

[9]See Thomas C. Oden, *Classic Christianity: A Systematic Theology* (New York: HarperCollins, 1992).

condition—a disease, because just as he fell through self-love, so do we also; a condition, because just as he became a slave and liable to death, so also are we both slaves and children of wrath ... and liable to death.[10]

Earlier we saw that Calvin writes of original sin as an "infection" that spreads from Adam to his progeny. The language of disease and infection used by these Magisterial Reformers should not displace the idea of original sin as an inherited corruption. Rather, like the case of the leper, they help to indicate why possession of original sin independent of actual sin renders a person unfit for the divine presence, through no fault of their own.

What, then, of those who possess original sin but never commit actual sin (our limit cases raised earlier)? Are they disbarred from the divine presence because they possess original sin even though they are not culpable for being in this moral state? It is certainly consistent with the logic of the moderate Reformed doctrine outlined thus far to reply in the affirmative to these questions. Perhaps those who fall under the description of these limit cases do indeed find themselves disbarred from the divine presence as a result. However, with William Shedd, I think this is a monstrous conclusion, one not worthy of God. We are told by the author of Ephesians to grasp "the breadth and length and height and depth" of the love of Christ (Eph 3:18). Earlier in the same epistle we read, "God, who is rich in mercy, out of the great love with which he loved us even when we were dead through our trespasses, made us alive together with Christ—by grace you have been saved" (Eph 2:4-5). But if God is able to make us alive in Christ while we are dead in our transgressions by sheer grace, why can he not save those "dead in their transgressions" because of original sin who have no capacity to exercise faith? Since the author of Ephesians tells us that faith itself is a gift of God, where that gift cannot be entertained because the person concerned is incapable of exercising faith, why would God not elect to save such people through Christ's atonement without faith? There is nothing to prevent God from doing so, nothing that can frustrate him in bringing this about. And, since God's grace and mercy are so great, he has the motivation to bring this about. He also has the means: the saving work

[10]Huldrych Zwingli, *Account of the Faith to Charles V* in *On Providence and Other Essays*, ed. Samuel Macauley Jackson (1922; repr., Durham, NC: Labyrinth Press, 1983), 40.

of Christ. Although Scripture does not provide a warrant for thinking that God does save through Christ those born with original sin that are incapable of faith, it seems to me that it does not foreclose such a possibility either. Given what we know from Scripture and tradition about the nature and purposes of God in salvation, and that God does not desire that anyone perish (2 Pet 3:9), not even the wicked (Ezek 18:23), there seems to be good reason to hope and expect that God does save such individuals as a class. These would be instances of persons with original sin rendered fit for the presence of God by having the benefits of Christ's work applied to them independent of the exercise of faith.

SOME OBJECTIONS TO THE MODERATE REFORMED DOCTRINE OF ORIGINAL SIN

This completes our exposition of the dogmatic claims that make up the moderate Reformed account of original sin. We are now in a position to consider some objections to this doctrine.

The first concern has to do with how this account is an improvement on the traditional Reformed doctrine that includes original guilt. For, on the face of it, it seems problematic to claim that fallen human beings are punishable for an inherited condition for which they are not culpable. However, as I have endeavored to argue, the idea that original sin is simply imputed by divine fiat to all human beings (barring Christ) is itself morally objectionable. Ascribing sin, and perhaps guilt, to one person on the basis of what some distant, long-dead ancestor has done seems monumentally unjust and immoral. Things are less objectionable where the arrangement is realist rather than merely representationalist—that is, where Adam and his progeny are regarded for certain purposes as one metaphysical entity rather than an arrangement in which Adam merely stands in for, or represents, the rest of humankind. But a metaphysically realist arrangement also requires some explanation and is not without theological cost. These costs are not incurred by the more modest theological claim that original sin is an inherited moral corruption. We inherit all sorts of genetic oddities from our forebears. Perhaps we also inherit various traits and dispositions as well. The moderate Reformed view supposes that original sin is a kind of moral analog to these things. Like being born in a state of slavery, being born in a state of sin is a condition we inherited from forebears for which we are not culpable. As the person born as a slave is rendered unfit to be given the status and privileges of a citizen without some act of redemption, so also human beings in a state of original sin are rendered unfit to be given the status and privileges of a citizen of the kingdom of God without some act of redemption. This explains why those in a sinful state may be disbarred from the presence of God even though they are not culpable for being in the state into which they were born. It also explains why actual sin provides additional reasons for preventing us from entering the presence of God without atonement being made. Thus, original sin is an inherited moral corruption for which fallen human beings are nonculpable yet rendered unfit for the divine presence, to which is normally added actual sin for which fallen human beings are culpable and worthy of condemnation in the absence of some act of atonement. This is clearly preferable to a doctrine of original sin that presumes I am guilty of Adam's primal sin.

A second concern is whether the moderate Reformed doctrine requires a historical Adam and Eve. I have already intimated in the foregoing that it does not have this requirement. In fact, the doctrine prescinds from making a judgment about whether human beings are descended from an aboriginal pair (monogenism) or from some larger population. It is consistent with the view that there was a historic pair, Adam and Eve, whose offspring we are, but this is not a requirement of the doctrine. It could be that we are descended from a community of around ten thousand early hominids, from which early humans emerged, as scientists working in this area conclude to be the case. That view is also consistent with the doctrine. My references to Adam in the foregoing should be understood as a place-holder. The use of the names Adam and Eve does not indicate commitment to a historic aboriginal pair in a primeval garden, although the view expressed is consistent with these claims. In the *Chronicles of Narnia*, children from our world who cross over to that fair realm are often referred to by Aslan and natives of Narnia as "sons of Adam" or "daughters of Eve," although this appellation is primarily metaphorical. They are not literally children of Adam and Eve but rather those who belong to the race of this fabled pair. By a similar token, someone today might be referred to as a child of Albion or as being related to good old Uncle Sam. But we do not presume that this should be taken literally. Rather, we take such appellations metaphorically. In a similar manner, the use of "Adam" and "Eve" in the context of the moderate Reformed doctrine of original sin does not necessarily indicate commitment to a historic pair from whom the human race has sprung (though it does not foreclose that option either).

A third, and closely related, concern is whether this doctrine fits with some account of the evolutionary development of the cosmos and humanity within it—what is often called evolutionary history. Here too, the moderate Reformed doctrine stops short of a firm commitment one way or another. However, it is not consistent with just any old doctrine of evolutionary history. Many accounts of the evolution of the various species on our planet, and of the cosmos as a whole, are metaphysically naturalist in nature. That is, they presume that once the physical factors involved in evolutionary processes are accounted for, explanation is exhausted. No supernatural agents or powers in addition to physical processes and entities need to be factored into the explanation of evolutionary processes. Thus, E. O. Wilson writes, "If humankind evolved by Darwinian natural selection, genetic chance and environmental necessity, not God, made the species."[11] Clearly, this sort of metaphysical naturalism is inconsistent with Christian doctrine as such and is therefore inconsistent with the moderate Reformed doctrine of original sin in particular. What is more, such metaphysically naturalist accounts of evolutionary history are nonteleological in nature. That is, they do not presume that there is some goal or outcome at which evolutionary processes aim. Such processes are said to be "blind," the outcome of chance, inherently random. But any account of human sin that is truly Christian will be teleological in nature because Christianity is teleological in nature: Christians believe that a divine intelligence stands behind the cosmos. He has created it, set it in motion, and overseen the physical processes by means of which human beings have come to exist, including their sinfulness, which requires salvation.

So the moderate Reformed doctrine of original sin is commensurate with some accounts of the evolutionary history of the world, and human beings in it, although any such explanation would need to be teleological and

---

[11]E. O. Wilson, *On Human Nature* (Cambridge, MA: Harvard University Press, 1978), xiii.

metaphysically supernaturalist in nature. But the moderate Reformed account is not committed to some doctrine of evolutionary history; it is also consistent with the idea that God specially created the world out of nothing and fashioned human beings from dust and ribs. There are good prudential reasons for adopting this sort of approach to controversial theological topics. To this end, it seems to me to be a good thing for a doctrine proposed as an explanation for something as controversial as the origins, nature, and transmission of human sin to be dogmatically minimalist in nature. The moderate Reformed doctrine prescinds from specifying a view on evolutionary history, and that is consistent with a dogmatically minimalist approach to original sin, deployed for prudential reasons. A diplomatic treaty commits the parties to carefully selected language so as to be acceptable to all signatories. Similarly, a dogmatically minimal account of original sin is likely to be acceptable to a wider range of those with a stake in the doctrine, both within the Reformed tradition and, perhaps, without. That, it seems to me, is a theological good worth pursuing.

A fourth and final objection concerns the Reformed bona fides of the moderate Reformed doctrine—in short, is it really a Reformed doctrine at all? Elsewhere I have attempted to provide reasons for thinking that the Reformed tradition tolerates more doctrinal breadth than is sometime thought, consistent with its confessionalism.[12] A similar sort of reasoning applies to the argument for the moderate Reformed doctrine of sin set forth here. That is, there is a range of views on this topic consistent with the Reformed tradition, and the view I have expressed here falls within that range. Some may worry that a view representing a minority report within a tradition should not be preferred to the majority voice. But, as I have argued here, there is good reason to take the moderate Reformed view seriously as well as good reason to worry about some important features of the sort of view more commonly regarded as the majority view in Reformed theology, which includes the notion of original guilt. But more fundamentally, perhaps, it is not clear (to me at least) that the views expressed here can really be

---

[12]See Oliver D. Crisp, *Retrieving Doctrine: Essays in Reformed Theology* (Downers Grove, IL: IVP Academic, 2011); *Revisioning Christology: Theology in the Reformed Tradition* (Farnham, UK: Ashgate, 2011); *Deviant Calvinism: Broadening Reformed Theology* (Minneapolis: Fortress Press, 2014); and *Saving Calvinism: Expanding the Reformed Tradition* (Downers Grove, IL: IVP Academic, 2016).

written off as a minority report when they are very similar to ideas found in a number of early Reformed confessions and two of the fountainheads of the Reformed tradition, particularly the views of Zwingli. Of course, I also think that the moderate Reformed doctrine is more defensible than other Reformed accounts, particularly those that include a doctrine of original guilt and commitment to a historic aboriginal pair, in part because it is a *moderate* doctrine—and doctrinal moderation is often a good thing. But, as I hope I have shown, it is also unambiguously a *Reformed* doctrine.

CONCLUSION

Some may worry that this reasoning seems almost entirely philosophical-theological and without detailed biblical exegesis. That is a good worry to have when doing Christian theology. But it is to mistake the kind of reasoning presented here. I am not offering in detail the biblical warrant for a particular doctrine of original sin, although I think the doctrine I have outlined can be supported from Scripture and have given some indication of this in my remarks about Romans 5. We might say that my contribution is an essay in doctrinal criticism, not in biblical theology or exegesis. To this end, I have attempted to provide a moderate account of original sin that is consistent with one strand of the Christian tradition (the Reformed tradition, broadly construed), although it is not the sort of view often reported as the Reformed doctrine of original sin. Yet, as I have tried to indicate, it is a minority report that is not without theological support from at least two of the Magisterial Reformers (Calvin and Zwingli) and several Reformed symbols (the Belgic Confession, Scots Confession, and the Articles of Religion). I am also concerned with finding an account of original sin that avoids some of the significant drawbacks to those versions of the doctrine that presume original sin is imputed from Adam to me and that I am guilty of Adam's sin—doctrines common among Reformed divines. This dovetails with my desire to isolate a doctrine that has ecumenical promise. Both Roman Catholic and Orthodox accounts of original sin do not include a doctrine of original guilt and are privative in nature: original sin is described as the privation of a state of original justice or righteousness, or as the loss of some morally exalted state with which the aboriginal human pair was created. The doctrine outlined here is closer to this sort of view than those versions of the doctrine that conceive of original sin as a moral corruption imputed to all humanity post-Adam, alongside the imputation of original guilt. For those concerned to find theological convergence between the different communions of the body of Christ, this may also be a reason for taking my argument seriously.

Finally, as I have summarized it, the moderate Reformed doctrine prescinds from any judgment about whether there is a specially created aboriginal human pair from whom all subsequent human beings are descended. So it does not presume monogenism (the view that we are descended from an aboriginal pair), although it is consistent with it. It also prescinds from any judgment about the origin of human suffering and misery and whether nature is created "red in tooth and claw." In other words, the doctrine is consistent with more than one story about both these worries, and to me that is a strength rather than a weakness.

3

A Wesleyan View

JOEL B. GREEN

For John Wesley's theological heirs, the pivotal significance of the doctrine of original sin is showcased especially in two ways. Exhibit A is the consistency with which Wesley spoke of original sin as integral to the analogy of faith; he thus regarded it as basic to his understanding of Scripture's unified witness. Exhibit B is his extensive defense of the doctrine in his 1757 treatise *The Doctrine of Original Sin: According to Scripture, Reason, and Experience*, which, at 522 pages, is the lengthiest of Wesley's many writings.[1]

Recognizing the significance of original sin for Wesley is not the same as achieving clarity regarding how Wesley understood the doctrine, nor does it predetermine in all its particulars what a Wesleyan perspective might look like for us, over two hundred years removed from Wesley's Great Britain. In this essay, then, I have set for myself three tasks: to sketch aspects of Wesley's understanding of original sin (compass points that might guide a contemporary, Wesleyan understanding of the doctrine); to interact with some of these elements as a New Testament scholar; and to explore how these considerations might shape a contemporary understanding of original sin.

WESLEY'S DOCTRINE OF ORIGINAL SIN

We begin by highlighting more fully the pivotal role the doctrine of original sin played for Wesley, which he himself documents in the aforementioned treatise. This is Wesley's response to John Taylor's book *The Scripture-Doctrine*

---

[1]John Wesley, *The Doctrine of Original Sin: According to Scripture, Reason, and Experience* (Bristol: E. Farley, 1757); Wesley's treatise is now introduced and printed in *The Works of John Wesley*, vol. 12, *Doctrinal and Controversial Treatises I*, ed. Randy L. Maddox (Nashville: Abingdon, 2012), 117-481.

of Original Sin Proposed to Free and Candid Examination (1740). Defending
the doctrine against Taylor's denial of the same on the basis of Enlightenment optimism, Wesley prefaces his account by indicating what is at stake
in the discussion. For him, Taylor's deist, rationalist position

> saps the very foundation of all revealed religion, whether Jewish or Christian.
> "Indeed, my L[ady?], said an eminent man to a person of quality, I can't see
> that we have much need of Jesus Christ." And who might not say, upon this
> supposition, "I can't see that we have much need of Christianity." Nay, not any
> at all, for "They that are whole have no need of a physician." And the Christian
> revelation speaks of nothing else but the great Physician of our souls.... If
> we are not diseased, we do not want a cure. If we are not sick, why should we
> seek for a "medicine to heal our sickness"? What room is there to talk of our
> being "renewed in knowledge or holiness, after the image wherein we were
> created," if we never have lost that image? If we are as knowing and holy now
> (nay, far more so) than Adam was immediately after his creation? *If therefore
> we take away this foundation, that man is by nature foolish and sinful, "fallen short
> of the glorious" image of "God," the Christian system falls at once—nor will it de-
> serve so honourable an appellation as that of a "cunningly devised fable."*[2]

Sans the doctrine of original sin, "the Christian system falls at once" and,
indeed, would not deserve even to be called "a cunningly devised fable"—
such claims speak to the pivotal nature of the doctrine for Wesley. This
eighteenth-century practical theologian was so unwavering in his affirmation of its importance that Wesley historian Ted Campbell justifiably
names original sin as one of Wesley's seven "essential doctrines."[3]

Using postliberal terminology, we might say that, for Wesley, original sin
was essential to the theological grammar of Scripture and life; or, using
premodern terms, we might say that Wesley's understanding of Scripture's
hypothesis (by which he identified Scripture's divine economy) fore-
grounded the doctrine. Wesley himself used the phrase "analogy of faith,"
popular among sixteenth- and seventeenth-century theologians, as a way of
referring to a doctrinal system that represented Scripture's wholeness, and

---

[2] Wesley, *Doctrine of Original Sin*, preface §4 (*Works*, 12:157-58), italics added.
[3] Ted A. Campbell, "The Shape of Wesleyan Thought: The Question of John Wesley's 'Essential'
Christian Doctrines," *Asbury Theological Journal* 59, nos. 1-2 (2004): 27-48 (here, 37-38); he thus
groups original sin with the Trinity, deity of Christ, atonement, biblical authority, justification by
faith, and regeneration.

he did so repeatedly. Perhaps none of these instances is more programmatic than his note on Romans 12:6. The English translation of this Pauline text provided in his *Explanatory Notes upon the New Testament* reads, "Having then gifts differing according to the grace which is given us, whether *it be* prophecy, *let us prophesy* according to the analogy of faith" (italics original).[4] Drawing on a parallel in 1 Peter 4:11, Wesley explains,

> St. Peter expresses it [that is, the analogy of faith], "as the oracles of God": according to the general tenor of them; according to that grand scheme of doctrine which is delivered therein, touching original sin, justification by faith, and present, inward salvation. There is a wonderful analogy between all these; and a close and intimate connexion between the chief heads of that faith "which was once delivered to the saints." Every article, therefore, concerning which there is any question should be determined by this rule; every doubtful scripture interpreted according to the grand truths which run through the whole.[5]

As this citation makes clear, for Wesley the analogy of faith—and, thus, a central ingredient of that analogy like original sin—is both derived from Scripture and ought to shape faithful reading of Scripture. Indeed, it is not too much to say, for Wesley, both that the whole Bible teaches original sin (as integral to the order of salvation, which is Scripture's *Sache*, or subject matter) and that this doctrine (again, as basic to Scripture's *Sache*) provides a normative guide for reading Scripture.

An Arminian account. Wesley followed the traditional, Western understanding of original sin rooted in Augustine, but with modifications. First,

---

[4]In the Authorized Version prevalent in Wesley's day, the phrase in question, κατὰ τὴν ἀναλογίαν τῆς πίστεως, reads "according to the proportion of faith," a reading also preferred by contemporary translators (e.g., Common English Bible, New Revised Standard Version). Wesley's reading is supported by the fact that ἀναλογία can signify not only "(mathematical) proportion" but also "correspondence," "resemblance," or "analogy." See Franco Montanari, *The Brill Dictionary of Ancient Greek* (Leiden: Brill, 2015), 142.

[5]John Wesley, *Explanatory Notes upon the New Testament* (1754; repr., London: Epworth, 1976), 569-70. Among the myriad places in his collected works where Wesley refers to those doctrines comprising the analogy of faith, original sin is a staple. This is because he understands Scripture's unity, especially as it witnesses the order of salvation, with its focus on the restoration of God's image following the effects of original sin. See Scott J. Jones, *John Wesley's Conception and Use of Scripture* (Nashville: Abingdon, 1995), 47-50; and Steven Joe Koskie Jr., *Reading the Way to Heaven: A Wesleyan Theological Hermeneutic of Scripture*, Journal of Theological Interpretation Supplement Series 8 (Winona Lake, IN: Eisenbrauns, 2014), 53-70.

with the Western church, Wesley affirmed total depravity, but with the Eastern church he spoke of sin as a disease (and, thus, of the therapeutic character of salvation [θεραπεία ψυχῆς, *therapeia psychēs*]). For example, in his sermon "Original Sin," we read,

> Keep to the plain, old "faith, once delivered to the saints," and delivered by the Spirit of God to your hearts. Know your disease! Know your cure! Ye were born in sin; therefore "ye must be born again," "born of God." By nature ye are wholly corrupted; by grace ye shall be wholly renewed. "In Adam ye all died"; in the second Adam, "in Christ, ye all are made alive." . . . Now "go on" "from faith to faith," until your whole sickness be healed, and all that "mind be in you which was also in Christ Jesus!"[6]

Second, Wesley moderated the consequences of Adam and Eve's sin, so that divine judgment was based on a person's own involvement in sin rather than on his or her inheritance from Adam and Eve. Consider, for example, his editorial work on the Anglican Church's Thirty-Nine Articles. Article 9 of this confession reads,

> Original sin standeth not in the following of Adam (as the Pelagians do vainly talk); but it is the fault and corruption of the Nature of every man, that naturally is engendered of the offspring of Adam; whereby man is very far gone from original righteousness, and is of his own nature inclined to evil, so that the flesh lusteth always contrary to the spirit; and therefore in every person born into this world, it deserveth God's wrath and damnation.[7]

In Wesley's redacted version, prepared for the Methodists in North America, we read,

> Original sin standeth not in the following of Adam (as the Pelagians do vainly talk), but it is the corruption of the nature of every man, that naturally is engendered of the offspring of Adam, whereby man is very far gone from original righteousness, and of his own nature inclined to evil, and that continually.[8]

---

[6]John Wesley, "On Original Sin," §3.5; in *The Works of John Wesley*, vol. 2, *Sermons II: 34–70*, ed. Albert C. Outler (Nashville: Abingdon, 1985), 185.
[7]"The Thirty-Nine Articles of Religion of the Church of English," in *The Creeds of Christendom: With a History and Critical Notes*, 3 vols., 6th ed., ed. Philip Schaff, rev. David S. Schaff (Grand Rapids, MI: Baker, 1983), 3:492–93 (citing the 1801 revision).
[8]John Wesley, *The Sunday Service of the Methodists in North America; with Other Occasional Services* (London, 1984), 309; cf. *The 2012 Book of Discipline of The United Methodist Church* (Nashville:

Wesley's doctrine of original sin thus maintained emphases on the corrupt nature of humanity and the pervasiveness of sin, but he excluded the idea that the transfer of original sin included the transfer of guilt. No one will receive eternal damnation because of Adam's guilt.

We might say that this admixture of Western and Eastern thought in Wesley's theology of original sin led him away from the notion that original sin was a "thing" humans inherited. Indeed, while Randy Maddox sketches Wesley's attempts to tie down the means by which original sin might be transmitted, he recognizes that, for Wesley, it was appropriate to refer to dual causation. "Wesley insisted that God can be the First Cause of human generation or corruption's transmission, while human beings or human nature are the efficient or natural causes." Accordingly, original sin was a way of referring to "the distortion of our nature resulting from being born into this world already separated from the empowering Divine Presence. *Deprived* of this essential relationship, our various faculties inevitably become *debilitated*, leaving us morally *depraved*."[9]

Third, Wesley's understanding of prevenient grace allowed him to affirm original sin *and* free will at the same time. Here Wesley's engagement with Taylor's optimism regarding the basic nature of humans comes into sharpest focus since this is where we see Wesley mapping a middle ground between Taylor's Pelagianism and the Calvinism against which Taylor contended. Wesley insisted that human nature was gravely impaired by the fall (the doctrine of original sin), but he also urged that God had already initiated, across the whole human family, his restoration of human capacities for responding to God by means of his grace (the doctrine of prevenient grace).[10] Against Taylor, then, Wesley viewed natural human moral psychology as deeply flawed, requiring renewal not simply by means of the powers of human reason but by the ongoing, renewing, enabling work of God's Spirit,

---

United Methodist Publishing House, 2012), §336 (p. 250). See Kenneth J. Collins, *The Theology of John Wesley: Holy Love and the Shape of Grace* (Nashville: Abingdon, 2007), 64.

[9]Randy L. Maddox, *Responsible Grace: John Wesley's Practical Theology* (Nashville: Kingswood, 1994), 80, 81; see esp. 78-81.

[10]"The free will of human beings in Arminius's theology and in classical Arminianism is more properly denoted *freed* will. Grace frees the will from bondage to sin and evil, and gives it ability to cooperate with saving grace by not resisting it. (Which is not the same as contributing to its work!)" Roger E. Olson, *Arminian Theology: Myths and Realities* (Downers Grove, IL: InterVarsity Press, 2006), 142.

who abundantly pours grace on all human beings. As Wesley opines, "But will *knowledge* balance *passion*? Or are 'rational powers' a counterpoise to sensual appetites? Will 'clear ideas' deliver men from lust and vanity? Or *seeing* the duty to love our enemies enable us to practise it?"[11] The anticipated response to each question is, of course, negative, with Wesley insisting that for him (but not for Taylor) the assistance of God's Spirit is required.

The work of "original sin." Reinhold Niebuhr famously acknowledged that "the doctrine of original sin is the only empirically verifiable doctrine of the Christian faith."[12] I mention Niebuhr not because he is a card-carrying Wesleyan but because his affirmation is one with which we can imagine Wesley agreeing. I also want to observe that what Niebuhr thus affirms falls well short of traditional views of the doctrine, with their interest in ancestral origins, transmission, and inherited guilt. (None of these is "empirically verifiable.")

That Wesley would have shouted a hearty amen to Niebuhr's statement is clear from the shape his argument takes in his treatise *The Doctrine of Original Sin: According to Scripture, Reason, and Experience.* Wesley develops his response to Taylor in four parts, but part one expresses Wesley's principal contribution, with the other three parts drawing heavily on earlier responses to Taylor by others. Moreover, it was part one that Wesley reformulated as a sermon—"Original Sin," published on its own in 1759 and in 1760 placed first in the fourth volume of his *Sermons on Several Occasions*—for widespread distribution among his preachers.[13] (They might not be expected to read his 522-page book, but they were surely expected to read his sermons.) Resisting all accounts of human dignity, virtue, and happiness, "as if it were all innocence and perfection," Wesley counters portraits of "the fair side of human nature" by discussing human nature after Adam and Eve but before Noah: "And God saw that the wickedness of man was great in the earth, and that every imagination of the thoughts of his heart was only evil continually" (Gen 6:5 AV). This, he urges, describes the human family to this very day. In fact, in the original title as Wesley published his treatise, the

---

[11]Wesley, *Doctrine of Original Sin*, Part II §5.2 (*Works*, 12:290).

[12]Reinhold Niebuhr, *Man's Nature and His Communities: Essays on the Dynamics and Enigmas of Man's Personal and Social Existence* (New York: Charles Scribner's Sons, 1965; repr., Eugene, OR: Wipf & Stock, 2012), 24 (citing the *London Times* with approval).

[13]Albert C. Outler, "Sermon 44: Original Sin: An Introductory Comment," in Wesley, *Works* 12:170-71.

word *and* was emphasized: *According to Scripture, Reason,* and *Experience.* This stylistic choice anticipated the case Wesley would develop—that it is easy to counter optimism regarding human dignity, virtue, and happiness by drawing attention to the surplus of sinful acts, past and present, typical of the human family.

This is not to say that Wesley concerned himself only or primarily with the ubiquity of sin. He followed what is for many a typical reading of salvation history. God created humanity in his own image, so humanity was "full of love," "full of justice, mercy, and truth," "pure from every sinful blot." Yet humanity was "not made immutable" but was "created able to stand, and yet liable to fall." God warned humanity of this possibility, but humanity ate of the forbidden tree and so fell from its "high estate." As God had warned, "in that day humanity did die: humankind died to God, the most dreadful of all deaths." Accordingly, the human family "lost both the knowledge and the love of God," "became unholy as well as unhappy," and "sunk into pride and self-will." Rebelling against God resulted in nothing less than "the loss of the life and image of God."[14] In other words, Wesley understood Genesis 3 as a fall narrative. With this story of sin's etiology, he could underscore the need for new birth. Similarly, Wesley's major writing on original sin was his attempt to ground the need for everyone to repent.

Wesley's understanding of original sin held together an emphasis on both human responsibility, characteristic of the Western church, and human recovery, characteristic of the Eastern church. This allowed him to cast God less as the judge of a human family implicated in Adam's guilt and more as a physician—a physician very much needed, to be sure, but also a physician already at work in the whole human family by means of the medicant of prevenient grace. Accordingly, human beings are judged not on account of the first couple's disobedience but in relation to their own responses to God's grace—responses that are made possible by the Spirit's work in the human family and not by humanity's inherent moral psychology. The narrative of paradise, paradise lost, paradise restored was for Wesley a way of underscoring both the need for and the possibility (or hope) of salvation.

---

[14] John Wesley, "The New Birth," in *Works* 2:186-201 (quotations from §§1.1-3).

RUMINATIONS ON SCRIPTURE

Although for many Western Christians today, Protestants especially, it seems obvious that Genesis 3 tells the story of humanity's fall and therefore serves as the fountainhead of the doctrine of original sin, this has never been a universally compelling reading. Interestingly, the doctrine is missing from the three ecumenical creeds of the Christian church (the Apostles', the Nicene, and the Athanasian Creeds), and the notions that the human family inherited Adam and Eve's guilt and that human beings, after the fall, were unable to choose the good are missing from the writings of the church's theologian exegetes in the post-apostolic era until the appearance of a late fourth-century commentary on Romans, attributed by Erasmus to an unknown churchman he called Ambrosiaster, whose reading of Romans influenced Augustine.[15] In this section, I turn to earlier readings of Genesis 3, first among Jewish writers outside the New Testament and then to two New Testament writers.

The significance of Adam's (and Eve's) sin: Second Temple Jewish texts. Most of the accoutrements of the traditional doctrine of original sin are likewise absent from Jewish writings of the Second Temple period—that is, writings from the early second century BC through the late first or early second century AD.[16] Among these texts, four speak to the question of the consequences of Genesis 3 for the human situation: the Life of Adam and Eve (also known as the Apocalypse of Moses; late first century AD?), 4 Ezra (end of the first century AD), 2 Baruch (late first or early second century AD), and Biblical Antiquities (also known as Pseudo-Philo; first century AD).

The Life of Adam and Eve tells the story of what happened after Adam and Eve were expelled from the Garden of Eden, with Adam and Eve

---

[15]For brief surveys, see John E. Toews, *The Story of Original Sin* (Eugene, OR: Pickwick, 2013), 48-72; Peter C. Bouteneff, *Beginnings: Ancient Christian Readings of the Biblical Creation Narratives* (Grand Rapids, MI: Baker Academic, 2008).

[16]For this material on Second Temple Jewish texts, I am summarizing material from Joel B. Green, "'Adam, What Have You Done?' New Testament Voices on the Origins of Sin," in *Evolution and the Fall*, ed. William T. Cavanaugh and James K. A. Smith (Grand Rapids: Eerdmans, 2017), 98-116 (see esp. 99-105). For surveys, see John J. Collins, "Before the Fall: The Earliest Interpretations of Adam and Eve," in *The Idea of Biblical Interpretation: Essays in Honor of James L. Kugel*, ed. Hindy Najman and Judith H. Newman, Supplements to the Journal for the Study of Judaism 83 (Leiden: Brill, 2004), 293-308; and John R. Levison, "Adam and Eve," in *Eerdmans Dictionary of Early Judaism*, ed. John J. Collins and Daniel C. Harlow (Grand Rapids, MI: Eerdmans, 2010), 300-302.

serving as representative humans going about the business of life. Antici-
pating his death, Adam tries to explain sickness and pain to their children.
In an account reminiscent of Genesis 3, Adam recalls that God brought
plagues on Adam because Adam had rejected God's covenant (8:1). Eve
bears particular responsibility in this story, though; in fact, she confesses to
Adam that "this has happened to you through me; because of me you suffer
troubles and pains" (9:2).[17] Later, she claims that "all sin in creation has
come about through me" (32:2-3). Eve's sin resulted from her encounter
with the serpent, whom she allowed into Paradise, who then "sprinkled his
evil poison"—that is, the venom of "craving" (ἐπιθυμία, *epithymia*),[18] "the
origin of every sin" (19:3). Eve's story of how she and Adam were deceived
was to serve as a prophylactic against future disobedience: "Now, then, my
children, I have shown you the way in which we were deceived. But you
watch yourselves so that you do not forsake the good" (30:1).

In 4 Ezra we find a series of interactions between Ezra and God (or the
angel Uriel), concerning Israel's exilic situation. Given the overwhelming
power of the inclination toward evil shared by human beings, why has God
abandoned his people? Ezra traces suffering and death to Adam's disobedience: "You gave him one command, and he disobeyed it, and so you immediately appointed death for him and for his descendants" (3:7);[19] then he
rehearses the story of God's people by tracing a series of events in which
people exercised their inclination toward doing evil and chose to disobey
God. He concludes,

> The first Adam, burdened with this inclination [to do evil], disobeyed you and
> was overcome, but so were all those descended from him. The disease became
> permanent; the Law was in the people's heart along with the wicked root, and
> that which was good departed and the wickedness remained. (3:21-22)

On the one hand, Ezra recognizes the culpability of a long line of human
beings: "Each nation lived by its own will, and people acted without giving
you a thought. They acted with scorn, and [the Lord] didn't prevent them" (3:8).

---

[17]English translations of Life of Adam and Eve are taken from M. D. Johnson, "Life of Adam and Eve:
A New Translation and Introduction," in *The Old Testament Pseudepigrapha*, 2 vols., ed. James H.
Charlesworth (Garden City, NY: Doubleday, 1983), 2:249-93; my references are to the Greek version.
[18]Johnson translates *covetousness* ("Life of Adam and Eve," 279).
[19]English translations of 4 Ezra follow the Common English Bible.

On the other hand, he is aware that Adam himself was burdened with an evil inclination: "A grain of evil seed was sown in the heart of Adam from the beginning, and how much godlessness it has produced until now and will produce until the time for threshing comes!" (4:30). Why does the heart lean toward evil (cf. 4:4)? Ezra is never told, although we do discover from 4 Ezra that the human inclination toward doing evil can and should be countered through the exercise of free will in the service of the law (e.g., 7:19-24, 118-26; 8:46-62; 14:34). Indeed, according to Uriel, humans can and should follow the path set out by Moses: "Choose life for yourself . . . so that you may live" (7:129; cf. Deut 30:19).

2 Baruch is a revelation concerning what would have been at the time of writing the recent destruction of Jerusalem in AD 70 and its ramifications for Jewish life. Seeking to make sense of this national trauma, the book mentions Adam in each of three dialogs between Baruch and God (13:1–20:6; 22:1–30:5; 48:26–52:7). In the first, God explains that the brevity of human life is due to disobedience to the law. In the second, Baruch requests that God demonstrate his power and glory by putting an end to death and restoring the dead to life (21:19-25). God's response emphasizes the results of Adam's sin: "For when Adam sinned and death was decreed against those who were to be born, the multitude of those who would be born was numbered. And for that number a place was prepared where the living ones might live and where the dead might be preserved" (23:4).[20] In the third exchange, Baruch exclaims, "O Adam, what did you do to all who were born after you? And what will be said of the first Eve who obeyed the serpent, so that this whole multitude is going to corruption?" (48:42-43). Lest we conclude that Baruch thus lays at Adam and Eve's feet responsibility for human sin and for divine judgment, we should note that Baruch demurs, speaking of all who fail to recognize God as their creator and who disobey the law (48:46-47). Although Adam brought mortality to this age, people are responsible for their future destinies. Baruch concludes, "Adam is, therefore, not the cause, except only for himself, but each of us has become our own Adam" (54:19).

---

[20]English translations of 2 Baruch are taken from A. F. J. Klijn, "2 (Syriac Apocalypse of) Baruch: A New Translation and Introduction," in *The Old Testament Pseudepigrapha*, 2 vols., ed. James H. Charlesworth (Garden City, NY: Doubleday, 1983), 1:615-52.

As "rewritten Scripture," Biblical Antiquities retells the biblical story from Adam to Saul's death. A pivotal reference to Adam appears in a re-counting of God's instruction to Noah after the flood. Speaking of "paradise," God said,

> This is the place concerning which I taught the first man, saying, "If you do not transgress what I have commanded you, all things will be subject to you." But that man transgressed my ways and was persuaded by his wife; and she was deceived by the serpent. And then death was ordained for the generations of men. (13:8)[21]

Speaking of Moses, whom Biblical Antiquities regards as the author of Genesis, the text continues, "And the LORD continued to show him the ways of paradise and said to him, 'These are the ways that men have lost by not walking in them, because they sinned against me'" (13:9). Thus, Adam's sin results in human mortality and God's people are themselves responsible for their own obedience (or disobedience).

Read side by side, these texts agree in two important respects: (1) Adam's (and/or Eve's) disobedience results in their own mortality and in the mortality of all who would come after them, and (2) human beings remain responsible for their own actions. When the question of sin's origin is mentioned, the answers differ. In the Life of Adam and Eve, the serpent gives Eve—and apparently the human family—the toxin of "craving" (that is, a heart bent toward evil). Similarly, in 4 Ezra, a characteristic feature of humanity is the "evil inclination," although its origins are unclear. This notion of an evil inclination is found in other Jewish texts as well. For example, countering any suggestion that God is the cause of sin, Sirach (second century BC) urges that God created humanity and left humans "to the power of their choices" (15:14); accordingly, sin arises from the exercise of volition in favor of evil rather than good, then from failing to control their cravings (ἐπιθυμία, epithymia; 5:2; 18:30; cf. 23:4-5)—but people have the native wherewithal to choose to follow God's commands and live faithfully (15:15). With formulations indebted to his Platonist sensibilities, Philo (first century AD) affirms that following God's instructions counters bodily

---

[21]English translations of Biblical Antiquities are taken from D. J. Harrington, "Pseudo-Philo: A New Translation and Introduction," in *The Old Testament Pseudepigrapha*, 2 vols., ed. James H. Charlesworth (Garden City, NY: Doubleday, 1983), 2:297-377.

pleasures and sets reason over irrational senses and excessive impulses (e.g., Special Laws 2:163). Similarly, 4 Maccabees aims to demonstrate that "godly thinking is supreme over emotions and desires" (1:1). In the Damascus Document, Qumran sectaries are instructed that they may choose what God loves and reject what God hates, "that you may walk perfectly in all His ways and not follow after the thoughts of the guilty inclination and after eyes of lust." In this case, though, the evil inclination is traced not to Adam and Eve, nor to the serpent, but to the "divine beings" or "Heavenly Watchers" of Genesis 6:1-6 (CD 2:15).[22] Throughout, however, humans remain free to choose the good, which is identified with God's instruction.

These brief comments on relevant Jewish texts are important primarily for the evidence they provide that, during the period within which the New Testament materials were being written, collected, and first interpreted, something like the traditional Christian doctrine of original sin was not influencing how Genesis 3 was being read, nor were Jewish readings of Genesis 3 giving rise to something like that doctrine. What about New Testament writers?

The letter of James. In James 1:2, the author counsels his audience to adopt a hopeful perspective in relation to the tests they experience: "My brothers and sisters, think of the various tests you encounter as occasions for joy."[23] After all, he continues, the testing of one's faith leads to its maturity and, indeed, to "the life God has promised to those who love him as their reward" (1:12). This raises the question of the source of testing, however, including the possible indictment against God as the cause of this testing. That Israel's Scriptures narrate God sending tests to his people (e.g., Gen 22:1) only presses the point.

As James responds in 1:13-18, we can see how his reflections have been guided by a reading of the early chapters of Genesis. That James works with Genesis is clear later in his letter, when he refers to "human beings made in God's likeness" (3:9; see Gen 1:26-27)—an important reference showing that, whatever the author's characterization of the human situation, they remain creatures in God's likeness. Closer to home, James refers in 1:17 to

---

[22]English translation in Geza Vermes, *The Complete Dead Sea Scrolls in English* (New York: Penguin, 1997), 128.

[23]Unless otherwise noted, I am following the Common English Bible.

"the Father, the creator of the heavenly lights," which recalls God's creative work in Genesis 1:3-5, 14-18. Similarly, James's claim that "every good gift" comes from God is reminiscent of repeated, divine affirmations of the goodness of creation (Gen 1:4, 10, 12, 18, 21, 25, 31). Moreover, the problem of testing has James reflecting on Genesis 3, even if he does not mention Adam and Eve by name. Working within the biblical tradition, he really has only three choices for identifying temptation's cause: God, Satan, or human beings. He flatly denies the first while emphasizing the third: "No one who is tested should say, 'God is tempting me!' This is because God is not tempted by any form of evil, nor does he tempt anyone. Everyone is tempted by their own cravings [ἐπιθυμία, *epithymia*]; they are lured away and enticed by them" (Jas 1:13-14). As Wesley observed in his comments on James, "We are therefore to look for the cause of every sin, *in*, not *out of*, ourselves."[24] Although James does not mention the second choice (Satan) in this section of the letter, he elsewhere leaves room for diabolical, hellish influence (cf. 3:6, 14-16).

The conundrum rests on the two seemingly contradictory ways James uses the term πειρασμός (*peirasmos*; plural, *peirasmoi*). Typically translated as "tests" or "trials" in 1:2-4, *peirasmoi* are to be the occasion of joy. This is because "the testing of your faith produces endurance. Let this endurance complete its work so that you may be fully mature, complete, and lacking in nothing." Typically translated as "temptations" in 1:14-15, one's own cravings (*epithymia*) give rise to *peirasmoi*; then, "once those cravings conceive, they give birth to sin; and when sin grows up, it gives birth to death." The Venerable Bede (AD 673–735) helpfully saw the problem, even if his reading of James's response needs some adjustment. "Up to this point," Bede writes, "he has discussed temptations which we bear outwardly with the Lord's assent for the sake of being tested. Now he begins to treat those which we sustain inwardly at the devil's instigation or even at the persuasive frailty of our nature."[25] Bede's interpretation introduces the devil, whereas here James has pinpointed what we might call "the persuasive frailty of our nature." More seriously, Bede identifies the second set of temptations as those "we sustain

---

[24] Wesley, *Explanatory Notes upon the New Testament*, 857.
[25] Bede the Venerable, *Commentary on the Seven Catholic Epistles*, trans. Don David Hurst, Cistercian Studies Series 82 (Kalamazoo, MI: Cistercian, 1985), 13.

inwardly," although for James it is our cravings, not these temptations, that are inward.

The basic contrast James draws is grounded not in an external-internal dualism but rather in different human responses to the phenomena he associates with the term *peirasmos*. In the face of *peirasmoi*, standing firm leads to the life God promised (1:12), but allowing one's cravings to control one's life leads to sin and death (1:14-15). James, we might say, is nimble in his use of the term *peirasmos*—which, in the biblical tradition, can refer both to diabolical temptation (which obstructs human flourishing) and to divine testing (which perfects human life and deepens human flourishing). Should the common experiences of exilic wanderers (1:1)—the cancers of distress, conflict, derision, marginalization, and pressure to apostasy—be characterized as testing or as temptation? The answer is an internal one, pivoting on whether these Christ-followers master their sinful dispositions or are mastered by them.

The two ways offered to James's readers may initially appear to recall what we found earlier in our brief sketch of perspectives from four Second Temple Jewish writings. However, their diagnosis of the human situation was more optimistic than James's. Echoing Deuteronomy 30:19-20, we might say that, like them, James sets before his audience life and death; yet unlike them he does not simply urge that they choose life, say, by following the Lord's instruction. Rather, he recognizes the overwhelming power of craving (*epithymia*), the evil inclination, which requires a remedy more potent than self-control or reason. On the one hand, human cravings (or desires) "give birth to sin; and when sin grows up, it gives birth to death" (Jas 1:15). On the other hand, God wants or desires "to give us birth by his true word, and here is the result: we are like the first crop from the harvest of everything he created" (1:18). God's choice or desire contrasts with human desire or craving. One leads to life, the other to death. Craving is countered by God's "true word . . . the word planted deep inside you—the very word that is able to save you" (1:18, 21), assuming, of course, that Christ-followers actually put that word into practice (1:22-27).

For James, exilic life presents opportunity for human craving, which gives way to sin and death. Neither exilic life's challenges nor God is the problem. The problem is internal, not external, to the human person: human craving.

Human hearts bend toward doublemindedness, favoritism, wrong speaking, arrogance, selfish ambition, violence. This is the way of earthly wisdom (3:14-16). The solution, although external (that is, God's "true word"), must similarly be internalized; the divine word must be received and put into practice so that it permeates one's thinking, feeling, believing, and behaving.

Paul and sin. The locus classicus for the doctrine of original sin has long been Romans 5:12, but this is due to a translation error. Let me first provide my translation: "Just as through one human being sin came into the world, and death came through sin, so death has come to everyone, since everyone has sinned." Ground zero is the last phrase of the verse, ἐφ᾽ ᾧ πάντες ἥμαρτον (*eph' hō pantes hēmarton*), which I have translated "since everyone has sinned." The fourth-century commentator Ambrosiaster, whom Augustine followed, took this Greek phrase as a reference in Latin to humanity's having sinned *in quo* (in whom)—that is, in Adam—and this led to a theological anthropology according to which the human family sinned in Adam. Sharing in his sin, they also shared in his guilt.

In the Pauline letters, the prepositional phrase *eph' hō* appears on three other occasions—in 2 Corinthians 5:4, where Paul writes that we groan and are weighed down *because* (*eph' hō*) we do not want to be stripped naked; in Philippians 3:12, where Paul writes that he pursues perfection so that he might seize it *because* (*eph' hō*) Christ has seized him; and in Philippians 4:10, where Paul rejoices in the Lord because the Philippians had renewed their concern for him—"Of course [*eph' hō*] you were concerned, but lacked the opportunity to show it." Pauline usage elsewhere thus speaks against the translation adopted by Ambrosiaster and Augustine. Contemporary translations of Romans 5:12 regard it as a marker of cause: "because all [have] sinned" (e.g., Common English Bible, New American Bible [2011], New English Translation, New International Version [2011], New Revised Standard Version, New Jerusalem Bible)—a reading long favored among grammarians.[26]

---

[26]Cf., e.g., James Hope Moulton, *Prolegomena*, vol. 1 of *A Grammar of New Testament Greek*, ed. James Hope Moulton (Edinburgh: T. & T. Clark, 1908), 107: "in view of the fact that"; Friedrich Blass, Albert Debrunner, and Robert W. Funk, *A Greek Grammar of the New Testament and Other Early Christian Literature* (Chicago: University of Chicago Press, 1961) §235(2): "for the reason that, because"; C. F. D. Moule, *An Idiom Book of New Testament Greek*, 2nd ed. (Cambridge: Cambridge University Press, 1959), 50: "inasmuch as, because"; Daniel B. Wallace, *Greek Grammar*

Paul still affirms that "through one human being [Adam] sin came into the world," and it is worth asking how this is so. Only rarely in letters attributed to Paul do we find the phrase "forgiveness of sins" (Col 1:14; Eph 1:7 read "forgiveness for our failures"), and this suggests that Paul's concern lies less with individual acts of disobedience than we might otherwise have imagined. The creaturely image introduced in God's response to Cain in Genesis 4:7 is suggestive: "Sin will be waiting at the door ready to strike! It will entice you." This image moves us in the direction of the perspective on sin that Paul develops in Romans 5–7, where sin exercises agency, with its power over human beings portrayed like that of a master or king. Humans are "controlled by sin" (6:6), the aim of sin is to "rule your body, so that you do what it wants" (6:12), people present "parts of [their] body to sin, to be used as weapons to do wrong" (6:13), people present themselves as slaves to sin (6:16), and the baptized were formerly enslaved to sin but are now liberated from its dominion (6:17-18, 20, 22). Accordingly, sin's power cannot be countered through obedience to God's instruction, not because God's instruction is flawed but because sin's pull prevails over human efforts. At the same time, Paul writes that, through Adam and from Adam, sin entered the world, death ruled, many people died, judgment came, many people were made sinners, and sin ruled in death (5:12-21). Piecing together what Paul writes, we might therefore say that, because of Adam, sin as a hegemonic force was let loose in the world and that Adam's disobedience set in motion a chain of consequences, one sin leading to the next, not because sin is basic to the human condition but because Adam set the pattern for all humanity.

We might wish for more from Paul. If so, we should also remind ourselves that Paul's questions and concerns are not always ours. At the end of the day, here in Romans, Paul is not actually concerned with the question of sin's etiology; he is not formulating a doctrine of original sin. Rather, here in Romans, he wants to demonstrate the common identity of Jews and Gentiles before God. In this argument, sin functions to level the playing field: "All have sinned and fall short of God's glory" (3:23). Just as there is no distinction between Jew and Gentile, but all are subject to sin's reign, so there is no distinction between Jew and Gentile, but "God's righteousness

---

Beyond the Basics: An Exegetical Syntax of the New Testament (Grand Rapids, MI: Zondervan, 1996), 342-43: "because."

comes through the faithfulness of Jesus Christ for all who have faith in him" (3:22), for "all who call on the Lord's name will be saved" (10:12-13).[27]

What about Genesis 3? For the doctrine of original sin, Genesis 3 typically bears a good deal of theological weight. This is the story of "the fall," after all—the juncture in the biblical narrative at which "sin" is introduced, the demarcation of the tectonic shift from a paradisal to an exilic state, the point after which God must undertake a kind of rescue mission. Strangely, then, the word *fall* is never mentioned in this chapter, and we search this account in vain for the term *sin*. Moreover, this way of reading the biblical narrative overlooks the potential of identifying God's mission with creation itself, opting instead for the view that God's mission awaits human transgression before it can be set into motion. Stranger still, perhaps, the Old Testament has almost nothing to say about Adam and Eve or their disobedience. Biblical theologian Gary Anderson goes further: "If the transgression of Adam really does usher in the reign of sin and death from which the rest of the biblical odyssey will seek redress, why is Adam's sin and its consequences *never* mentioned until the writings of Paul?"[28] Not without good reason could Anderson write a book titled *Sin: A History* without a single reference to Genesis 3.[29] Indeed, when reading the chapters that immediately follow in Genesis, prior to the opening of the Abraham story in Genesis 12, the disobedience of Adam and Eve is simply the first in a succession of stories of human failure—Adam and Eve, Cain, the Nephilim, Babel—with the situation aptly summarized by the narrator in 6:5: "The LORD saw that humanity had become thoroughly evil on the earth and that every idea their minds thought up was always completely evil." To be sure, Genesis 1–11 demonstrates something like the viral spread of sin, but this speaks more to the relational and ubiquitous character of sin than to its etiology.

---

[27]Cf. Michael Wolter, *Paul: An Outline of His Theology*, trans. Robert L. Brawley (Waco, TX: Baylor University Press, 2015), 372-73.

[28]Gary A. Anderson, "Original Sin: The Fall of Humanity and the Golden Calf," in *Christian Doctrine and the Old Testament: Theology in the Service of Biblical Exegesis* (Grand Rapids, MI: Baker Academic, 2017), 59-60. In the Old Testament, Adam is mentioned only twice in connection with sin, with neither text carrying the significance allotted Genesis 3 by the doctrine of original sin: (1) Job wonders whether, like Adam, he has concealed his offense (Job 31:33; some translations refer to humanity rather than to Adam) and (2) speaking of God's people, Hosea writes, "Like Adam they broke the covenant" (Hos 6:7).

[29]Gary A. Anderson, *Sin: A History* (New Haven, CT: Yale University Press, 2009).

Anderson's question, quoted above, can be parsed into two—the first regarding what to make of Genesis 3, the other concerning why Paul read Genesis 3 as he did. We have already addressed the second question by reminding ourselves of the nature of Paul's argument in Romans. If Paul had been concerned to highlight Israel's sinful inclinations, he would have needed to look no further than the story of the golden calf (Ex 32), which, unlike Genesis 3, does function for the Old Testament as a kind of origin story for Israel's idolatry. Taking this path, though, he would not have been able to posit universal sin as the equalizer between Jew and Gentile. Israel may indeed be prone to sin, but this diagnosis is not exclusive to the Jews. An inclination to waywardness is characteristic of all peoples, as the theological anthropology of Genesis 3 shows.

What to make of Genesis 3 is another matter, and for this we take our point of departure from two observations. The first is that the narrative encompassing 2:4–3:24 does not actually follow the creation account constituting 1:1–2:4, at least not in terms of story time. Rather, these two accounts narrate a single story from two different viewpoints—the one more majestic, even liturgical, and the other more earthy, this worldly. The second concerns the nature of humanity. Whereas the first account has humanity being created in God's own image, so that humans are "like God" in significant ways, the second account has humanity seeking to be like God. Gordon McConville identifies as "the central issue in reading the two creation accounts together" this latter point—namely, "what it means to say that human beings are in any sense 'like God.'"[30]

Taking a circuitous route through recent Old Testament scholarship to get there, McConville offers a reading of Genesis 1–3 that suggests how the story of Adam and Eve might be read archetypically, along the lines of what we find in the history of their interpretation among Paul, James, and the writers of the Jewish texts previously noted. Reading the language of the *imago Dei* in terms of humanity's "presencing God" in the world God has created, McConville thus highlights God's blessing on humanity and humanity's vocation both to admire creation and to share in his vision and aim for it. If God's good creation was completed with the appearance of

---

[30]J. Gordon McConville, *Being Human in God's World: An Old Testament Theology of Humanity* (Grand Rapids, MI: Baker Academic, 2016), 39.

humanity, however, it was also disturbed by the presence of this new agency. Humans, he writes, are a destabilizing factor in God's world: "Genesis 1-3, therefore, depicts the human condition in its conflicted relation to good and evil, life and death," with "humans . . . entrusted with presencing God in the world yet . . . subject to a fatal misreading of what this means as subjective reality."[31] From this perspective, the life of human beings is deeply paradoxical, caught, as it were, between these two portraits: being like God and misconstruing the possibilities and limitations of God-likeness.

Genesis 1-3 provides little foundation for the traditional doctrine of original sin as this emerged in Augustine and was continued by his heirs. Neither does the Old Testament as a whole, nor the New Testament. Scripture does not refer to the fall of humanity, nor does it bear witness to the salvation-historical narrative that the notion of a fall presumes, nor does it speak of Adam's (and Eve's) sin as an inheritance, nor does it explore sin's (ultimate) etiology, nor does it posit sin and sin's guilt as integral to the human condition. Although the Jewish texts from the Second Temple period we surveyed countenance obedience to God's instructions as the corrective to sin (or to the inclination to sin), both James and Paul testify to a more radical view of sin that requires divine intervention if human beings are to be freed from sin's power and enabled to serve God. James's reflections on creation assure his audience that human craving, the evil inclination (and not God), stands behind temptation, sin, and death. Paul reflects on Adam both to mark the onset of the human journey into sin and to identify Adam as a kind of trailblazer whom all people, Gentile and Jew, have followed into sinfulness. Both Paul and James thus emphasize sin's corporate dimension and assume sin's heritability—not in the sense of passing sin down biologically but in the sense of pattern and influence.

ORIGINAL SIN?

Following his sketch of the growth of traditional notions of original sin, Veli-Matti Kärkkäinen lists associated beliefs requiring reconsideration: a problematic reading of Genesis 2-3, together with the idea that humanity originated with one couple who once lived in a perfect state of innocence

---

[31]McConville, *Being Human in God's World*, 41, 43.

and immortality; hereditary views of sin's transmission; universal human guilt and condemnation on account of the disobedience of the first couple; and the doctrine's overly individualistic account of sinfulness.[32] Because he regards the doctrine as inescapably implicated in such troublesome beliefs, Kärkkäinen rejects the language of original sin and develops his own account under the heading "the misery of humanity." This is a useful summary that indicates why traditional notions of original sin have been set aside in recent years.

Some aspects of the doctrine have been under scrutiny for a long time, perhaps none more controversial than how best to explain the transmission of original sin from one generation to the next. Wesley himself claimed that he knew only that original sin was passed on, not how (although he was not above speculating on this latter point too). Wesley rejected the traditional idea that humans inherited Adam's guilt and judgment. And Wesley held together the effects of original sin *and* the exercise of free will, with the capacity to respond faithfully to God's goodness enlivened through God's prevenient grace; this means that, for Wesley, humans are responsible for their own waywardness. Ultimately, we might say that the importance of the doctrine for Wesley resided in its soteriological significance since his real concern was affirming the universality of sin as the grounds on which he could then affirm the universality of need, of grace, and of hope of healing.

To these Wesleyan compass points we should add two other methodological considerations—namely, (1) the open arms with which he greeted the natural sciences, exhibited in his willingness to read Scripture alongside the "book of nature," and (2) the esteem with which he held the Bible. To some, these two starting points may seem paradoxical, but this is not how Wesley saw them. When confronted by a tension between accounts of God's revelation in the natural world and God's revelation in Scripture, he did not simply allow one to trump the other but rather opened himself to consider fresh interpretations that honored both. In a telling example, Wesley was aware that some educated people in his day questioned reports of Jesus's miracles of healing and exorcism. In a note on Jesus's commission to the disciples that they should "cast out devils" (Mt 10:8 AV), Wesley conceded

---

[32]Veli-Matti Kärkkäinen, *Creation and Humanity*, vol. 3 of *A Constructive Christian Theology for the Pluralistic World* (Grand Rapids, MI: Eerdmans, 2015), 395 (see 389-95).

that some said that diseases ascribed to the devil in the Gospels "have the very same symptoms with the natural diseases of lunacy, epilepsy, or convulsions," leading them to conclude "that the devil had no hand in them." Wesley continues,

> But it were well to stop and consider a little. Suppose God should allow an evil spirit to usurp the same power over a man's body as the man himself has naturally, and suppose him actually to exercise that power; could we conclude the devil had no hand therein, because his body was bent in the very same manner wherein the man himself bent it naturally?
>
> And suppose God gives an evil spirit a greater power to affect immediately the origin of the nerves in the brain, by irritating them to produce violent motions, or so relaxing them that they can produce little or no motion, still the symptoms will be those of over-tense nerves, as in madness, epilepsies, convulsions, or of relaxed nerves, as in paralytic cases. But could we conclude thence, that the devil had no hand in them?[33]

Phrases like "violent motions" and "over-tense [or relaxed] nerves" reveal Wesley's acquaintance with neurological theories emerging in the seventeenth and eighteenth centuries; more generally, we witness here his interest in taking seriously the importance of science for biblical interpretation. In this case, Wesley refused to choose between neural activity and the work of demons, or between God's two books, the book of Scripture and the book of nature.

Returning to the doctrine of original sin, Wesley had an avocational interest in the natural sciences, so it is worth asking how he might have responded to perspectives on human origins that developed over the past two hundred years. Evolutionary biology continues to rewrite the specifics of the human story, but even in its broad strokes this story stands in significant tension with some of the fundamentals of the traditional doctrine of original sin, including the idea that the human family can be traced back to a single couple and the possibility of dividing human history into two "eras" (before and after "the fall").[34]

How might Wesley have responded had he been confronted with what some presume is the last nail in the coffin of the doctrine of original sin,

---

[33]Wesley, *Explanatory Notes upon the New Testament*, 53.

evolutionary biology? Given his methodological commitments, we might more easily imagine his rethinking the doctrine than anticipate his outright rejection of either Scripture or science.

Taken together, these data and ruminations prove to be hospitable to a fall narrative, although not the one traditionally associated with the doctrine of original sin.[34] In this alternative account, we might imagine our early ancestors as creatures whose lives were not yet clouded by the haze of spiritual darkness or the muddle of decisions that eventually would envelop the human family as it turned away from God. They would nonetheless have been subject to innate tendencies to act toward their own benefit, whether harmful or helpful to others. These innate tendencies would not have been uniquely "human" qualities, since they would have been characteristic of animal life before and alongside the emergence of our human ancestors. However, they would have acquired a peculiarly moral dimension within communities of self-aware, self-conscious human ancestors among whom moral choices transcended instinctual behavior. Called to serve as agents of God's presence among the wider human family, as well as in relation to the cosmos, these ancestors were nonetheless subject to temptation and the desire to turn away from God's voice and were vulnerable to the perversions, violence, abuse, and self-centeredness bequeathed to them by means of their ancestors' modeling and patterns of interacting, familying, and socializing. Strikingly, however, these desires and perversions, this waywardness, does not write the last chapter of this alternative narrative, since our ancestors also engaged in a range of altruistic practices, including selfless behavior in the service of the most vulnerable. For Wesleyans, this is nothing other than what one might expect of a human family whose moral psychology has been invaded and enlivened by God's prevenient grace—not simply God's goodness made available to the righteous and the wicked but, indeed, God's goodness enabling faithful response to God's initiative. For Wesleyans, such persons are on a soteriological journey that could lead to new birth and to inward and outward holiness.

---

[34]Here I am indebted especially to Daryl P. Domning and Monika K. Hellwig, *Original Selfishness: Original Sin and Evil in the Light of Evolution* (Aldershot, UK: Ashgate, 2006); Kärkkäinen, *Creation and Humanity*, 387-411; and Anthony C. Thiselton, *Systematic Theology* (Grand Rapids, MI: Eerdmans, 2015), 155-56.

This narrative would be generous toward several elements associated with the doctrine of original sin—the emergence of sin as a pervasive quality of human experience, sin's personal and structural nature, and sin's character as a disease that permeates the human family relationally and contextually. It would also account for the plentiful evidence throughout history and across the globe that "man is very far gone from original righteousness, and of his own nature inclined to evil, and that continually" *and* for the plentiful evidence throughout history and across the globe of human beings behaving, as it were, against their nature, as agents of God's presence in the world.

4

An Eastern Orthodox View

ANDREW LOUTH

INTRODUCTION: THE ORTHODOX DILEMMA

One problem faced by Orthodox seeking to participate in almost any discussion of theological topics with fellow Christians of Western traditions is that the linguistic and conceptual geography appears strange. Terms are used that are difficult to translate into Greek, the originary language of Eastern Orthodoxy, something made even more difficult when one is considering the way in which these theological terms or concepts relate to one another. The theological terrain, mapped out by the concepts generally expressed (for the West) in Latin, often seems quite unfamiliar. To ask what the Orthodox make of original sin is to ask, first of all, for a translation of an unfamiliar concept into something recognizable on the terrain of Orthodox theology, shaped as it is by Greek terms and concepts. Of course, it was the other way round in the formative years of the church; then the terminology of theology was primarily Greek—one might indeed argue that the aboriginal language of the Christian church, once it realized its mission to the nations, is Greek; indeed, Latin was late to emerge.

So it was that Latin thinkers struggled to represent Greek terms and distinctions in Latin, something that was often very difficult. Latin theologians were aware of this: Augustine is quite conscious that the terminology of Greek trinitarian theology, involving the distinction between *hypostasis*, the word that came to be used for the members of the Trinity, and *ousia* ("being" or "essence") or *physis* ("nature"), used for the divine unity, was poorly expressed by the traditional language of Latin trinitarian theology, which distinguished between *persona* and *substantia*. Indeed, confusion was in danger of being further confounded by the fact that *substantia* in Latin, representing the unity of the Godhead, corresponded most closely to the Greek *hypostasis*, used in Greek theology to represent the three members of the Trinity: Father, Son, and Holy Spirit.

"Fall" and "original Sin": this sounds like something that all (or virtually all) Christians hold in common. However, even if the notion of the fall is something shared (and perhaps we shall see that even here there are significantly different nuances), original sin, as it came to be understood in Western theology, seems to be a development peculiar to the West. The term *original sin* (*peccatum originale*) belongs to a particular Western context; nor is it easy to translate into Greek. I suppose the most direct translation would be ἀρχικὴ ἁμαρτία, an expression, to my knowledge, never found in Greek, and not without reason, for it would suggest that sin (ἁμαρτία, *hamartia*) is itself a fundamental principle (ἀρχή, *archē*), which would be tantamount to Manichaeism, perhaps the most fundamental heresy of all to the Greek patristic mind. The term in Greek corresponding most closely to *peccatum originale* is προπατορικὴ ἁμαρτία, the sin of the forefathers or ancestral sin (first attested, according to Lampe, in the sixth or seventh century). Although this expression corresponds to something of the meaning of *peccatum originale*, there are significant differences, as we shall see.

TWO THEOLOGICAL TRAJECTORIES: FROM CREATION TO DEIFICATION, FROM FALL TO REDEMPTION

This might seem a very particular lexical matter, barely touching the real issues of broader import. And indeed there are broader issues: from my perspective—that of one who is now a priest of the Russian Orthodox Church but who until his midforties was an Anglican, who learned his theology in English and Scottish universities, and who served as an Anglican priest for nearly twenty years, teaching theology for most of them—it seems to me that fall and original sin is Western theology's starting point. It is concerned with understanding how the human, fallen away from God and communion with him, is redeemed by God's becoming human and living a human life, finally offering himself to death on the cross, and through the resurrection unleashing on humankind a new, abundant life that transcends death. Even as I write that, I find myself wondering, Am I not reading too much of what I have experienced in Orthodoxy back into my perception of Western theology, fearful of caricaturing the West by emphasizing perceived differences? For I almost wrote that Western theology is concerned with the process by which fallen humanity is redeemed from sin by the death of Christ on the cross. But to suggest that, say, Lutheranism narrows the focus of theology in such a way does not, to my mind, survive listening to the *Et resurrexit* from Bach's B Minor Mass (even though the end of his St. Matthew Passion might seem to suggest that all is complete with the death of Christ).

If my perception has anything in it, then what I am suggesting is that Western theology tends to narrow the focus of theology to the redemption of fallen humanity. How does Orthodoxy escape from this? Fundamentally, I suggest, by beginning in the beginning—with creation, and within that creation the fashioning of the human. That is, we begin with the fashioning of the human in the image of God—a fashioning with the purpose, on God's part, of bringing the human into a likeness with him that is so profound, so deep, that to grasp the fullness of what is understood, Greek Christianity came to use the language of deification, θέωσις (*theōsis*). The purpose of the incarnation is not just to overthrow the entailment of Adam's sin but to bring humankind to share in the divine life, to make humans "participants of the divine nature" (2 Pet 1:4). As St. Athanasius famously put it, the Word of God "became human, so that the human might become God."[1]

It is not that Western theology fails to see that the fruits of the incarnation go beyond redemption, beyond canceling out the effects of the fall; in several ways there are strands in Western theology that recognize this gladly. Perhaps the most famous expression of this occurs in the Easter Proclamation, the *Praeconium Paschale*, sung at the Easter Vigil in the Western rite and dating back to the fourth century, perhaps even composed by St. Ambrose: *O felix culpa, quae talem ac tantum meruit habere Redemptorem*—"O happy fault, which merited to have such and so great a Redeemer." This has led some to speak of a "fortunate fall," as the fall prepared the way for a redemption (and a Redeemer) much greater than the

---

[1]Athanasius, *On the Incarnation*, 54.

fall itself. As Gerhart Ladner put it, "The reform of man then is both return to Paradise and attainment of a much higher state which, even if Adam had not sinned, he could never have reached by himself."[2] A similar notion is found in the Middle English poem "Adam lay ibowndyn" (Adam lay bound):

> Ne hadde the appil take ben, the appil take ben,
> Ne hadd never our Lady a ben hevene qwen.[3]

Nevertheless, it seems to me that what we find here is not a perception of the inadequacy of the fall-redemption movement but the exploration of some surprising consequences of just this movement. What we find in the Greek patristic tradition—and in modern Orthodox theologians such as Sergii Bulgakov, Vladimir Lossky, and Dumitru Stăniloae—is a sense that the lesser theological arc (as we might call it) of fall-redemption is subordinate to the greater theological arc of creation-deification. As Vladimir Lossky put it,

> Considered from the point of view of our fallen state, the aim of the divine dispensation can be termed salvation or redemption. This is the negative aspect of our ultimate goal, which is considered from the perspective of our sin. Considered from the point of view of the ultimate vocation of created beings, the aim of the divine dispensation can be termed deification. This is the positive definition of the same mystery, which must be accomplished in each human person in the Church and which will be fully revealed in the age to come, when, after having finally reunited all things in Christ, God will become all in all.[4]

Another way of putting this contrast between East and West would be to say that the West comes to see the engagement between God and the human as concerned with sin and its consequences: original sin expresses the consequences of the fall, which renders humanity guilty before God and subject to a just punishment. In contrast, the East sees sin in a cosmic light:

---

[2]Gerhart B. Ladner, *The Idea of Reform: Its Impact on Christian Thought and Action in the Age of the Fathers* (Cambridge, MA: Harvard University Press, 1959), 146. I think Ladner misunderstands the Greek Fathers in attributing to them no more than a return to Paradise.
[3]See, e.g., *The Oxford Book of English Verse*, ed. Christopher Ricks (Oxford: Oxford University Press, 1999), 12 ["Never had the apple taken been, the apple taken been / Never had our Lady been made heavenly queen"].
[4]From his essay "Redemption and Deification," in *In the Image and Likeness of God* (Crestwood, NY: St. Vladimir's Seminary Press, 1974), 110.

sin has disordered God's creation and through this disorder or disharmony introduced corruption and death. Fallen humanity is seen not primarily as guilty, bound up in Adam's sin, but rather subject to death and to the corruption or decay, of which death is consequence and seal. Death rather than guilt haunts fallen humankind: it threatens with meaninglessness all human endeavor and is an aspect of, and a symbol of, the way in which the fallen world—and not just fallen humanity—is out of joint, shot through with shafts of unmeaning.

ATHANASIUS AND ANSELM

Something of the contrast I am seeking to make can be illustrated by comparing classic theological texts from the Greek East and the Latin West: Athanasius's *De Incarnatione* and Anselm's *Cur Deus homo*. Both thinkers consider why Adam's repentance would not suffice to cancel his sin. Athanasius introduces the question thus:

> What should God have done? Demand repentance from humans for their transgression? For one might say that this was fitting for God, that as they had become subject to corruption by the transgression, so by repentance they might return to incorruption. But repentance would not have saved God's honour, for he would still have remained untruthful unless humans were in the power of death. Repentance gives no exemption from the consequences of nature, but merely looses sin. If, therefore, there had only been sin and not its consequence of corruption, repentance would have been very well.[5]

The same thought—that repentance might suffice—occurs to Boso, Anselm's interlocutor in *Cur Deus homo*: "I would think that I cancel this sin by a single moment of repentance," to which Anselm replies, *Nondum considerasti, quanti ponderis sit peccatum* (You have not yet considered how heavy a weight is sin).[6] With these words we come to the axial notion of Anselm's treatise: his conviction of the profound gravity of sin. We need to consider, Anselm insists, the way in which disobedience to God—sin—is proportionate to the honor of God and therefore of infinite gravity: the infinite

---

[5]Athanasius, *De Incarnatione 7*, in Athanasius, *Contra Gentes and De Incarnatione*, ed. and trans. Robert W. Thomson (Oxford: Clarendon Press, 1971), p. 151 (modified).

[6]*Cur Deus homo*, 21 (Janet Fairweather's translation in *Anselm of Canterbury: The Major Works*, ed. Brian Davies and G. R. Evans, Oxford World's Classics [Oxford: Oxford University Press, 1998]), 305.

recompense required is beyond the means of a finite creature. This sounds, superficially, very like Athanasius, who, at least in the translation I have used, also speaks of God's honor. The Greek, however, is τὸ εὔλογον τὸ πρὸς τὸν Θεὸν (*to eulogon to pros ton Theon*), which perhaps means more precisely "the fairness that belongs to God"; Athanasius's point is that, having said that eating of the fruit of the tree in the garden would lead to death, God cannot go back on his word: his "fairness" here is a matter of his truthfulness. But this is not all Athanasius has to say; he also asserts that repentance would only have affected Adam's standing before God and would not have dealt with the consequences of his sin, which was the unleashing of corruption and death—φθορά (*phthora*) and θάνατος (*thanatos*)—on the cosmos.

Anselm's concern is solely with the standing of finite human beings before their infinite Creator. Athanasius's concern is more ontological; it is not a matter of the standing of humans before God but rather the consequences for the way things are following Adam's sin. And this is because of the cosmic dimension of Athanasius's thought and that of the Greek fathers generally. In a much-quoted passage from one of St. Gregory the Theologian's homilies (really two, for he seems to quote it, or at least repeat it, himself!), the creation of humankind is described in these terms:

> The Word and Fashioner created the human, a living being, one from both, that is, from the invisible nature and the visible; and taking the body from already pre-existing matter, he put into it from himself breath, which the scriptural account knows to be the intellectual soul and image of God, [making] a kind of second cosmos, little in great, standing upon the earth, another angel, worshipper of mixed parts, contemplator of the visible creation, initiate of the intelligible, ruler of those on earth, ruled over from above, earthly and heavenly, passing away and immortal, visible and intelligible, a mean between greatness and lowliness, the same both spirit and flesh, spirit on account of grace, flesh on account of pride, the one that he might abide and glorify his benefactor, the other that he might suffer and when suffering remember and be chastened, aspiring to greatness, a living being guided in this life and transformed in the age to come, and—the furthest reach of mystery—by his inclination to God deified.[7]

---

[7]Gregory of Nazianzus, *Homily* 38. 11: in Grégoire de Nazianze, *Discours 38–41*, ed. Claudio More-schino, Sources Chrétiennes 358 (Paris: Cerf, 1990), 124–26 (*Hom*. 38. 11 recurs in more or less the

The human being was created like this, in the image of God and mediating between the spiritual and the material, in order to fulfill a role in the cosmos. Thus, humanity's turning away from God was not just a personal matter; it had cosmic consequences, for humanity could no longer fulfill its role as a little cosmos (μικρὸς κόσμος; *mikros kosmos*) in whom the manifold variety of the created order was held together. As a result of humanity's failure to fulfill its role as the bond of the cosmos (σύνδεσμος τοῦ κόσμου; *sundesmos tou kosmou*), the cosmos itself was visited by corruption and death.

Anselm, following a long tradition in the West, conceives of the primal sin and its consequences in terms of the fracturing of humanity's relationship with God; Athanasius, and following him the Greek patristic tradition in general, conceives of the primal sin and its consequences in cosmic terms—the primal sin has not only fractured the relationship between the human being and God but also disturbed the harmony of God's creation, leaving it to corruption and death. One can, I think, go a step further. For Anselm the primal sin leaves humankind in a state of guilt before God that finite humanity cannot assuage, for it requires an infinite recompense; for Athanasius the primal sin unleashes corruption and death that affects the whole of the cosmos—the human is powerless in the face of this disaster; he lives in a ruined cosmos that is disintegrating and at odds with itself.

ANCESTRAL SIN VERSUS ORIGINAL SIN

We have seen that the Greek East came to speak of "ancestral sin" (προπατορικὴ ἁμαρτία; *propatorikē hamartia*), whereas the Latin West, after Augustine and the Pelagian controversy, came to use the term *original sin* (*peccatum originale*). What is the difference?

To answer this, we perhaps need to step back and ask more about the context in which they function. The fall and original sin can be seen as elements of an attempt, in Milton's words, to "assert eternal providence, And justify the ways of God to men": to solve, to use a Greek term, the problem of theodicy. As such they are part of an intellectual strategy of fundamentally Platonic inspiration; the evils of this world are not the responsibility of

---

same form in *Hom.* 45. 7 [Patrologia Graeca. Edited by Jacques-Paul Migne. 162 vols. Paris, 1857-1886. 36. 632AB]).

the gods (or God) but the result of human choice (or at any rate the free choice of rational creatures): αἰτία ἑλομένου· θεὸς ἀναίτιος (*aitia helomenou; theos anaitios*; "the blame lies with the one who chooses; god is blameless"; *Rep.* 10:617D). Essays in theodicy are found throughout the Christian tradition, both East and West. St. Basil the Great's sermon "That God Is Not the Author of Evil" is perhaps the most influential essay in theodicy in the Greek East; in modern Orthodox theology, both Bulgakov and his (younger) mentor Florensky struggled with theodicy. Bulgakov's first considerable work of Christian theology, *Unfading Light* (1917), and Florensky's most famous work, *The Pillar and Ground of the Truth* (1914), are both essays in theodicy (the latter explicitly so described). In the context of such theodicy, the fall and original sin are parts of an attempt to account for the fact that God's creation, presumed to be free from evil as it left God's hands, is manifestly free from evil no longer: the entry of evil is called the fall, and the principal, inescapable way by which evil has spread throughout the world is dubbed original sin.

We might start from this point: the world is manifestly evil; all of us human beings are caught up, inexorably it seems, in the spread of evil. John Donne, in his poem "A Hymne to God the Father," captures well the way in which we are caught in a web of sin (which is more than our personal sin) that we further:

Wilt thou forgive that sinne where I begunne,
  Which is my sin, though it were done before?
Wilt thou forgive those sinnes through which I runne,
  And doe them still: though still I doe deplore? . . .

Wilt thou forgive that sinne by which I'have wonne
  Others to sinne? and, made my sinne their doore?
Wilt thou forgive that sinne which I did shunne
  A yeare, or two: but wallow'd in, a score? . . .

At the end of each of these stanzas, there is a refrain:

When thou hast done, though hast not done,
  For, I have more.[8]

---

[8]John Donne, *The Divine Poems of John Donne*, ed. Helen Gardner (Oxford: Clarendon Press, 1978), 51.

What is it we are accounting for? The notion of ancestral sin sees each of us humans as born into a web of sin: the accumulated sin, and its consequences, of all our forefathers and foremothers. We find ourselves, inexorably, participating in this web of sin, for the sins of all the generations that have gone before us have eroded whatever examples of good conduct we might have had; furthermore, they have lent the weight of tradition to standards of behavior that we may be able to recognize as inadequate or pernicious but which nevertheless enjoy the power of custom. This way of looking at our ingrained tendency to sin does not deprive human beings of free will, although to seek goodness under such conditions is a matter of unremitting struggle. Furthermore, it needs to be remembered that, in the Orthodox tradition, the notion of ancestral sin is complemented by the realization that we live in a cosmos that is disrupted, out of joint, without the mediating role of the human as image of God, microcosm, and mediator.

Those who endorse original sin find this analysis inadequate: it seems to leave open the possibility (even if totally exceptional) of someone living a blameless life. Pelagius seems to have thought it possible to live such a life, or at least he thought it possible—even required—to live a life free from sin after having received forgiveness of sin through the grace of (adult) baptism. For Augustine, such a position bore no relation to reality—indeed, he considered it blasphemous. For him, we are each guilty of a sin we did not personally commit: the sin of Adam in which we are in some way seminally implicated. The logic of this position grew out of Augustine's opposition to Pelagius; the power of his concept of original sin was enhanced by his analysis of the fallen human condition, both in his *Confessions* and, more profoundly, if that is possible, in his *Enarrationes in Psalmos*. Take, for example, this passage from his homily on Psalm 100 (Ps 101 in the Hebrew enumeration):

> For at the present, while you do not see my heart and I do not see yours, it is night. You sought I do not know what from someone. You did not get it; you thought yourself despised, but maybe you were not despised; for you do not see the heart—and suddenly you blaspheme. In the night pardon is to be given you when you go astray. Someone loves you, I do not know who, and you think that he hates you; or he hates you, and you think that he loves

you; but whatever it is, it is night. Do not fear, trust in Christ; in him grasp the day.[9]

Here we find Augustine exploring the darkness of the human condition, a darkness made by our separation each from one another, enclosed as we are in the solitude of our hearts, which are inaccessible one to another. This sense of the darkness of the human condition and the frailty of the human will lies behind his notion of original sin, but here Augustine, as pastor and preacher, does not systematize his insight. That is what he does—in the controversy with Pelagius and his supporters—when he traces the cause of the moral darkness we inhabit back to our complicity in the primal sin of Adam, "that sinne where I begunne, Which is my sinne, though it were done before," in Donne's words. This sense of our identity with Adam and his sin is a profound insight, and later we shall see other ways of developing it. But Augustine wants to nail it; it is not enough for it to be a matter of the influence of Adam and his successors, of an accumulation of sins committed in the past and their influence—our complicity with Adam's sin is such that we share in his guilt and thus stand before God as guilty, with no defense. *Omnes enim fuimus in illo uno, quando omnes fuimus ille unus*—"In that one man were we all, when we were all that one man."[10] It must be ontological, concerned with the way things are, with the way we are, not just a matter of influence and example.

For Augustine the solution is the notion of original sin: the sin of Adam passed on to all his descendants or heirs by some kind of inheritance—not just of frailty or some taint of disease but the inheritance by which we are born guilty before God, deserving punishment. For Athanasius, I have argued, the weight of this ontological complicity in the effects of sin is borne by the cosmic disaster that Adam's sin has caused, because by sinning and severing his link with God, the cosmic role of the human has been broken and the cosmos reduced to a ruined state. This sense of the cosmic seems not to have been available to Augustine; it has been replaced by his profound

---

[9]Augustine, *En. in Ps. 100* 12.20–6, in Eligius Dekkers and Johannes Fraipont, eds., CCSL 39 (Turnholti: Brepols, 1956).

[10]Augustine, *De Civitate Dei* 13.14, quoted by Gerald Bonner, *Saint Augustine of Hippo: Life and Controversies* (London: SCM Press, 1963), 371. For Bonner's account of original sin, on which I have relied, see pp. 370-82.

sense of interiority, something explored at length and in a variety of ways in his *Confessions*. The ontological belongs to the realm of the interior: the ontological entailment of Adam's sin must belong to this realm, too, so original sin is seen as passed down from parents to children—ultimately from Adam—as some aboriginal taint, and more seriously, because it must be personally owned, as an original guilt.

The key text that Augustine cites in support of his theory of human seminal identity with Adam in his primal sin is, famously, Romans 5:12, in the Latin read by Augustine as follows: *Propterea sicut per unum hominem in hunc mundum peccatum intravit, et per peccatum mors, et ita in omnes homines transivit, in quo omnes peccaverunt* (Therefore, just as through one man sin has entered into this world, and through sin death, so also it [death] passed to all men, in that all sinned). However, Augustine read those last four words differently. He took *in quo* to refer back to *unum hominem* (that is, Adam) and understood the text to say, "in whom [that is, Adam] all sinned." A good deal of comment on this passage and Augustine's use of it seems to me to be wide of the mark. It is not a matter of the Latin being a mistranslation of the Greek; it is a perfectly acceptable translation of the Greek, a fairly literal rendering customary with the Scriptures (Jerome, aware of the dangers of excessive literalism, did not change this in his Vulgate version). The Greek for those last four words is ἐφ' ᾧ πάντες ἥμαρτον (*eph' hō pantes hēmaton*). The Latin translator has done his best. With its limited vocabulary compared with Greek, Latin often has to make do with *in* for two Greek words, ἐν (*en*) and ἐπί (*epi*), which mean "in" and "on," respectively, hence the translation is rendered *in quo*. In the Greek original of Romans 5:12, it is generally agreed that ἐφ' ᾧ (*eph' hō*) is a contraction of ἐπὶ τούτῳ ὅτι (*epi toutō hoti*), meaning "for this reason that" or simply "because" (reading *eph' hō* as "because," as Meyendorff remarks,[11] is the norm among the Greek and Byzantine fathers who, after all, spoke Greek as their

---

[11]John Meyendorff, *Byzantine Theology: Historical Trends and Doctrinal Themes* (London: Mowbrays, 1975), 144. Meyendorff also speaks of a Greek understanding of the phrase as "because of death all sinned" (on analogy with 1 Cor 15:22 ["in Adam all die"]), but he gives no reference to any Greek father, and I cannot see how taking ᾧ as masculine, and thus referring back to θάνατος, can justify the rendering "because of death," as it is ἐφ' ᾧ that can mean "because," not ἐπί on its own. The idea that the consequences of the fall are seen rather in death (and corruption) than in sin is, however, characteristic of the Greek fathers, as we have seen.

native language), and this meaning can be represented in both Latin and English as "in that," *in quo.*

Augustine's taking *in quo* to refer back to *unum hominem* may be bizarre, but it is Augustine's misconstrual of the Latin, not a mistake in the Latin translation (the same translation of ἐφ' ᾧ by *in quo* occurs in Phil 3:12, which can hardly be taken in any other way than "in that," "because"). Nor should it be said that Augustine *based* his understanding of original sin on this text. The reasons for his embracing this doctrine are as outlined above. To explain, against the Pelagians (or his understanding of them), why all stand before God guilty, even newborn babies, by a tight understanding of human seminal identity with Adam, Romans 5:12 is read by Augustine in the way he does because it seems to express in lapidary fashion this sense of human identity with Adam in his sin.

Is the Augustinian doctrine of original sin to be regarded as a more radical version of the Greek doctrine of ancestral sin? I do not think Augustine ever considers this question, as the doctrine of original sin serves the purpose of rendering all guilty before God, and therefore in need of grace that must be given freely (*gratia gratis data*), that is essentially undeserved, and that no one can elicit or attract. Anselm, however, does consider this question, and it is clear to him that the sins of our ancestors after Adam are irrelevant; it is our complicity in Adam's primal sin that leaves us guilty, deprived of justice: "I see no reason why the sins of our near ancestors should be imputed to the souls of their descendants. . . . This destitution of justice has descended to all infants from Adam, in whom human nature had robbed itself of that justice."[12] The effect of this is to exalt Adam's primal sin to a state of splendid isolation. Adam was created perfect; he sinned and brought about the fall; in the incarnation Christ redeemed fallen humanity—theology is confined to what, from the point of view of Orthodox theology, I have called the "lesser arc," stretching from fall to redemption.

ORTHODOX UNDERSTANDING OF THE FALL AND ITS CONSEQUENCES

I would argue that the Orthodox failure to endorse the Western doctrine of original sin has an impact on the understanding of the fall, for fallen

---

[12] *On Virginal Conception and Original Sin*, 24 (Camilla McNab's translation in *Anselm of Canterbury: The Major Works*, 383).

humanity is not to be regarded as bereft of God, utterly severed from him, in the way that original sin seems to suggest. From a Western point of view, several aspects of Orthodox faith and practice must seem strange. For example, on the Sunday before Christmas we commemorate "all the righteous who were pleasing to God, from Adam down to Joseph the Betrothed of the Mother of God." Adam—one of the righteous who were pleasing to God? Is he not the one who made the whole human race *displeasing* to God? But the Christian calendar is the calendar of the church of the resurrection; it surveys everything from the perspective of the resurrection. The icon called *The Resurrection* (Ἡ Ἀνάστασις; *Hē Anastasis*) does not depict Christ emerging from the tomb but rather Christ, having broken down the gates of hades, leading out all those confined there, beginning with Adam and Eve, whom he grasps by their wrists. Adam is seen as one saved by Christ's victory over death on the cross—indeed, the first to be released from hades. Elsewhere in the Orthodox church year, called the Sunday of the Last Judgment or Forgiveness Sunday, we commemorate Adam on the Sunday immediately before the beginning of Lent (which begins in the Eastern calendar on a Monday). He is commemorated as repentant, sitting outside the closed gates of Paradise, weeping for his sins. In the *doxastikon* at Vespers for the Sunday we sing,

> Adam sat before Paradise and, lamenting his own nakedness, he bewailed: Alas! I was persuaded by evil deceit and led astray, and removed far from glory. Alas, in my simplicity I was stripped naked and am now in want. O Paradise, no longer shall I enjoy your delights; no longer shall I behold the Lord, my God and Maker; to the earth I shall go back, from which I was taken. O merciful and compassionate One, I cry to you: Have mercy on one who has fallen.

Adam has sinned and been expelled from Paradise, but he is depicted as repentant, begging God for mercy. He is the archetypal sinner but also archetypal in his repentance. For we do not contemplate Adam as an "other" but rather see ourselves in him: sinful, fallen, and repentant. The *apolytikion* for the Forefeast of the Feast of the Nativity runs:

> Bethlehem prepare; Eden is opened for all. Make ready Ephratha, because the tree of life has flowered in the Cave from the Virgin. For her womb has

been revealed as the spiritual Paradise in which is the plant of life; eating from it we shall live; we shall not die like Adam. Christ is born to raise up his image which before was fallen.

Orthodoxy approaches the fall and its consequences through an array of images, mostly biblical, not through some narrowly defined doctrine. And these images are understood from the perspective of the cross, the Tree of Life. Adam is not so much the primal ancestor as our contemporary in the risen Christ. In the Catholic Church the only saints from the Old Testament commemorated in the calendar are (oddly) the Seven Maccabean Martyrs on August 1st (or were, until they were removed from the universal calendar in 1969, after the Second Vatican Council). In the Orthodox calendar, many saints from the Old Testament are commemorated: the patriarchs, Moses, and many of the prophets. The celebration of some of these is very popular, particularly the prophet Elijah. This seems to me to betoken a rather different attitude to postlapsarian history, not virtually bereft of God but a world in which God never left himself without witnesses. In the Anaphora (or Eucharistic Prayer) of St. John Chrysostom (the one most commonly used) we read, "You brought us out of non-existence into being, and when we had fallen you raised us up again, and left nothing undone until you had brought us up to heaven and granted us your Kingdom that is to come."

In the Anaphora of St. Basil the Great, the creation of humankind and the fall and its consequences are dealt with at greater length:

> For you fashioned a man by taking dust from the earth, and honoured him, O God, with your own image. You placed him in the Paradise of delight and promised him immortal life and the enjoyment of eternal blessings, if he kept your commandments.
>
> But when he disobeyed you, the true God, who had created him, and when he had been led astray by the deception of the serpent and been slain by his own transgressions, you banished him by your just judgment, O God, from Paradise into this world, and returned him to the earth, from which he had been taken; while, in your Christ, you established for him the salvation which comes through rebirth. For you did not utterly turn away from your creature, O Good One, nor forget the work of your hands, but you visited us in divers manners through your compassionate mercy. You sent Prophets,

you performed deeds of power through your saints, who have been well-pleasing to you in every generation; you spoke to us through the mouth of your servants, the Prophets, announcing to us beforehand the salvation that was to come; you gave the law as a help; you appointed Angels as guardians.

But when the fulness of time had come, you spoke to us through your Son, through whom you had also made the ages.[13]

We certainly live in a fallen world, yet it is still created and still bears the marks of its maker. The world cannot be considered as bereft of God, nor can humankind; however far we might have become estranged from God, he will not abandon us. The whole created order is still created for union with him, and the human is still destined for the role God intended. Christ, the God-man, has restored this possibility to humankind; he has not fulfilled it, leaving nothing for humanity to do. Rather, in fulfilling the human role, he has made it possible for humans to find their true destiny, which consists in sharing in the divine life (deification) and in this way being enabled to fulfill the essentially human role as priest of creation, enabling the whole created order to function in its true theophanic mode.

MODERN ORTHODOX THOUGHT ON "ORIGINAL SIN": STĂNILOAE AND BULGAKOV

Modern Orthodox theologians treat this in different ways, but they are one in seeing the question of the fall and sin in the broader and deeper context of creation and deification. Let me briefly take examples from two thinkers, each often claimed to be the greatest Orthodox theologian of the last century: the Russian Sergii Bulgakov and the Romanian Dumitru Stăniloae. In the section of his *Orthodox Dogmatic Theology* (in English, *The Experience of God*) called "The World: Creation and Deification," Stăniloae, so far as I can tell, does not use the expression *original sin* at all, as such, although he has a great deal to say about the state of fallen humankind. Toward the end of this section there is a chapter called "The Fall" in the English translation (the Romanian original is a little more long-winded: "The Fall of the Forefathers and Its Consequences"). Here, in the course of an elaborate analysis of the fallen human condition, there is constant stress on the fact

---

[13]Translation of both liturgical texts by the late Archimandrite Ephrem Lash (slightly modified in the case of the Anaphora of St. Basil).

that the world, including humankind, is created by God and that, however disastrous the effects of the fall, its status as created is still manifest. So Stăniloae says,

> We note that in the Orthodox view, the world after the Fall did not take on a totally and fatally opaque image, nor was human knowledge wholly restricted to a knowledge that conformed to an opaque, untransparent image of the world. Humans can penetrate this opacity in part by means of another kind of knowledge, and indeed, they often manage to do this, but they cannot wholly overcome this opacity and the knowledge that conforms to it.[14]

And a little later,

> Creation has been ordered in such a way that it might be a place where God can speak and work with this purpose in view and where we can respond to God through our words and deeds and set out on the path of this developing communion that God has willed. Creation fulfils its purpose when it continues to remain a place wherein our human being can undertake a dialogue of some sort with God. For this dialogue can grow only if the world continues to be seen, at least in part, as a gift of God, a foundation for the higher gift of salvation through which the world will be delivered from its present state of corruptibility and death.[15]

Bulgakov shares this sense that, as created, the world cannot but speak of God—that, touched by the creative hand of God, it is by nature holy. Bulgakov expressed this in terms of his doctrine of Sophia, the wisdom of God (a doctrine certainly controversial among Orthodox). In contrast to Stăniloae, Bulgakov seems to speak directly of "original sin." So, at least, is the impression given by the English translation of his great dogmatic trilogy, *On Godmanhood*.[16] However, the Russian term behind the translator's *original sin* is первородный грех (*pervorodny grekh*), which is not exactly original sin but rather "sin of the first-born" or perhaps less clumsily "primal sin." Bulgakov knows well and discusses the Augustinian notion of

---

[14]Dumitru Stăniloae, *The Experience of God: Orthodox Dogmatic Theology* (Brookline, MA: Holy Cross Orthodox Press, 2000), 2:172.
[15]Stăniloae, 172-73.
[16]The English translation by Boris Jakim is published in three volumes: *The Bride of the Lamb* (Grand Rapids, MI: Eerdmans, 2002); *The Comforter* (Grand Rapids, MI: Eerdmans, 2004); and *The Lamb of God* (Grand Rapids, MI: Eerdmans, 2008).

peccatum originale, but his notion, though complex, is clearly different. It is, however, central and important: "The dogma of original [primal] sin is the axis of Christian soteriology. This dogma states that, with the fall of Adam in Eden, the whole human race fell, to be redeemed later by the new Adam, Christ."[17]

As we have seen, Augustine wants to assert something more precise than simply seeing Adam as the origin of the fallen state of humankind: fallen humanity is guilty before God, its relationship to God is severed, its being in the image of God is either lost or totally nugatory. This is not what Bulgakov maintains. As with Stăniloae, he believes that although the human is at odds with itself and has lost a sense of the cosmos as speaking unambiguously of God (it has become opaque, as Stăniloae puts it), something remains of the link between God and humankind that is manifest in the *imago Dei*.

> In his fall, man did not destroy the image of God in himself but only obscured and weakened it. Likewise nature, when it was separated from man, did not lose its sophianic foundation or content, although its countenance was obscured. The world remains God's creation, and the eternal word about creation, "let there be," always resounds in the world. Thus, even after the fall of the world, the Divine Sophia shines in it as God's revelation. . . .
>
> And this Wisdom of God, manifested in the world, is the inexhaustible source of the inspiration of life with the nature that elevates, purifies, strengthens, and saves fallen man. This is the everyday experience of all of human kind. And this sophianicity of the world is the foundation of that which, in nature, is its proper, although impersonal, life: "hypostaticity" that does not know its hypostasis but is capable of being hypostatized and of living its life for man, for angels, and for God. Man is only dimly conscious of this life of rocks, minerals, water, and plants, although he does have access to some extent to the life of the animal world. This life of nature, being the Glory of God in creation, sings this glory to the Creator, and the heavens truly confess this glory.[18]

Bulgakov's earliest reflections on original sin in relation to Western theology are to be found in the first of his works written in the West: *The*

---

[17]Bulgakov, *Bride of the Lamb*, 164.
[18]Bulgakov, *Lamb of God*, 152-53.

Burning Bush: On the Orthodox Veneration of the Mother of God.[19] In this book he explores Roman Catholic Mariology, especially the doctrine of the immaculate conception, arguing that it is based on a fundamental theological error.[20] This critique, however, is principally directed not so much at the tenets of such Mariology as at the notion of *natura pura* (pure nature) that was important for the kind of scholasticism Bulgakov had encountered in the West. Pure nature was conceived of as nature in itself, untouched by God and without any orientation toward him. The notion had evolved in the context of the Western understanding of nature and grace that originated with Augustine. The idea of pure nature evolved to preserve the notion of the gratuity of grace to prevent any idea that nature, in itself, could naturally evoke the response of God's grace.

Bulgakov's fundamental objection to this, though he expresses it mainly in an allusive rather than a direct way, is that the idea of nature untouched by God is fundamentally un-Christian. If nature is created by God, it is profoundly touched by God, and however distorted it might be as a result of the fall, it exists because it is created by God—and therefore touched by God and loved by him. So we find Bulgakov saying that in Paradise "God comes in the cool of the day to talk with man, as with a friend, and that 'conversation' was no *donum superadditum* in relation to his uncorrupt nature, but on the contrary, that conversation was something quite normal."[21] It seems to me that his rejection of the notion of *natura pura* is the other side of his profound sense, already mentioned, of the holiness of nature. It is a fault in us, because of the fall, to experience nature bereft of God; the reality is quite other. It is also worth remarking that this very notion of *natura pura* was the focus of Henri de Lubac's attack on the debased scholastic theology of his day in his *Surnaturel* (1946), for which he was disciplined. It is striking how far Bulgakov's criticisms anticipate those of de Lubac, which seem now more acceptable by modern Roman Catholic theology.[22]

---

[19]See Sergii Bulgakov, *The Burning Bush: On the Orthodox Veneration of the Mother of God*, trans. Thomas Allan Smith (Grand Rapids, MI: Eerdmans, 2009), although I have used the Russian original: Protierei Sergii Bulgakov, *Kupina Neopalimaya* (Paris, 1927).

[20]For what follows see my article "Father Sergii Bulgakov on the Mother of God," *St Vladimir's Theological Quarterly* 49 (2005): 145-64, of which I have made extensive use.

[21]Bulgakov, *Kupina Neopalimaya*, 25.

[22]On this issue, see John Milbank, *The Suspended Middle: Henri de Lubac and the Debate Concerning the Supernatural* (London: SCM Press, 2005).

THE SINLESSNESS OF MARY?

For his understanding of the Mother of God, Bulgakov looks to "the liturgy inspired by the Spirit and the prayerful life of dogma." So it is to the liturgical texts that he turns:

> In its innumerable services devoted to the Mother of God, the Holy Orthodox Church teaches firmly and clearly about the complete sinlessness of Mary in her birth, her holy childhood and adolescence, in the Annunciation, in the Birth of her Son, and in her whole life.[23]

He begins by setting out some principles in relation to the question of the Virgin Mother's sinlessness:

1. Mary is without personal sin.
2. She is, however, not "alone without sin," for that is Christ's prerogative, and further, unlike Christ she suffered natural death, the consequences of Adam's original sin.
3. She calls God her Savior in the Magnificat.

It follows from these three principles that Mary's state is not a sinless natural state but rather the result of her personal attitude to sin, her personal overcoming of sin. Bulgakov goes on to ponder how one subject to original sin, as Mary was, could nevertheless be sinless. He begins from the doctrine of human creation in God's image; from this it follows that the soul has a trihypostatic form or image and that humankind was to exercise the role of microcosm in relation to the cosmos. This he sets against the Western scholastic notion of humanity as *natura pura* and argues that there is no creation without God and no human life without a relationship with God, either affirmed or repudiated. So he characterized the fall of humanity in these terms:

> Thus first-formed man in his nature is neither mortal nor given to concupiscence [both characteristics of humanity as *natura pura*], since in his nature is included a blessed life with God and in God, since he was made in the world for God. But, as a created being, he knows in himself created weakness and the instability of nature; in him is hidden the possibility of Life not only in

---

[23]Bulgakov, *Kupina Neopalimaya*, 13, followed by a footnote listing liturgical texts, running to four and a half pages.

God and for God, but in the world and for the world. And in original sin man extinguishes in himself the blessed life, cuts off direct blessed communication, "conversation," with God, he commits murder against himself, changing from being man the friend of God and becoming a natural being immersed in the cosmos.[24]

Thus the fall affects humankind's relationship with God and our relationship with the world. On the one hand, fallen humanity has lost contact with God by repudiating him, the source of its life, and in doing this it disrupts the harmony of soul and body, which opens up the possibility of death—the separation of soul and body. On the other hand, humankind appears to itself to be the ontological center of the world and begins to lord it over the cosmos, to exploit the cosmos for its own ends. So Bulgakov can say that, as a result of the fall, "the world falls into *orphanhood*, it no longer has anyone to look after it. The fall into sin is manifest as a cosmic catastrophe, 'cursing' the earth."[25] Another consequence of the fall that Bulgakov dwells on, which is a consequence of the disruption of the harmony between soul and body, humankind and the cosmos, is the creation of a polarity between individual and nature. On the one hand, there are isolated, self-oriented individuals, and on the other, "a certain ontological solidarity of the whole human race, substantiated by its metaphysical unity, not that 'everyone is guilty before all' (as Dostoevsky said), but everyone—and each one—doing things for himself and his own sake, does them in and for the whole of humanity,"[26] with disastrous consequences. Individuals, then, are trapped in the necessary universality of their nature.

This polarity of individual and nature brought about by the fall has destroyed God's original creation, the human hypostasis *freely* summing up in itself as microcosm the manifold variety of the cosmos, which hypostasis Bulgakov calls "the centre of love, a wise ray of Sophia."[27] It is, however, into this state of polarity that we are born, and each of us realizes for himself or herself the original sin of Adam by his or her personal sin. Moreover, it was into this state of polarity that the Mother of God was born, and if she is

---

[24]Bulgakov, *Kupina Neopalimaya*, 26-27.
[25]Bulgakov, *Kupina Neopalimaya*, 27.
[26]Bulgakov, *Kupina Neopalimaya*, 31-32.
[27]Bulgakov, *Kupina Neopalimaya*, 35.

sinless, then she is sinless in this fallen world. The personal sinlessness of the Mother of God is therefore different from the sinless state that Eve lost:

> First-formed Eve did not know the weight of original sin, which pressed on the Virgin Mary herself. For this reason, too, the primal sinlessness of Eve remained untested, unjustified, free; in contrast the freedom from personal sin of the Virgin Mary manifests not only her personal victory (*podvig*), but also the victory of the whole Old Testament Church, of all the forefathers and fathers in God, that is the summit of the ascent of the whole human race, the lily of paradise that blossomed on the tree of humanity.[28]

The sinlessness of the Mother of God is not some natural state miraculously created by God (as Bulgakov understood the Roman Catholic doctrine of the immaculate conception to assert) but rather the result of God's providence, working through the history of salvation and culminating in her personal faithfulness. It is such that Mary is glorified by all Christians.

The doctrine of the immaculate conception of the Virgin Mary is not accepted by the Orthodox Church. Yet, as Meyendorff has observed, "the Mariological piety of the Byzantines would probably have led them to accept the definition of the dogma of the Immaculate Conception of Mary as it was defined in 1854, *if only* they had shared the Western doctrine of original sin."[29] But exempting the Virgin Mary from original sin must mean exempting her from the effects of the fall; in some way she is separated from the rest of the human race, who experience the fallen state through participating in (being guilty of) original sin. Paintings of the immaculate conception, depicting the Virgin Mary raised up, on the moon, or borne up by *putti*, seem to emphasize her separation from the rest of humanity. In contrast, the Byzantine liturgical texts (though plundered for the Latin feast of the immaculate conception) see Mary as part of humanity, in particular the crowning glory of the Old Testament church, emphasizing that she belongs to the Jewish race: "the beauty of Jacob," as she is called in one of the liturgical hymns. Although confessed as sinless, the Virgin is not regarded as exempt from the consequences of sin. She lived in a sinful world and suffered temptation as we all do. For if her Son was "tested as we are,

---

[28]Bulgakov, *Kupina Neopalimaya*, 70.
[29]Meyendorff, *Byzantine Theology*, 148.

yet without sin" (Heb 4:15), she can hardly have been exempt. Maybe here original sin meets its reductio ad adsurdum, if it means that the Savior and his mother must be considered free from original sin, for they were not exempt from the struggle against temptation that is part of the fallen human lot.

CONCLUSION

In another context the "dogma of original sin" has been invoked. I refer to the several mentions of "the dogma of Original Sin" in *Speculations* by T. E. Hulme,[30] "who also had an aptitude for theology," as T. S. Eliot remarked.[31] These mentions, all very similar in tone, regard the dogma of original sin as characteristic of what he calls the classical view of humankind, in contrast to the romantic view (introduced, he maintained, by the Renaissance). It was embraced by modernists such as Ezra Pound and T. S. Eliot as an element in their rejection of Romanticism. Hulme himself expresses the difference between these two views in these terms:

> Put shortly, these are the two views, then. One, that man is intrinsically good, spoilt by circumstance; and the other that he is intrinsically limited, but disciplined by order and tradition to something fairly decent. To the one part man's nature is like a well, to the other like a bucket. The view which regards man as a well, a reservoir full of possibilities, I call the romantic; the one which regards him as a very finite and fixed creature, I call the classical.[32]

Hulme wrote this just before or during the First World War (in which he was killed in 1917); one can see the attraction it had to the modernists. I would suggest, however, that the truth Hulme wants to affirm is better served not by the dogma (as he called it) of original sin but by the sense conveyed by the view of humankind as created by God and destined for deification. For humans understood in this way are regarded as made for a lofty destiny that they have denied themselves in their pursuit of making themselves rather than finding themselves in communion with their Creator.

---

[30]T. E. Hulme, *Speculations: Essays on Humanism and the Philosophy of Art*, ed. Herbert Read, 2nd ed. (London: Routledge and Kegan Paul, 1936).
[31]T. S. Eliot, *The Use of Poetry and the Use of Criticism*, 2nd ed.(London: Faber and Faber, 1964), 149.
[32]Hulme, *Speculations*, 117.

Original sin, primal sin, ancestral sin: all speak of a destiny lost or denied by human sin, either that sin committed by all Adam's descendants in the first forefather, or the accumulation of sin over the ages, or both. As I have argued, the fundamental difference between East and West lies in two factors: first, the conviction that God's creation remains his and cannot be fundamentally overthrown by creaturely error or rebellion, and second, the view, maintained more firmly in the East, that humankind was created in and for the cosmos and that humanity's fall involves the cosmos, which thus loses its coherence that depends on the human role as microcosm and mediator. It is the recovery of the cosmic, I would argue, that both reveals the true gravity of human sin, as the desertion of the place in the cosmos God intended for humankind, and preserves a confident conviction that God is God rather than some superior being entangled in the fate of the cosmos of which he is the source.

There is another rarely used expression in English to denote original or primal sin (*OED* gives no other example in this sense). In the poem on the life of the Virgin Mary, written by the nonjuring bishop Thomas Ken in retirement after being deposed from the see of Bath and Wells (a poem more easily found in a hymnbook than in a collection of poetry), one of the stanzas runs,

> As Eve when she her fontal sin reviewed,
> Wept for herself and all she should include,
> Blest Mary with man's Saviour in embrace,
> Joyed for herself and for all human race.[33]

"Fontal sin": "original" sin in the sense of the sin that comes from the source or fount of humankind, and fontal in the sense of the sin taken away by the baptismal font, not just looking backward to the origin but forward to participation in the death and resurrection of Christ in baptism, setting out on the path of discipleship that leads to union with God and deification.

---

[33] *The English Hymnal* (London: Oxford University Press, 1915), no. 217.

5

A Reconceived View

TATHA WILEY

THE NEED FOR RECONCEIVING ORIGINAL SIN

The Christian doctrine of original sin has fallen on hard times. To many people, it seems to parse the human condition in outdated categories that make little sense in our contemporary scientific worldview. It seems rooted in a mythical story. Its classic interpretation does not fit well with current biblical scholarship. And it has been articulated in ways that seem to deny the goodness of human sexuality and even of being human.

Yet, contrary to much of the world, which has dismissed the doctrine and moved on, I believe that the doctrine retains relevance and potential for our day. But it has undergone a crisis of meaning. Fundamentally it is at odds with how contemporary science and scholarship understand our universe, human life, development, and culture. For nearly two hundred years, our world has been described as "evolutionary."[1] Christian theology has had ample time to adjust to this world, but some Christians think it an insult to God to reconceive the mysteries that the doctrine points to. Instead they insist on living in a fictional world.

Of course, there are many, even conflicting, reasons for this theological situation. Rooted in Enlightenment critiques of religion, modern secular thinkers have framed the discussion about God, sin, and salvation in terms of scientific credibility. They offer reasons for disbelief—for instance, that "God" is a projection of some aspect of the human (Ludwig

---

[1]See, e.g., the work of John Haught, especially his *God After Darwin: A Theology of Evolution* (Boulder, CO: Westview, 2000).

Feuerbach).[2] The idea of original sin, including its biblical warrant, seems incongruous to many of our contemporaries. They dismiss the Genesis story as an account of human origins—although often we find that contemporary atheists and scientists know the Bible only through a fundamentalist reading of it and are unaware of historical criticism. Yet their basic point is sound: that the Genesis story, employed by Christians as the factual, historical, biblical ground of original sin, can hardly bear the weight that Christians have put on it.

Because it is a lynchpin of our Christian understandings of Christ and redemption, an outmoded conception of original sin can threaten contemporary reception of the whole Christian message. The form of the doctrine accepted by the Council of Carthage (411–418 CE)[3] was largely Augustine's formulation of original sin—itself built on centuries of evolving thought—and other key doctrines came to be explained by it:

- Ecclesiology: Why the church? *To take away the stain of original sin.*

- Sacraments: Why baptism? *To mediate Christ's forgiveness and reconcile the baptized to God.*

- Soteriology: Why Christ? *Christ forgives Adam's sin, which we inherited at birth.*

This traditional concept of sin and atonement requires a historical Adam and an actual sin. But the New Testament certainly is not limited in its soteriological options, and it is only since the fifth century that this one doctrine dictated the answers to all the questions.[4]

---

[2]I offer a fuller discussion of the fate of the concept of sin in modernity in Tatha Wiley, *Original Sin: Origins, Developments, Contemporary Meanings* (Mahwah, NJ: Paulist Press, 2002), 103-26.

[3]The council took Augustine as their theological authority, affirming, among other things, that Adam had been given the gift of original justice but had lost that gift with sin. The council inferred an inherited sin from the church's long tradition of infant baptism. The council repudiated Pelagian optimism about the natural goodness of human nature and the human ability to avoid sin. Instead, with the help of Augustine's traducianism, the council affirmed that human beings have Adam's sin at birth. All are sinful and in need of salvation. The Council of Orange (529) affirmed Augustine's views on original sin but rejected the extremism that his thought evoked—for example, that human freedom had been completely destroyed. With Orange, patristic debates about original sin ended. The doctrine became pivotal within the whole constellation of Christian doctrinal commitments.

[4]Biblical scholars challenge us to reappropriate the meaning of redemption in real social transformation. Walter Wink writes that "the study of Jesus has recovered the social and political referent of Jesus' preaching," concluding that "the gospel is not a message of personal salvation from the world, but a message of a world transfigured right down to its basic structures." Walter Wink, *Engaging the*

Of paramount importance for the doctrine of original sin was the historicity of Adam and Eve. The assumption about their historicity as sole progenitors of all humanity held by the patristic theologians can no longer be maintained in light of modern empirical sciences and modern history. Literary critics, too, including biblical scholars, shifted from classifying the Genesis narrative of human origins as history to seeing it as myth.

Yet the church has often resisted modern science, historiography, and literary criticism. Pius IX convoked the first Vatican Council primarily to define papal infallibility as a dogma (that is, as an affirmation that must be believed). It was an antimodern council, attacking modernity for its liberalism, rationalism, and materialism. Along the way, the attending bishops addressed the value and criteria of scientific truth in relation to faith. They set a high hurdle for science while displaying a complete misunderstanding of it: *To be true, scientific conclusions must conform to church doctrine.*[5] By contrast, the chief value in modern empirical science is verification by a return to the data (Is this hypothesis true?), so the council's demand engendered deep conflict between scientific and religious worldviews.

By the time of the Second Vatican Council (1962–1965), the independence of scientific inquiry—and the independence of the universe itself—was affirmed, and the demand that scientific conclusions support church dogma was dropped. *Gaudium et Spes*, "The Pastoral Constitution on the Church in the Modern World,"[6] one of Vatican II's most important documents, specifically addressed the transition of scientific understanding from a static to a dynamic worldview: "For by the very circumstance of their having been created, all things are endowed with their own stability, truth, goodness, proper laws and order" (#36).

Even today, not all Christian denominations have reconciled themselves with modern science, and very few have done what is needed with regard to

---

Powers (Minneapolis: Fortress Press, 1992), 51. Wink contrasts the reign of Rome as a domination system with Jesus' vision of the reign of God as an *alternative* system, a domination-free order (107-37).
[5]This was especially true of the accounts of human origins and original sin. Cf. Ludwig Ott, *Fundamentals of Catholic Dogma*, ed. James Canon Bastible (St. Louis, MO: B. Herder Book Company, 1962; originally published in German in 1955). Ott writes, "Since Adam's sin is the basis of the dogma of Original Sin and Redemption the historical accuracy of the [biblical] account as regards the essential facts may not be impugned. According to a decision of the Biblical Commission in 1909, the literal historical sense is not to be doubted in regard to the following facts." (106).
[6]Walter M. Abbott, SJ, *The Documents of Vatican II* (New York: Guild Press, 1966), 183-308.

original sin. Often preachers and others simply do not talk about original sin. Very few see how original sin is intertwined with other beliefs and controls the meaning of those beliefs. It seems that there is nothing more to be said about this doctrine today. But what original sin crucially sought to explain is the mystery of sin and evil and how they can be partially understood in the framework of Christian belief. Given that our worldview is so different from the ancient one, we need to start from a different place in our search for an explanation of this deep and perennial mystery of our lives and our faith.

UNDERSTANDING EVOLUTION AND
THE EVOLUTION OF UNDERSTANDING

This essay proposes a reconceptualization or reframing of this vital doctrine. For this explanation, I draw on the work of noted theologian and philosopher Bernard J. F. Lonergan, SJ (1904–1984).[7] In particular, Lonergan offers an understanding of history and a contemporary anthropology that are fruitful for reconceiving the mystery of sin and evil. About the development of knowledge, Lonergan writes,

> For human concepts and human courses of action are products and expressions of acts of understanding; and as understanding develops over time, such development is cumulative, and each cumulative development responds to the human and environmental conditions of its place and time.[8]

We live in a post-Darwinian world. That reality has radically changed the way we view the universe. We think in terms of millions or billions of years now instead of generations or even centuries. We cannot make the same assumptions we once did. Evolution has influenced all aspects of culture. The scientific insight that we have evolved from the same watery origins, for example, has prompted us to question and purge our cultures of their inherited racism. But while there has been a strong scientific consensus about evolution, there has been much religious resistance to it.[9] Some Christians

---

[7]I am especially indebted to him for an understanding of human knowing in its development, structure, differences as common sense and theoretical, interferences, and so on. Of primary importance in his work are two major books: *Insight: A Study of Human Understanding* (New York: Philosophical Library, 1957); and *Method in Theology* (New York: Herder & Herder, 1972).
[8]Lonergan, *Method in Theology*, 30.
[9]See Tatha Wiley, *Creationism and the Conflict over Evolution*, Cascade Companions (Eugene, OR: Wipf & Stock, 2008).

act as if they think this evolutionary world is a surprise for God instead of a discovery by us. If we do not believe this kind of world exists in God's mind, does that not mean *we* are the unbelievers? And if God is God, there can be no surprises. God's understanding is unrestricted. This bears repeating. God understands everything there is to be understood.

In contrast, our human understanding is restricted. There are always further questions and more to be understood. As Lonergan says above, our understanding is cumulative and develops over time. One important change is from conceiving of things as "out there" or "in here" to how they are in themselves. When questions no longer ask about "things in relation to me" but rather ask about "things in relation to themselves," a differentiation of consciousness occurs that takes us from the realm of common sense to that of theory. For original sin, this occurred in the appropriation of Augustine's framework into a systematic framework in the Middle Ages. I argue that a further differentiation is now needed for original sin, from systematizing the traditional concepts to grounding our apprehension of our root sin in the categories of consciousness. We need to analyze the problem of sin and evil by way of transcendental method—that is, through categories directly verifiable in our own experience and the structures of human consciousness. This will be the shift from theory to interiority.

We cannot take any human explanations, including doctrinal ones, for granted as permanent. We once had a comfortable view of the world we thought was not just true but reality itself—creation, fall, redemption, judgment: how could it be otherwise?—that now seems, in crucial ways, irreconcilable with how we understand reality today.

Some still think, with Genesis 1, that creation occurred in seven days.[10] If a "day" in the biblical account is not twenty-four hours, they will say, then maybe each day stands for a million days or a billion years. Anything to keep the creation story somehow reconcilable with the insights of modern science and to be able to think that the Bible was right all along. We cherish the Genesis story as the narrative underpinning of the account of original sin made famous by Augustine. But explanations are time-bound. No matter

---

[10]It is interesting to note that, in his work finished in 415, *On the Literal Meaning of Genesis: A Commentary in Twelve Books*, Augustine dismissed the idea that God actually created the world in the six days depicted in the Genesis narrative.

the conceptual formulations, they are not the mystery itself. When they no longer make sense of the reality we experience and are no longer found compelling, they have to be changed. The real world, Lonergan writes, is what is to be known through the totality of true judgments.[11] Scientists give theologians knowledge of the actual universe. When the scientific context changes, our understanding of doctrines changes too. As Lonergan says, "For doctrines have meaning within contexts, the on-going discovery of mind changes the contexts, and so, if the doctrines are to retain their meaning within the new contexts, they have to be recast."[12] *Recast*, not simply rewritten. We have to find a new starting point, new terms and relations, for our explanation to be compelling for a new context.

But there is a further consideration: our doctrinal formulations must comport not only with our scientific worldview but also with what we today understand to be authentic values. Many theologians have authentically appropriated a doctrine with unauthentic elements—counterpositions, in Lonergan's terms. Augustine never did deal with Pelagius's question about how sin, which is an event of wrongdoing of some sort, can be transmitted biologically. Nor did he ever have to address the way in which he associated marital sex with lust, effectively making sexual relations sinful. Then, by maintaining Genesis 2–3 as his foundational story, Augustine elevated Eve's punishment—that she was subject to her husband's rule—into a divine mandate for female submission and an expression of God's own will for women. The church stood firmly behind not just the subordination of women but the whole patriarchal structure of both family and state for nearly two thousand years. Finally, the doctrine has ensured that access to salvation was restricted to those baptized in the Roman Catholic Church—meaning that no other religious body can offer its adherents salvific hope. These unauthentic consequences of the traditional conception of original sin impugn its theological validity and its pastoral appropriateness.

In the following brief sketch, we will explore the idea of our root sin, review the classic doctrine, and examine the role of systematic meaning and

---

[11]Bernard J. F. Lonergan, "Insight: Preface to a Discussion," ch. 10 in *Collection*, 2nd ed., ed. Frederick E. Crowe and Robert M. Doran (Toronto: University of Toronto Press, 1993), 158.

[12]Lonergan, *Method in Theology*, 305; cf. p. 28.

theory before turning to the world of interiority and Lonergan's account of the problem of sin and evil as a basis for reconceiving "original sin."

OUR ROOT SIN

What do we mean fundamentally by *sin?* What is our root sin?

The biblical writers' efforts to understand sin were many, and they used numerous terms for sin—for example, sin as missing the mark, sin as rebellion, or sin as lawlessness. In Genesis 3, sin is a violation of superiority and authority. It is disobedience of a superior's command. The point is that the command is to be followed no matter what, whether it makes sense or not, whether it seems important or not. This is an individualistic notion of sin. It cannot accommodate the social meaning of sin.

Genesis 2–3, the story of Adam and Eve, is a symbolic narrative of creation and the first sin. The symbolic apprehension of the world and of being human is expressed in myth. Scholars date the narrative in the tenth century BCE. The first creation story in Genesis 1, dated in the sixth century BCE, is also myth, more poetry than narrative. They are both prescientific and prephilosophical apprehensions of creation and the roots of sin and evil.[13] The language and thought are ordinary, what Lonergan calls the undifferentiated mode of consciousness, or common sense.

The prophet Amos did look at things through a social lens. He was concerned about the exploitation and oppression of the poor by the rich. His remarks are biting, calling elite women "you cows . . . who oppress the poor, who crush the needy" (4:1). He says they would "sell the righteous for silver, and the needy for a pair of sandals" (2:6). In Amos, sin is injustice. God is known through justice.

The New Testament also employs many concepts of sin, including the Gospel of John's novel understanding of sin—namely, unbelief in Jesus. But it is Paul who puts his finger on what is perhaps our root sin. Scholars have

---

[13]Much of the church has accepted Genesis 1, the seven-day creation story, as symbolic. But that has not been the case with Genesis 2:1-3. This despite the scholarly consensus that the Genesis text contains no equivalent to what later is called original sin, nor even a "fall" as such. See, authoritatively, Claus Westermann, *Genesis 1–11: A Continental Commentary* (Minneapolis: Fortress Press, 1994), 247-48, 275-76, 278. Of course, it is disingenuous of theologians to acknowledge the symbolic character of Genesis 1–3 while still basing their whole understanding of original sin on them through such categories as *pre-* and *postlapsarian.*

long concluded that Paul did not have any notion of inherited sin, which is a strictly postbiblical idea.[14] Yet he knew that even the most routine of our experiences is complex, and if we are to understand why we do evil, insight into this experience is crucial:

> I do not understand my own actions. For I do not do what I want, but I do the very thing I hate. Now if I do what I do not want, I agree that the law is good. But in fact it is no longer I that do it, but sin that dwells within me. For I know that nothing good dwells within me, that is, in my flesh. I can will what is right, but I cannot do it. For I do not do the good I want, but the evil I do not want is what I do. Now if I do what I do not want, it is no longer I that do it, but sin that dwells within me. (Rom 7:15-20)

Rather, Paul thinks of the "root sin" as *privilege*. In a passage that scholars believe is a fragment from a baptismal ceremony,[15] he declares, "There is no longer Jew or Greek, there is no longer slave or free, there is no longer male and female; for all of you are one in Christ Jesus" (Gal 3:28).

The women and men who were joining Paul's communities would have said this during baptism. (They were not revolutionaries but perhaps were more radical than we have heretofore thought.) What would a world without ideologies of superiority—without religious exclusivism, slaveholding, and male privilege—be like? Without going into detail, we can say that Paul's convictions about sin were existential, communal, and eschatological.[16]

Religious judgments, though, are ambiguous. Some express genuine insights into the human good and sin; others subvert the good by ideologies of various sorts. This is true even in the Bible.[17] As we have said, Eve's punishment, that her husband would "rule over her," reinforced in God's name the male privilege and patriarchy that had already existed for centuries. Similarly, another text, from a deutero-Pauline letter, is remarkable for,

---

[14]See, e.g., Robert Jewett, "Romans," in *The Cambridge Companion to St. Paul*, ed. James D. G. Dunn (Cambridge: Cambridge University Press, 2003), 91-104. "This is the purpose of the Adam/Christ comparison; not to develop a new 'doctrine' of original sin but to show how the new 'reign' of grace and righteousness extends its influence over 'all people' (5:17, 21)" (96).

[15]Hans-Dieter Betz, *Galatians*, Hermeneia (Philadelphia: Fortress Press, 1979), 197.

[16]See the characterization of Paul's communities in Tatha Wiley, *Paul and the Gentile Women: Reframing Galatians* (New York: Continuum, 2005).

[17]I have addressed the problem of how to deal with unauthentic aspects of revelatory texts in "Canon and Conscience: A Feminist Perspective," *Word and World* 29, no. 4 (Fall 2009): 357-66.

among other things, its betrayal of the most characteristic conviction of the apostle Paul—justification by faith:

> I permit no woman to teach or to have authority over a man; she is to keep silent. For Adam was formed first, then Eve; and Adam was not deceived, but the woman was deceived and became a transgressor. Yet she will be saved through childbearing, provided they continue in faith and love and holiness, with modesty. (1 Tim 2:12-15)

Is the author *describing* reality or what he *wishes* were so? Either way, the author of 1 Timothy is part of the reappropriation of male privilege in early Christianity.[18] The Pauline communities were noted for their involvement of women in leadership (cf. Rom 16). In addition to his reversal on salvation, the author makes the surprising assertion that Eve sinned but Adam did not. In the Genesis story, each violates the divine command—she actively, he passively. Instead of through their faith, women are saved, this author maintains, through their acquiescence in their biological role in reproduction, which the culture lays out as their proper function.

With biblical scholarship behind us, we can say with confidence that the Bible contains many, even competing, notions of sin; that biblical accounts of sin are largely symbolic and metaphorical; that neither the Hebrew Bible nor the New Testament contains what we would call a developed doctrine of original sin; and that any use of the biblical narratives in a theological construction of sin must also employ a hermeneutics of suspicion about its historical value and ideological elements.

THE WORLD OF THEORY

An example: The doctrine of God and creation. In relation to sin, the turn toward theory came with the development of the concept of original sin. I would like to introduce that development first by noting another, closely related turn toward theory, in the development of the Christian doctrine of God. I will link these remarks with evolution because it has been such a problem for both our understanding of creation and of original sin.

---

[18]For an effort to sort out authentic and unauthentic elements in the Pauline and deutero-Pauline letters, see my *Encountering Paul: Understanding the Man and His Message*, Come and See Series (Lanham, MD: Rowman & Littlefield, 2010).

In conceiving God as creator, the patristic writers started not with the details of the creation stories but with the judgment most obvious in Genesis 1: that there is an ultimate source for everything that is. Over several centuries and in conversation with ancient philosophy, through "faith seeking understanding," they sought the intelligibility of this judgment. The exigence to understand raised further questions, so they introduced technical terms to express their thinking when the more metaphorical terms no longer sufficed.

When they began to conceive of God theologically as spirit rather than as matter, the turn toward theoretical meaning had been made.

The church fathers and the medieval theologians made the further transition—a transition of *mind*—from imaging and imagining God to explaining God (or as Thomas would say, explaining what God is not), with the help of philosophical categories. God is the *efficient cause* of the universe. God brings the universe into being with all the secondary causes within the universe. In such a theoretical context, "creation" refers to *a relation of dependence*, not to an event in the past, as is portrayed in the symbolic narrative. Creation is not about God making things. As Lonergan writes, "Only absolute being is the sufficient ground for the production of being."[19]

Indeed, for Thomas Aquinas, "creator" is the fundamental meaning of God. It means that all things stand in a relationship of absolute dependence on God. This relation is not "out there" but intrinsic to creatures. Existence is contingent. Created beings *have* being, while God *is* being. God gives existence to what was not.

To talk about creation and its ultimate source, premodern theologians explored the concept of causality. Why does the explanation of an infinite regression of causes not work? What is the evidence? We can have the image (somewhat) of causes extending into the distance, but that does not explain the universe nor satisfy our desire to understand. The data of the universe are contingent. Things do not cause themselves.

But we can go beyond images to posit a *relation* between a contingent universe and its cause. For it to be cause of the whole, it would have to be an uncaused (or absolute) cause, distinct from the universe. We can affirm,

---

[19]Bernard J. F. Lonergan, "On God and Secondary Causes," in Crowe and Doran, *Collection*, 56.

even if we cannot *imagine*, an uncaused cause. "God knows all things in God's own essence," as Lonergan explains:

> I would affirm that *world-order is prior to finite nature*, that God sees in his essence, first of all, the series of all possible world-orders each of which is complete down to its least historical detail, then only consequently inasmuch as natures, their properties, exigences, and so on.[20]

He continues,

> Coherently with this position I would say that the finite nature is the derivative possibility, that it is *what it is because of the world-order* and that the world is what it is, not at all because of finite natures, but because of divine wisdom and goodness.[21]

When we understand the doctrine of creation in this way, the alleged contradiction of creation and evolution disappears.[22] Are they opposed to one another? If one's idea of creation is Genesis 1, then yes, they must be alternatives. But if one shares the consensus of the scientific community at large that the evidence for evolution is "overwhelming," then Genesis 1 and evolution must be truths on completely different planes. One is a symbolic apprehension, the other a scientific apprehension of the origins of the universe and of human beings. They should not be compared, nor do they represent two alternatives from which we must choose.

In fact, Genesis 1 is not even explaining creation. Nor is the Big Bang explaining creation. The Big Bang is about development. In Christian understanding, creation is not a myth, nor is it a historical event, nor is it a scientific theory. As we have stressed, creation is the *relation* between finite and infinite reality. It accounts for *being* (all that is). As creator, God gives *existenc*e (that is, actual being of each thing in time) to the universe. God wills an evolutionary world order in its entirety. World order is ontologically prior to *things*. God did not create things one way and then evolution arose and took over. It bears repeating: there are no surprises for God.

---

[20]Bernard J. F. Lonergan, "The Natural Desire to See God," in Crowe and Doran, *Collection*, 85.
[21]Lonergan, "Natural Desire to See God," 88.
[22]See Lonergan, "Natural Desire to See God," 90: "Hence there will be only one act of will, one freedom of exercise and one freedom of specification if, as God knows all existing things by knowing one concrete world order, so also God wills all existing things inasmuch as he wills one concrete world order." See also fuller discussion of these issues in my *Creationism and the Conflict over Evolution*.

Original sin in a framework of theory. The turn toward systematic meaning in relation to sin itself began for the patristic writers with accounting for the proclamation about Jesus.[23] They started with the faith conviction that Christ was redeemer of all. It was an exclusive proclamation that left no room for salvation from any other source. As Acts proclaimed about Jesus, "There is salvation in no one else, for there is no other name under heaven given among mortals by which we must be saved" (Acts 4:12).

This fundamental conviction of the indispensability of Jesus would be reinforced by Origen's dictum, "Outside the Church there is no salvation." If all humanity needs salvation through Jesus, they reasoned, then all of humankind must be sinful. But why? What is the cause of the universality of human sin? They found the principle of explanation in an inherited sin. Sin is passed down as an actual sin from the first parents of all. The fact that they located the cause in a "something" shows how close the systematic meaning was to common sense, but nonetheless they were on their way. To avoid blaming God for sin and evil, they devised an anthropology of perfection. Two nonbiblical terms were used to denote the anthropology of perfection and the way we are now: *prelapsarian* and *postlapsarian.*

Pre-fall and post-fall humanity. The patristic writers thought that prior to sin, God had helped Adam and Eve to choose the good. In particular, God had enhanced their moral capacity with the "gift" of what they called original justice or integrity. It was a gift because it was not a permanent part of human nature. In the medieval parlance, using the conceptual distinction between supernatural and natural, original justice was a supernatural gift that could—and would—be taken away. In disobeying God, Adam and Eve lost this gift. Using the supernatural category clarified how human nature, on its own, did not include such integrity.

After the fall, the rational and moral capabilities proper to human nature remain. But they are diminished by sin, and, in Augustine's view, human beings no longer have the power to do the good, even if they have chosen it. They need the help of cooperative grace, another nonbiblical term.[24]

---

[23]For a fuller account of the development of the doctrine of original sin in the patristic and medieval periods, see Wiley, *Original Sin*, chs. 2–4.

[24]Lonergan pegs the meaning of operative and cooperative grace in more familiar terms: "Operative grace is religious conversion. Cooperative grace is the effectiveness of religious conversion, the

The biblical story provided patristic theologians with the authoritative warrant and narrative basis for the doctrine. The church fathers considered it both a historical account and divine revelation. As history, it told them "what had happened." As divine revelation, it told them that women were created second and sinned first, to paraphrase 1 Timothy. (Interestingly, Augustine thought that women would have been subject to men even without sin.) As revelation, it told them the consequences of sin—the punishment of Eve to be subject to her husband, the joint (and permanent) punishment of concupiscence, the loss of immortality, and the loss of the supernatural gift of original justice. Original sin was code for all of this.

Augustine speculated that all of humankind was sinful because each human had inherited sin through biological procreation.[25] The meaning of *original* in this context is not "first" but "inherited" sin. This is unique to Christianity.[26] This was the reason for the necessity of redemption and thus the necessity of Christ. Many Christians continue to think of redemption and Christ in this way, and that it must be thought this way.

Besides the idea that all have inherited Adam's sin at birth, there are further implications: the church has a monopoly on salvation. All humankind is in need of the one church and its baptism.

There were a few demurrals. Augustine's opponent, Pelagius, and Augustine both thought that sin was universal: Augustine, inevitably so; Pelagius, practically so. But Pelagius believed that Augustine confused two distinct realms of human existence: the realm of freedom, which chose evil, and the biological realm of procreation.[27] Augustine was untroubled by Pelagius's objection. Nor did he see that he made marital sex sinful not only by thinking of it as lust but by making procreation the carrier of original sin.

---

gradual movement towards a full and complete transformation of the whole of one's living and feeling, one's thoughts, words, deeds, and omissions." *Method in Theology*, 241.

[25]On Augustine, see the fuller treatment in Wiley, *Original Sin*, 56-75. Augustine interpreted the Adam and Eve story in three works on Genesis: *On Genesis Against the Manichees* (387); *Literal Commentary on Genesis, an Incomplete Work* (392); and *Literal Commentary on Genesis* (begun in 401; finished in 415).

[26]To my knowledge, no other religion accounts for sin in this precise way, although the idea of karma has some similarities.

[27]The medieval theologian Abelard plaintively said about Adam and Eve, "Could God just not have forgiven them?"

What scared Augustine about Pelagius's view was that if a person *could be righteous*—if a person could *avoid* sinning—then there would be no absolute necessity for Christ. The fundamental Christian proclamation (that is, that all humankind needs Christ's forgiveness of sin) would be false. Pelagius did not discount the possibility.

In Augustine's account, the permanent punishment that God imposed on Adam and Eve for their sin was concupiscence. The effect of concupiscence is that our desires are "disorderly." In fact, for Augustine concupiscence is disordered desire, a much broader category than simply sexual desire. He writes in the *Confessions*, "For you have imposed order, and so it is that the punishment of every disordered mind is its own disorder" (11.19). For example, where the will should be subject to reason, it is not. As Paul himself had said, there exists a difficulty in *doing* the good that one chooses. The cumulative effect of concupiscence in the historical realm is what Augustine described as moral impotence. He saw his age as corrupted by rampant evil. In his view, human nature is not neutral, open toward good or evil, but biased toward evil. While human beings technically retained freedom of choice (*liberum arbitrium*), after Adam's sin it is freedom to choose evil.

In the medieval period, Anselm makes the advance to an explicitly theoretical framework by linking original sin to the natural/supernatural distinction and an almost feudal or juridical conception of the God-human relationship.[28] As creature and subordinate, Adam owed God submission of his will. By violating God's command, Adam failed to give honor where honor was due. His disobedience required repayment—as a crime would—but repayment to a divine being was too large for even humankind as a whole to meet. As both God and man, Jesus Christ could satisfy this debt owed to God. With his forgiveness, Jesus restored to human beings the possibility of reaching union with God, the transcendent end for which human nature was created.

Anselm defined true human freedom as the absence of sin, which is honoring God properly. Yet Augustine had understood the condition of

---

[28]On Anselm, see G. R. Evans, *Anselm and a New Generation* (Oxford: Clarendon Press, 1980); and R. W. Southern, *Saint Anselm: A Portrait in a Landscape* (Cambridge: Cambridge University Press, 1990). For fuller discussion, see Wiley, *Original Sin*, 76-83.

original sin (*peccatum originale originatum*) as a *something* in contrast to a *privation*, as it is in Anselm. For Augustine, original sin was the culpable inclination of the will against God (*amor sui, cupiditas*). His theological expressions shared the metaphorical character of the biblical tradition. He describes the problem of sin, for example, as the enslavement of the human will to evil.

For the later medieval theologian Thomas Aquinas, sin is an ontological problem, a problem of nature rather than exclusively a moral problem, as it was for Augustine. At the center of Thomas's theology is not the fall but the supernatural destiny of human nature.

The natural desire of humans is to know God.[29] In Thomas's view, this desire cannot be fulfilled by natural means, because the fulfillment of the desire is a transcendent end. Neither can human reason independently discover the truth that human existence is fulfilled only by union with God. It has to be revealed—hence Jesus. Thomas transposed Paul's existential language of the power of sin and the Spirit, as well as Augustine's incipient theoretical appropriation of grace (operative and cooperative grace), into a metaphysical conception of divine grace as the means by which finite nature can reach its supernatural end.[30]

Luther's challenge. The term *Pelagian* became a favorite weapon of the Reformation as Catholics and Protestants hurled it back and forth as the worst thing they could say about one another.

In the sixteenth century, the Reformer Martin Luther recovered Augustine's notion of original sin and discarded Anselm's and Thomas's metaphysical conceptions. For Luther, in part based on his exegesis of Scripture and his profound personal experience, original sin was not just a moral problem (as it was for Augustine), nor an ontological problem (as in Anselm and Aquinas), but a *religious* problem—one concerning the

---

[29]Aquinas's discussion of original sin is in the *Summa Theologica* (New York: Benziger Brothers, 1947), I-II, q. 81-83 (Hereafter *ST*). Thomas writes, "The privation of original justice, whereby the will was made subject to God, is the formal element of original sin." *ST* I-II, q. 82, art. 3. On the history of the theology of grace, see Quentin Quesnell, "Grace," in *The New Dictionary of Theology*, ed. Joseph Komanchak et al. (Collegeville, MN: Liturgical Press, 1987), 437-50. For Thomas specifically, see 440-41. Thomas refers to original sin as a "sin of nature" in *ST* q. 82, art. 1, ad 2m and q. 82, art. 4.
[30]"Therefore the last end of man is not the good of the universe, but God himself." Aquinas, *ST* I-II, q. 2, art. 8.

relationship of humans with their Creator. He resonated fully with the teaching of Paul, especially about the bondage of the will and the impossibility of human avoidance of sin. For Luther, original sin is the irresistible tendency toward evil. Not distinguishing between concupiscence and sin itself, Luther saw this propensity as affecting all actions and relationships. For him, justification involves forgiveness of original sin but not a removal of the sin itself nor its effects on human nature.

Justification by faith alone, Luther's Archimedean point, challenged the claim of the church to mediate salvation exclusively, through administration of the sacraments. So while Luther had no demurral about the reality of original sin, he reconceived it in a way that repudiated the medieval model and its claims to ecclesial hegemony.

By contrast,[31] with only slight modifications, the Council of Trent (1563) affirmed the "something" (a culpable inclination of the will) of Augustine and the "privation" (loss of original justice) of Anselm. Thomas had already provided a synthesis of the two understandings. The council affirmed, under pain of *anathema*,

- that Adam lost the supernatural gifts of holiness and justice when he disobeyed God's command and that he therefore suffered death and his nature was changed;

- that Adam's sin affects all humankind, not just Adam;

- that Adam's sin was transmitted through procreation and that it is forgiven only by Christ, through baptism;

- that infants are born with original sin and must be baptized; and

- that original sin is taken away entirely through the grace of Christ in baptism, but concupiscence remains as the inclination to sin.

Trent's formulation became the dogma of the Roman Catholic Church. The doctrine of original sin did not undergo any further changes in the Catholic tradition and was unquestioned until the modern period.

---

[31]For fuller treatment of Martin Luther's understanding, especially in contrast to Trent, see Wiley, *Original Sin*, 88-93. John Calvin also abandoned the metaphysical framework and spoke of the effect of original sin as the total depravity of humanity, although Calvin did disagree with Luther in affirming the possibility of humans doing the good. See David Steinmetz, *Calvin in Context*, 2nd ed. (Oxford: Oxford University Press, 2005), 262-63.

FROM THEORY TO INTERIORITY: RECONCEIVING THE DOCTRINE TODAY

Over the twentieth century, several theologians made valiant attempts to reinterpret the doctrine of original sin for our own particular age. In the view of the late Dutch theologian Piet Schoonenberg, "Even if we prescind from any original sin and its influence on us, this solidarity [in sin] exists."[32] He did not mean that we need a replacement myth but that we need a compelling account of this solidarity in sin for an evolutionary world. When we do that, we are not giving an account of original sin as such but an account of the mystery of sin and evil. Original sin, the concept of an actual sin transmitted in procreation that affects our ability to avoid sinning or alters our nature, was a formulation for premodern time, but it has lost its explanatory power.

Two other notable theologians who have tackled the challenge were Reinhold Niebuhr and Rosemary Radford Ruether.[33] Niebuhr emphasized egoism, while Ruether identified patriarchy in all its forms as our original sin. Recently Jim Wallis has written a book in which he named racism as America's original sin. But we need a new, more comprehensive understanding of the problem of radical evil for a new age, not just a new metaphor for original sin. Terrence Tilley has put the case starkly: "The reception of the tradition involves changing the tradition if the tradition ... is to endure."[34] In an evolutionary world, there is no place for the garden, and the picture of our fully mature first parents no longer fits with what we know about the development of *Homo sapiens.* If the tradition is to endure, it must change.

Lonergan derives the categories needed to shift the analysis of the mystery of sin and evil from the world of theory to the world of interiority. He calls this transcendental method, the basic pattern of operations of the human mind. Minds are individual, but the data and structure of consciousness are both individual and universal. In other words, when we start from such an empirical anthropology, we have moved beyond symbolic

---

[32]See his *Man and Sin: A Theological View* (Notre Dame, IN: University of Notre Dame Press, 1965).
[33]For Reinhold Niebuhr, see especially his *The Nature and Destiny of Man* (New York: Charles Scribner's Sons, 1941), vol. 1, esp. chs. 7–10. Rosemary Ruether's now-classic critique and interpretation of original sin is in *Sexism and God-Talk: Toward a Feminist Theology* (Boston: Beacon, 1983).
[34]Terrence W. Tilley, *Inventing Catholic Tradition* (Maryknoll, NY: Orbis, 2000).

or even a metaphysical theoretical basis to one that allows us to speak about individual conscious acts and also about the historical process they produce. Lonergan traces the source of right and wrong decisions in both individual and collective spheres:

> For both individual conscience and the ethics of the social order, right decisions result from the cumulative attentiveness to situations, intelligence in thinking about possible courses of action, reasonableness in judgments of fact, and responsibility in carrying out actions appropriate and beneficial for the situation. Inadequate, wrong, or evil decisions result from a mixture of inattentiveness, oversight, irrationality, and irresponsibility.[35]

The contemporary understanding of the person is different from a metaphysical anthropology, which simply took human nature as the same in all places and times. This new view not only allows for a pluralism of cultures but also aims to pinpoint the tensions and norms that all humans of whatever culture or developmental period struggle with. Transcendental method "endeavors to envisage the range of human potentiality and to distinguish authentic from unauthentic realization of that potentiality. On this approach, being human is ambivalent: one can be human authentically, genuinely, and one can be human unauthentically."[36]

In *Method in Theology*, Lonergan locates the problem of human living in "sustained unauthenticity."[37] In *Insight* he states, "Essentially the problem lies in an incapacity for sustained development."[38] When we know what he means by *unauthenticity*, we will see why "sustained unauthenticity" is a verifiable category useful for approaching the problem of sin and evil.

Empirical anthropology as the basis for understanding sin and evil. An empirical anthropology derives its terms from conscious intentionality. It "prescinds from the soul, its essence, its potencies, its habits, for none of these are given in consciousness."[39] They are abstract terms. We know what they mean, but they are not experiential realities. Lonergan is concerned rather

[35]Lonergan, *Insight*, 628.
[36]Bernard J. F. Lonergan, "The Response of the Jesuit as Priest and Apostle in the Modern World," ch. 12 in *A Second Collection*, 2nd ed., ed. William F. J. Ryan and Bernard J. Tyrrell (Toronto: University of Toronto Press, 2016), 140.
[37]Lonergan, *Method in Theology*, ch. 1.
[38]Lonergan, *Insight*, 630.
[39]Bernard J. F. Lonergan, "The Subject," in Ryan and Tyrrell, *Second Collection*, 63.

with the data of conscious intentionality. Behind all the special methods—for example, in the natural sciences—lie the procedures of the human mind. Intentionality is a dynamic process, putting itself together. Lonergan distinguishes four levels of consciousness: empirical, intelligent, rational, and responsible. The first three levels are cognitional and the fourth an existential one of decision and loving. The fourth level is where we make the existential discovery both that our authenticity, as Lonergan says, is precarious, always a withdrawal from unauthenticity, and that through our choices and decisions we make ourselves who we are.[40]

Later in life, Lonergan divided the fourth level into two levels, with loving, religious experience and religious conversion identified as a fifth level. Because moral decisions open persons to interpersonal relations, there arises a further exigence to be loving. And because the human desire for truth and value is not restricted to the natural order but open to transcendent mystery, the indwelling of the divine is experienced in interiority as the summons to be holy.[41]

Lonergan's understanding of sin grew more existential over the course of his life. In *Insight*, "basic sin" was a problem of rationality: "Basic sin is a failure of rational consciousness."[42] It is the failure to make one's doing consistent with the grasp of a rational (thus moral) course of action. In *Method in Theology*, basic sin is an existential problem: it is the self-contradiction produced by the refusal or absence of self-transcendence.[43] Saying that sin is more than moral evil, Lonergan identified sin as fundamentally a "radical dimension of lovelessness"[44]—that is, the failure to love that typifies unauthenticity.

It is important to sketch these levels further in order to ground the dynamics in which authenticity and unauthenticity emerge. The structure of knowing and doing is dynamic. Through the four levels of operations, we successively transcend ourselves to comprehend and affirm reality and then choose among the values we discern for acting on it. Lonergan calls the groups of operations or activities "levels" because it is a "fuller self" that we

---

[40]Lonergan, *Method in Theology*, 55.
[41]See discussion of this fifth level in Wiley, *Original Sin*, 188.
[42]Lonergan, *Insight*, 666.
[43]Lonergan, *Method in Theology*, 364.
[44]Lonergan, *Method in Theology*, 243.

encounter as we experience each in ascending order. The first group of operations is sensing the data of our experience. We then question the data of our experience. What? Why? How? So the second group of operations includes questioning for understanding. Along with questioning are the operations of wondering, thinking, conceptualizing, and the central act of understanding, insight. A third group of operations checks our understanding: Is it so? We need sufficient evidence to determine the truth and what is real. It yields judgments of fact.

The fourth group of operations is not cognitional but existential. Here we ask questions of value and responsibility. What should I do? What is worthwhile? At this level alternatives are posed, choices made, decisions settled, and responsible actions are envisioned and done. Here the decisions are incomplete until they are put into action. We *do* the responsible course of action. In the largest sense, we exist for moral self-transcendence. Lonergan explains the relationship between the three cognitional levels and the more existential one:

> We experience and understand and judge to become moral: to become moral practically, for our decisions affect things; to become moral interpersonally, for our decisions affect other persons; to become moral existentially, for by our decisions we constitute what we are to be.[45]

Moreover, he says, human beings are responsible "individually, for the lives they lead and, collectively, for the world in which they lead them."[46]

Starting from interiority gives Lonergan a distinctive notion of the person. In his view of the person, "authentic being is self-transcendence." We are what we are made to be when we are understanding correctly, deciding responsibly, and fulfilling our decisions in responsible courses of action.

The empirical basis in interiority also gives Lonergan the norms for the whole structure of knowing and doing. The momentum and dynamism are given by the transcendental notions or "exigences" that Lonergan expresses by these short sayings corresponding to the levels: Be attentive! Be intelligent!

---

[45]Bernard J. F. Lonergan, "Mission and the Spirit," in *Third Collection*, ed. Frederick E. Crowe, SJ (New York: Paulist Press, 1985), 29.
[46]Paraphrasing Lonergan from "The Subject," in Ryan and Tyrrell, *Second Collection*, 80.

Be rational! Be responsible! Be loving![47] Authenticity results from prolonged fidelity to these exigences of consciousness. Infidelity to them generates unauthenticity. By authenticity, Lonergan transposes what the biblical and theological tradition called righteousness or holiness. By unauthenticity, he meant sin.

Our authentic development requires three reorientations, each of which is an element of God's remedy for human sinfulness. Lonergan calls them "conversions"—intellectual, moral, and religious.

Intellectual conversion occurs when we transcend the myth that knowing is like seeing. It is the discovery of the process of self-transcendence that constitutes knowing. Understanding alone is incomplete since insights may be wrong. Questions for understanding advance to questions for judgment: Is it so? Knowing is understanding correctly—that is, through correct affirmation of an insight. Understanding and appropriating this process enables a radical reorientation of our intellectual lives and endeavors.

In the reorientation of the moral realm, too, there is conversion, or the discovery of the process proper to moral self-transcendence and decision-making and moving from decisions based on interests, satisfactions, and pleasure to decisions based on value.

Lonergan describes religious conversion as an "other-worldly love."[48] It is a reorientation generated and sustained by the indwelling presence of divine mystery. There are many kinds of love—of a man for a woman, a parent for a child, and so forth—and Lonergan speaks warmly of these. But ultimately, whether experienced as an undertow or a dramatic event, religious conversion is about falling in love with divine mystery.

The absence of correct understanding or of achieving the human good—whatever the interference—is of great consequence for individual as well as collective development in history. Growth in authenticity requires the reorientations effected by religious, moral, and intellectual conversion. Their absence breeds justification of ideologies of superiority (shades of Paul) and the resulting inequalities in political, economic, and religious power.

---

[47]In classical terms, these are figured as transcendent notions, i.e., what is intended by consciousness. The transcendental notions promote the level, as he calls the different, successive groups of conscious operations. When objectified, the transcendental notions are the intelligible, the real and the true, and the good.

[48]Lonergan, *Method in Theology*, 289.

To fail in self-transcendence is to fail to meet these exigences of interiority. As Lonergan says above, there is "a mixture of inattentiveness, oversight, irrationality, and irresponsibility."

Sin is alienation from one's authentic being. It justifies itself by ideology.[49] The *basic form of ideology*, Lonergan says, is any doctrine that justifies alienation. From these basic forms, all others can be derived. The basic forms of ideology corrupt the social good.

Moral impotence, Augustine's term, is the *social surd* in Lonergan. The social order no longer corresponds to any one set of genuine insights. It is rather an ambiguous mixture of rationality and irrationality. It is partly the product of intelligence and reasonableness and partly the product of aberration from them. The social surd is a "false fact"—that is, "the actual existence of what should not be."[50] The facts in the situation "more and more are the absurdities that proceed from inattention, oversight, unreasonableness and irresponsibility." It is at the root of historical change: "As self-transcendence promotes progress, so the refusal of self-transcendence turns progress into cumulative decline."[51]

Why do we fail at the one task that truly matters, that of becoming fully human? It is in answering this question that the arduous job of recasting the doctrine into terms drawn from the world of interiority yields the most fruit for connecting doctrine to life. Our root sin is sustained unauthenticity. In the traditional paradigm, abstract terms did not shed light on our experience. We were almost destined to be alienated from God since we were born with sin, and, while we retained freedom of choice, it was, as Augustine taught, after Adam, only the freedom to choose evil.

In terms of interiority, however, infidelity to the norms of consciousness is empirical and experiential. There is much to interfere—interests, biases, privileges—with becoming authentically human, but we are not *destined* for sustained unauthenticity. Moreover, by exploring the biases and infidelities, we can see how unauthenticity infects not just individual but also social and cultural spheres, and even civilizations.[52]

---

[49]Lonergan, *Method in Theology*, 364.
[50]See Lonergan, *Method in Theology*, 55.
[51]Lonergan, *Method in Theology*, 55.
[52]See particularly Lonergan, *Insight*, chs. 6 and 7.

Further, such an account comports more directly with contemporary New Testament scholarship and our understanding of the teaching of Jesus. Progress, decline, and redemption; the presence of self-transcendence; the absence of transcendence; and the transformation of the world: Jesus dealt with these very realities in his *basileia* preaching. *Basileia* is often translated "kingdom" or "reign," but it also means "empire." As mentioned earlier, Walter Wink said, "The gospel is not a message of personal salvation from the world, but a message of a world transfigured right down to its basic structures." Jesus contrasted two empires: the one that is and the one that should be. The latter is God's empire; the former is Rome's. The chief value in God's empire is inclusion, in contrast to the exclusionary practices of Rome. Redemption from evil reverses sinful personal relations and social structures. His gospel was good news for the poor. He advocated equality and compassion. The fragment from the Jesus followers' baptismal ceremony that Paul included at Galatians 3:28 characterized a world without privilege: "There is no longer Jew or Greek, there is no longer slave or free, . . . for all of you are one in Christ Jesus." Three ideologies of superiority are identified— three distortions of the world. God's *basileia* is a world freed from hunger and poverty, one that embraces genuine values to generate political strategies and economic policies that restore well-being to the subordinated and dispossessed. Jesus' parables, healing, relationships, and preaching all contributed to his message. For us, as our redeemer and way to God, he faced the cross fully in love with God.

CONCLUSION

The explanation of the mystery of sin and evil by an inherited sin was compelling for nearly two thousand years. Its failure to compel today is to be expected. Its narrative basis can no longer be seen as a historical account but is a symbolic narrative, an all-too-human story that is a mixture of the author's oversights and insights. If we remain locked into the traditional formulation of original sin, it is often because the doctrine of the incarnation seems to dominate our theology and require it. Original sin has held the center for centuries with other doctrines revolving around it. We need a new center that uses an empirical anthropology, expands that to include historical process, respects the features of the world as we find it today, eliminates gender bias, affirms our humanity, and rethinks the salvific significance of the world's other religious traditions.

Thus, I am urging a further development of the doctrine. As it once transitioned from a largely metaphorical, symbolic apprehension to one more grounded in theory, so now the doctrine needs to transition through a further differentiation to be based in the verifiable categories of interiority, in which we find "sustained unauthenticity"—the human inability to sustain authenticity—to be the core meaning of our "root sin."

PART TWO

RESPONSES

6

An Augustinian-Reformed Response

HANS MADUEME

After reading the splendid essays by my four interlocutors, I was reminded why some theologians find the traditional doctrine of original sin implausible. However, a brief meditation on the Christian faith instructs us that "plausibility" is not a static concept and depends on a wide range of factors. Believers, for example, confess the triune God, the incarnation of God's Son, his death and resurrection, and the indwelling Holy Spirit. Yet nonbelievers reject such truths as deeply implausible. Conflicts over the plausibility of a wide range of doctrinal facts are also (regrettably) common between fellow believers, and it is often difficult to figure out what lies at their root.

At the best of times, doctrinal disagreements are not straightforward. They often turn on different judgments about divine revelation, responsibility to received traditions, the evidential support for scientific theories, and the like. So it is with the doctrines of the fall and original sin. In what follows, I will try once more to show why I believe an Augustinian-Reformed perspective best reflects God's revelation in Scripture. For the record, I am closest to Oliver Crisp and furthest from Tatha Wiley (with Andrew Louth and Joel Green somewhere in between). In a different forum, I might have been more inclined to build bridges and stress areas of commonality. But that is not my mandate nor the purpose of this particular volume, so I beg the reader's indulgence.

ENGAGING WILEY

In Tatha Wiley's account, a post-Darwinian, scientific understanding of the world compels us to reject the traditional doctrine of original sin. For example, she writes,

> What original sin crucially sought to explain is the mystery of sin and evil and how they can be partially understood in the framework of Christian belief. Given that our worldview is so different from the ancient one, we need to start from a different place in our search for an explanation of this deep and perennial mystery of our lives and our faith. (104)

The point recurs throughout her essay: "We once had a comfortable view of the world we thought was not just true but reality itself—creation, fall, redemption, judgment: how could it be otherwise?—that now seems, in crucial ways, irreconcilable with how we understand reality today" (105). The idea of original sin, she argues, is built on exegesis that has been called into question by science and historical criticism of the Bible. Wiley looks instead to the pre-Augustinian tradition for alternative foundations on which to develop a new conception of original sin.

I am mystified, however, that Wiley feels the need at all to reconceive a doctrine of original sin. She believes Adam and Eve never existed, Genesis 1–11 is not historical, Paul's views about Adam should be rejected, and so on, thereby denying the canonical data that informed the doctrine of original sin in the first place. Wiley wants the key insights of original sin without the historical and metaphysical baggage, having her cake and eating it too. I am delighted she still cares about original sin, but it is not clear to me why she does. Her own commitments sever the roots from which the doctrine first bloomed.

The problem is partly epistemological. Wiley privileges current scientific claims and human experience: "Our doctrinal formulations must comport not only with our scientific worldview," she claims, "but also with what we today understand to be authentic values" (106). She takes as a given that doctrine *must* change in light of the scientific consensus, although she never wrestles with the implications of her position for doctrinal development. Her method gives science unprecedented dogmatic power and threatens the very idea of Christianity as a revelatory faith. In Wiley's defense, some of my other interlocutors resonate with her on this point (although less radically); she is just the most forthcoming.

Wiley uses Bernard Lonergan to move the doctrine of original sin from
"theory" to "interiority." This shift opens up an understanding of sin "through
categories directly verifiable in our own experience" and leads her to invoke
Lonergan's notion of "sustained unauthenticity." She then correlates this
picture with New Testament themes, including "a world freed from hunger
and poverty, one that embraces genuine values to generate political strategies and economic policies that restore well-being to the subordinated and
dispossessed" (123). Despite some welcome notes, there is strikingly no
mention of human depravity, repentance, divine wrath, and the like; one is
left wondering if her revision of sin merely reflects her modern values. She
tells us to privilege "our own experience" and "structures of human
consciousness," but why should we think those are a reliable basis on which
to build a new doctrine of original sin? Perhaps they are unreliable.

These problems are exacerbated by her doctrine of Scripture. For example,
she lauds a "hermeneutics of suspicion" and identifies "unauthentic aspects
of revelatory texts" (108); she advises readers to "sort out authentic and unauthentic elements in the Pauline and deutero-Pauline letters" (109). Unlike
individualistic readings that "cannot accommodate the social meaning of sin,"
she focuses on the prophet Amos because he looked "at things through a
social lens" (107). Indeed, she claims that the root sin for Paul was *privilege*;
in her words, "we can say that Paul's convictions about sin were existential,
communal, and eschatological" (108). But this selective reading of Paul, like
all advocacy hermeneutics, leads to a "canon" within the canon. As one scholar
avers, "Such study can never have God's voice come to it except to confirm
what it thinks already."[1] I do not mean to be uncharitable, but Scripture has
become a mirror that reflects Wiley's own cultural assumptions.

ENGAGING GREEN

Joel Green gives two main objections to a doctrine of the fall.[2] First, he
contends that the words *fall* and *sin* are absent from Genesis 3. Second, he

---

[1]John Goldingay, "Hearing God Speak from the First Testament," in *The Voice of God in the Text of
Scripture: Explorations in Constructive Dogmatics*, ed. Oliver Crisp and Fred Sanders (Grand Rapids,
MI: Zondervan, 2016), 75.

[2]He also argues that the Augustinian way of reading the Adam story "overlooks the potential of
identifying God's mission with creation itself, opting instead for the view that God's mission awaits
human transgression before it can be set into motion" (71). But this seems like a non sequitur. A

thinks the Old Testament itself "has almost nothing to say about Adam and Eve or their disobedience" (71). Such weak claims are common among biblical scholars. Green's objection succumbs to the word-concept fallacy, since the absence of the word *fall* is irrelevant to whether the concept itself is present in Genesis 3. At the risk of being pedantic, such focus on words alone can lead to superficial readings of the Bible; by that metric, the church was wrong to confess the Trinity since the word is absent from Scripture. As C. John Collins observes, Genesis 3, as with the rest of Scripture, relies far more on showing than on telling.[3]

The claim that the Old Testament is largely silent on Adam and Eve is debatable. Apart from direct references to our first parents, there are broader allusions to the Eden story that are relevant.[4] Green may be right that the Old Testament has little to say *explicitly* about Adam and Eve, or their disobedience. But there is much that God reveals *implicitly* in the biblical story. And even if we concede Green's point for the sake of argument, Blocher reminds us that "frequency of occurrence [should] not be the sole measure of importance; its place in the canon is significant. It is obvious that the Eden story is no peripheral anecdote or marginal addition; it belongs decisively to the structure of Genesis and to that of the Torah."[5] The fall doctrine makes explicit what is already implicit in Scripture, and without it the rest of the biblical narrative makes little sense.

Green also claims there is no fall doctrine in early church history. He notes that three ecumenical creeds—Apostles', Nicene, and Athanasian—make no mention of the doctrine. But this argument says too much and too little. It says too much because those same creeds ignore other doctrines that were also central to the early understanding of Christianity; the absence of those doctrines hardly implies they were unimportant for early Christians. (None of those creeds mentions the doctrine of Scripture; are we to think early Christians lacked a notion of scriptural authority?) Green's argument

---

robust doctrine of the fall need not conflict with recognizing God's mission of creation (I return to this point in my response to Louth).

[3]C. John Collins, *Reading Genesis Well: Navigating History, Poetry, Science, and Truth in Genesis 1–11* (Grand Rapids, MI: Zondervan, 2018), 175–79.

[4]E.g., see C. John Collins, *Did Adam and Eve Really Exist? Who They Were and Why You Should Care* (Wheaton, IL: Crossway, 2011), 51–71.

[5]Henri Blocher, *Original Sin: Illuminating the Riddle* (Grand Rapids, MI: Eerdmans, 1999), 32.

also says too little, for it is likely that the creeds assume the fall without trying to demonstrate it. For example, in the Nicene Creed, the Son of God came down from heaven "for our salvation," implying there is something we need saving from. The need for salvation is woven throughout the Athanasian Creed (e.g., see the phrases "Whosoever will be saved"; "everlasting salvation"; and, "except a man believe truly and firmly, he cannot be saved"). Again, what are we being saved from? All these references are admittedly consistent with human sinning as such, but early Christians assumed that sin had an origin; creation was originally good and reflected the goodness of God. As they saw it, Adam's first sin is vital to the biblical story.[6] Even the slender Apostles' Creed mentions "the forgiveness of sins"—that clause in its historical context probably assumes the fall. As J. N. D. Kelly remarks, its original referent was "the cleansing effect of baptism."[7] Augustine invoked this very practice of infant baptism as proof that original sin was held throughout the Catholic Church.[8]

But was Augustine right? Green claims that Augustine's doctrine of original sin, especially his exegesis of Romans 5:12, originated from Ambrosiaster's commentary on Romans. Prior to Ambrosiaster, Green argues, the doctrine of inherited guilt is "missing from the writings of the church's theologian exegetes in the post-apostolic era" (62). He is not alone in blaming Ambrosiaster for Augustine's reading of Romans 5:12; indeed, current patristic literature is on Green's side.[9] However, I am uncertain

---

[6]Since at least the latter part of the second century, Christians appealed to Adam's fall to preserve the goodness of God's original creation and thereby foil the Manichaean doctrine of evil; the early creeds presuppose this theodicy. Cf. N. P. Williams, *The Ideas of the Fall and of Original Sin* (London: Longmans, Green & Co., 1927), 183-84.

[7]J. N. D. Kelly, *Early Christian Creeds*, 3rd ed. (New York: Continuum, 2006), 384. By the middle of the fourth century the phrase took on the additional meaning of forgiveness through confession and absolution.

[8]One can also argue that the early creeds were never intended as complete accounts of Christian doctrine (the "what" of our faith); their purpose, especially at baptism, was to pledge allegiance to the three divine persons whom we trust (the "who" of our faith). They were not meant to be doctrinally exhaustive. See, e.g., Donald Fairbairn, "*Fides Quae Creditur?* The Nicene Background to the Reformation," in *Reformation Celebration: The Significance of Scripture, Grace, Faith, and Christ*, ed. Gordon Isaac and Eckhard Schnabel (Peabody, MA: Hendrickson, 2018), 191-203.

[9]For a review of the debate, see Dominic Keech, *The Anti-Pelagian Christology of Augustine of Hippo, 396–430* (Oxford: Oxford University Press, 2012), 107-15. For recent studies on this question, see *inter alia* Aäron Vanspauwen and Anthony Dupont, "The Doctrine of Original Sin Amongst Augustine's African Contemporaries: The Case of Evodius of Uzalis' *De fide contra Manichaeos*,"

what to make of these attempts to reconstruct the source material in Augustine's exegesis of Romans 5. Augustine likely gleaned something from Ambrosiaster, but it was not a neat line; in my view, these modern conjectures do not undermine Augustine's plain claims to have derived his views from Scripture and the broad consensus of church fathers before him.[10] In a typical instance, Augustine denies any novelty to his doctrine, one that he says was held by "many holy, outstanding, and renowned teachers of the catholic truth: Irenaeus, Cyprian, Reticius, Olympius, Hilary, Gregory, Basil, Ambrose, John, Innocent, Jerome, and other companions and colleagues of theirs, as well as the whole Church of Christ."[11] While it is a minority report in the literature, I am drawn to the older judgment of Bernard Leeming:

> Augustine insisted that his doctrine on original sin was held by all Christians, handed down as part of the faith, so that not even heretics and schismatics held anything else. If he spoke the truth, and who can doubt it?—then we have an explanation of the origin of his opinions; and a possible explanation likewise of the same doctrine appearing in Ambrosiaster some fifty or sixty years earlier. He in turn derived it from the common teaching. Herein also lies the explanation of certain similarities between Augustine and Ambrosiaster.[12]

Current scientific understanding does most of the heavy lifting in Green's provisional picture of original sin (76). Yet his evolutionary proposal is still haunted by the perennial questions that plagued Pelagius and Augustine. If Green acknowledges universal sinfulness, then how does he explain *why* everyone sins? Positing innate sinfulness as the answer raises questions about the nature of sin. For example, does sin result from evolutionary development? Or is sin a description of biologically inherited tendencies? Green jeopardizes the goodness of God to the extent that God *created* humanity innately sinful. Perhaps Green thinks that biologically mediated inclinations and tendencies are *not yet* sin; they become sin only when we

---

Zeitschrift für antikes Christentum 21, no. 3 (2017): 459-71; and Anthony Dupont, "Original Sin in Tertullian and Cyprian: Conceptual Presence and Pre-Augustinian Content?" *Revue d'Études Augustiniennes et Patristiques* 63, no. 1 (2017): 1-29.

[10]I am grateful to Pete Sanlon for helpful dialogue on this question.

[11]Augustine, *Answer to Julian* 2.10.37, in *Answer to the Pelagians*, vol. 2 (Hyde Park, NY: New City, 1998).

[12]Bernard Leeming, "Augustine, Ambrosiaster and the Massa Perditionis," *Gregorianum* 11, no. 1 (1930): 74.

act on them by our free will.[13] But that merely pushes the question back to free will; that is, why do all human beings use their free will sinfully? The free will argument falls apart if there are no sinless people (apart from Christ)—*universal* sinfulness cannot be explained by free will alone.

I agree with Green that theological reflection should not overlook the created order, but he seems to conflate scientific consensus and the book of nature. Green's assumption that current evolutionary biology—which claims that all organisms on earth descended from a single common ancestor, the Last Universal Common Ancestor—is epistemically secure is debatable.[14] Christian doctrines like the fall and original sin should receive their primary definition from Scripture, not from fallible scientific theories. At the same time, taking divine revelation seriously does not commit believers to an "encyclopedic" fallacy in which we expect the Bible to speak infallibly on any topic that has no bearing on salvation. The Bible is not that kind of book. Nevertheless, in laying out the way of salvation Scripture *does* speak authoritatively to nonsalvific domains of knowledge that are implicated in the gospel story; those biblical insights will sometimes overlap with, and even correct, our best scientific theories.[15] The canonical witness to the fall rightly sets limits on scientific theories of human origins.

In short, Green's doctrine of Scripture is too thin epistemologically. That said, he could strengthen his position by adopting "limited" inerrancy,

---

[13]See, e.g., Frederick Tennant, *The Origin and Propagation of Sin*, 2nd ed. (Cambridge: Cambridge University Press, 1906), 172-73.

[14]For some of the diversity of opinion in theoretical and historical biology, see Colin Patterson, "Evolutionism and Creationism," *The Linnean* 18 (2002): 15-33; Carl Woese, National Academy microbiologist and biophysicist, writes, "The time has come for Biology to go beyond the Doctrine of Common Descent. Neither it nor any variation of it (invoking, say, several primordial forms) can capture the tenor, the dynamic, the essence of the evolutionary process that spawned cellular organization." "On the Evolution of Cells," *Proceedings of the National Academy of Sciences of the United States of America* 99, no. 13 (2002): 8745. See also Malcolm Gordon, "The Concept of Monophyly: A Speculative Essay," *Biology and Philosophy* 14 (1999): 331-48. Among Christians, of course, evolution is a source of ongoing debate. See, e.g., Norman Nevin, ed., *Should Christians Embrace Evolution? Biblical and Scientific Responses* (Nottingham, England: Inter-Varsity Press, 2009); J. P. Moreland, Stephen Meyer, Chris Shaw, Ann Gauger, and Wayne Grudem, eds., *Theistic Evolution: A Scientific, Philosophical, and Theological Critique* (Wheaton, IL: Crossway, 2017).

[15]This claim is obviously contested among theologians, but I take it to be the traditional position *and* true to Scripture's self-understanding. For a recent defense, see Mark Thompson, "The Divine Investment in Truth: Toward a Theological Account of Biblical Inerrancy," in *Do Historical Matters Matter to Faith? A Critical Appraisal of Modern and Postmodern Approaches to Scripture*, ed. James Hoffmeier and Dennis Magary (Wheaton, IL: Crossway, 2012), 71-97.

restricting biblical authority to soteriological elements only.[16] While limited inerrancy has serious defects, this move would give his position greater self-consistency. Otherwise his doctrine of original sin is caught, awkwardly, between two worlds. On the one hand, he accepts much of evolutionary biology; on the other hand, he tries to demonstrate its consistency with the doctrine of sin, but since he glosses over significant areas of conflict, his synthesis is not persuasive. His doctrine of original sin, informed primarily by science instead of divine revelation, has a different epistemic norm from the traditional doctrine. Limited inerrancy would be a better reflection of the logic of his proposal, although it is a solution with its own insuperable problems.

ENGAGING CRISP

Oliver Crisp rejects the notion of original guilt. The idea that God imputes Adam's guilt to all his descendants is unjust, he thinks, thus theologically invalid. But Crisp's intuitions about divine justice are not obviously true, and they likely reflect modern—and misleading—assumptions about fairness.[17] I agree with him that the divine imputation of guilt, if there is such a thing, would be radically different from normal human ascriptions of guilt and culpability. But that mere fact alone is no argument *against* imputed guilt. After all, many areas of theology, clearly attested in Scripture, have no analogy in human experience—for example, the Trinity, the hypostatic union, and the sinlessness of glorified saints, to name just three. That we have no analogous ways of conceiving such dogmatic realities does not render them untrue. If original guilt is a sure deliverance of divine revelation, that is all the grounding we need.

But Crisp denies that inherited guilt has biblical warrant. On Romans 5:12-19, he writes, "It is not at all clear to me that this passage implies original guilt. It may be consistent with something like the Augustinian realist picture of how sin is transmitted." And, more stridently,

---

[16]As Galileo put it, "The intention of the Holy Spirit is to teach us how one goes to heaven and not how heaven goes." "Galileo's Letter to the Grand Duchess (1615)," in *The Galileo Affair: A Documentary History*, ed. and trans. Maurice Finocchiaro (Berkeley: University of California Press, 1989), 96.

[17]See, e.g., Alasdair MacIntyre, *Whose Justice? Which Rationality?* (Notre Dame, IN: University of Notre Dame Press, 1988), 1-11, 326-48.

"Original guilt does not rest on a strong biblical foundation. The main text used to defend the doctrine, Romans 5:12-19, does not appear to teach anything like a doctrine of original guilt" (44). I think Crisp is mistaken. Romans 5:12-19 suggests that our burden of original guilt is inseparable from the redemption secured by Christ's atonement. The parallelism between Adam and Christ in Romans 5:12-21 (esp. vv. 18-19) intimates the imputation of Adam's guilt and the imputation of Christ's righteousness.

Besides, the truth of original guilt does not rest solely on one or two contested proof texts; rather, it synthesizes themes from the whole Bible and is integrally connected to other cardinal doctrines.[18] The Old Testament sacrificial system, instituted for all Israelites indiscriminately, implied that *all* were guilty—including children. Christ's atonement was both necessary and sufficient for all humanity (2 Cor 5:15), again because *all* are guilty—not just infants but even those with cognitive disabilities who cannot commit, or are limited in committing, actual sins. No one can be justified by keeping the law (cf. Rom 3:20; Gal 2:16), for we are all judged already guilty and condemned (e.g., Ps 51:5; Eph 2:3). Original guilt is implied in the nature of the gospel itself, with Christ's atoning sacrifice intended precisely for people who are in Adam and thus under the curse of eternal death. Inherited guilt is primarily a doctrinal, not exegetical, exposition of what it means canonically to say that everyone comes into the world from birth condemned before God.[19] Crisp fails to recognize, much less critique, this deeper doctrinal warrant.

Crisp also alleges that the Scots Confession, the Belgic Confession, and the Thirty-Nine Articles of Religion do not teach the doctrine of original guilt. But this claim is misleading, as we shall see, beginning with the Scots Confession. Crisp is correct that inherited guilt is absent, but we should not make too much of that. Does the omission of a doctrine by a confessional statement imply that its drafters rejected it? Not necessarily. Are we to think that the confession's silence on divine impassibility and omniscience, say, implies that Scottish divines denied those attributes of God? Confessions

---

[18]On this conceptual point, see Ben Dunson, "Do Bible Words Have Bible Meaning? Distinguishing Between Imputation as Word and Doctrine," *Westminster Theological Journal* 75 (2013): 239-60.

[19]For a Reformed perspective on original guilt and infant baptism, see J. Mark Beach, "Original Sin, Infant Salvation, and the Baptism of Infants: A Critique of Some Contemporary Baptist Authors," *Mid-America Journal of Theology* 12 (2011): 47-79.

do not work that way; they are written primarily for historical context, not doctrinal completeness.

All the same, the Belgic Confession depicts infants as infected with a condition "in their mother's womb," a condition described as "so *vile* and *abominable* in the sight of God" (article 15, my emphasis); according to article 20, "God therefore manifested His justice against His Son when He laid our iniquity on Him ... *who were guilty and worthy of damnation*" (my emphasis)—the two articles taken together seem to imply original guilt. As for the Anglican Articles of Religion, there is no ambiguity with article 2:

> The Son, which is the Word of the Father, begotten from everlasting of the Father, the very and eternal God, and of one substance with the Father, took Man's nature in the womb of the blessed Virgin, of her substance: so that two whole and perfect Natures, that is to say, the Godhead and Manhood, were joined together in one Person, never to be divided, whereof is one Christ, very God, and very Man; who truly suffered, was crucified, dead, and buried, to reconcile his Father to us, and to be a sacrifice, *not only for original guilt*, but also for all actual sins of men.[20]

Contrary to Crisp's assertions, then, original guilt is more prevalent in Reformed confessions than he recognizes.

There is much to commend dogmatic minimalism of the general type Crisp proposes, "an approach to a particular doctrine that attempts to affirm as 'thin' an account as is doctrinally possible yet consistent with wider theological and confessional commitments" (37). Deployed legitimately, dogmatic minimalism is motivated by genuine ambiguity or silence in the text; in some cases, scientific questions can rightly drive us back to the text to perceive real textual ambiguities that had always been there but were previously missed. However, if I am right that the Scriptures are not ambiguous about the historicity of Adam and Eve, then using dogmatic minimalism to justify an agnostic approach to these matters is unwarranted, notwithstanding the current scientific consensus on human origins.

A final concern with Crisp's doctrine of original sin relates to divine justice. Although we are blameless for Adam's first disobedience, he avers,

---

[20]John Leith, ed., *Creeds of the Churches*, 3rd ed. (Louisville: Westminster John Knox, 1982), 267, my emphasis. Crisp misses this reference because he has only article 9 ("Of Original or Birth-sin") on his radar.

we still inherit a state of moral corruption and are blameworthy for sins that arise inevitably from it. On this view, however, I would like to know why God condemns us for our actual sins. Since Crisp believes that we are blameless for our vitiated condition, why are we blameworthy for sins that arise *inevitably* from that very condition? That seems unjust, for Crisp's position implies that I sin by necessity *through no fault of my own*. To be sure, sin is a *contingent* truth; it is not essential to original human nature. But sin does become a consequent necessity *after* Adam's fall, hence the universality of sin; fallen human beings sin by necessity. If I am right, then Crisp needs to explain why this situation is not monumentally unjust.

ENGAGING LOUTH

Andrew Louth claims that Western theology should emphasize death—not sin and guilt—as the crux of the human dilemma. As he puts it,

> Death rather than guilt haunts fallen humankind: it threatens with meaninglessness all human endeavor and is an aspect of, and a symbol of, the way in which the fallen world—and not just fallen humanity—is out of joint, shot through with shafts of unmeaning. (82)

Sin, he says, is a consequence of human mortality and corruption. However, his position contradicts the apostolic witness. According to Paul, "the wages of sin is death" (Rom 6:23), and again, "sin came into the world through one man, and death came through sin, and so death spread to all *because* all have sinned" (Rom 5:12, my emphasis). Death results from sin, ultimately Adam's sin (cf. Gen 2:17). Louth's assertions about the priority of death are difficult to square with these explicit biblical statements, nor do they make sense of Christian experience. We are not drawn to sin by the fear of our own death.

This predicament relates to Louth's understanding of ancestral sin, which he defines as follows:

> The notion of ancestral sin sees each of us humans as born into a web of sin: the accumulated sin, and its consequences, of all our forefathers and foremothers. We find ourselves, inexorably, participating in this web of sin, for the sins of all the generations that have gone before us have eroded whatever examples of good conduct we might have had; furthermore, they have lent

the weight of tradition to standards of behavior that we may be able to recognize as inadequate or pernicious but which nevertheless enjoy the power
of custom. (86)

In contrast, Louth critiques original sin as exalting "Adam's primal sin to
a state of splendid isolation." Adam gets all the action; the sins of our "forefathers" and "foremothers" are irrelevant in the Augustinian scheme. Louth
finds the Augustinian picture too gloomy and pessimistic, unduly obsessed
with the fall-and-redemption motif, all of which marginalizes creation.
Eastern theology to his mind preserves the more optimistic balance of
creation-and-deification.

Augustinians should heed these helpful cautions, but they are overstated.
There is no necessary correlation between holding to original sin and mar-
ginalizing creation. Even if Augustinians sometimes overemphasize original
sin at the expense of creation, that is no fault of the doctrine of original sin.
And counterexamples abound; for example, the neo-Calvinism of Abraham
Kuyper and his heirs emphasizes common grace (with its rich creation
motifs) *and* a robust Augustinian hamartiology—the same can be said for
other Augustinian theological traditions.

Furthermore, it is not true that Augustinians trivialize the sins of our ancestors after Adam (as if only Adam's sin matters); in fact, a robust doctrine of
original sin *already* incorporates the main insights of ancestral sin. As I understand original sin, the sins of our ancestors and the unimaginable consequences
of sin that precede us are an *enabling occasion* for individual innate corruption
to express itself in actual sins. Ancestral sin is not the originating sin—Adam's
first sin holds that pride of place—but it *does* multiply sin and misery, affecting
us for ill in countless ways, as Louth helpfully describes.

Not so helpful, however, is his insistence that humanity moves from a
lower (created) to a higher (deified) state. This picture, so central to Eastern
Orthodoxy, invites the worry that God gave us less than his best at creation.
Louth renders God partly responsible for the deficient condition of original
humanity, for Adam and Eve were imperfect from the beginning and thus
needed to ascend to a higher state. Part of the genius of the fall doctrine is
that it sidesteps this troubling scenario.

On a final note, the corruption-only position of ancestral sin is a flawed
doctrine; it discounts the truths of imputation (and realism) implied in

passages like Romans 5:12-21 and 1 Corinthians 15:21-22 as well as the broader doctrinal synthesis of the whole Bible on which imputed guilt rests (see my remarks to Crisp). I ask Louth, Are there any human beings apart from Christ who were perfectly sinless? Answering yes would suggest he has a defective hamartiology and Christology. Scripture is clear that with the exception of Christ *all* humans are sinners (e.g., Rom 3:9-20; 1 Jn 1:8); if we presume there *were* any sinless people, as perfectionists have claimed, such naiveté detracts from the glory of the incarnation and belittles the gravity of sin. I suspect Louth agrees. In that case, it must be our inherited corruption that makes sinning inevitable. But then how is this scenario just? Since no human is responsible for innate corruption, in his view, and since that same corruption leads inevitably to sin, it is unclear how ancestral sin fares any better than original guilt. The concerns surrounding divine justice remain.

CONCLUSION

I thank my four dialogue partners for the privilege of thinking through these difficult questions together. I have benefited from this exchange. I am also sobered, though not surprised, that none of them see a future for the doctrine of original guilt—these days a doctrine more despised is hard to find.

For it is beyond doubt that nothing shocks our reason more than to say that the sin of the first man has rendered guilty those who, being so removed from this source, seem incapable of participation in it. This transmission seems not only impossible to us but also very unjust. For what is more contrary to the rules of our miserable justice than to damn eternally an infant incapable of will, for a sin wherein he seems to have so little a share, that it was committed six thousand years before he was in existence? Certainly nothing offends us more rudely than this doctrine; yet, without this mystery, the most incomprehensible of all, we are incomprehensible to ourselves. The knot of our condition takes its twists and turns in this abyss, so that man is more inconceivable without this mystery than this mystery is inconceivable to man.

I hope Pascal, of blessed memory, will forgive me for passing off his wisdom as my own. As with original guilt, so here: mea culpa.[21]

---

[21]The entire preceding paragraph quotes directly from Blaise Pascal, *Pensées*, trans. W. F. Trotter (Mineola, NY: Dover Publications, 2003), 121-22.

7

A Moderate Reformed Response

OLIVER D. CRISP

In my constructive contribution to this volume, I set out and defended what I called the moderate Reformed doctrine of original sin. In this response, I will offer some reflections on the essays of my fellow contributors, with particular emphasis on ways in which their views converge or diverge from my own. I remind the reader at the outset that my contribution was offered as a piece of constructive dogmatic theology in the Reformed tradition—that is, one way of thinking about the doctrine of original sin from a Reformed perspective, taking seriously the dogmatic or confessional tradition that has shaped Reformed theology. I was also concerned to provide a doctrine that was (a) in conformity with Scripture and (b) ecumenically oriented. I was clear that my constructive view was only one possible Reformed view, although it does have considerable support in early Reformed theology, including the work of Zwingli and Calvin, and the Scots Confession, the Belgic Confession, and the Articles of Religion.

I begin with some remarks about the essays closest to my own, theologically speaking, before working my way toward those where there is greater theological distance. In this way, the reader will be able to quickly assess the extent to which my own views differ from those of my coauthors.

RESPONSE TO MADUEME

In many respects the essay by Hans Madueme is the one closest to my own. He is, after all, a theologian who also self-identifies with the Reformed tradition. His essay is, in many ways, a good example of a more conservative Reformed view of original sin than my own. It includes the notion of original guilt and assumes the theological viability of a historic fall, aboriginal pair, and monogenism (the idea that all humans are descended from a single male-female couple). I admire the attempt to stay in step with the tradition and to revise as little as possible. However, I have several worries with his essay.

The first of these is a theological consideration having to do with the place of Reformed theology relative to the rest of the catholic church. Considerable diversity exists within the "great tradition" of theological reflection on the doctrine, a fact that Madueme frankly admits at points, even as he stakes his claim on a particular version of Augustinianism. There are divergent accounts of the doctrine in the history of the church, and serious divisions remain across confessional lines, as the other essays in this volume make plain. The Reformed version of Augustinianism is one venerable tradition of interpretation—but only one. It is one voice among many, including the Orthodox and Roman Catholic (who make up the majority of Christians in history and on the planet today) and the variety of views represented within Protestantism. Have the Reformed got it all right? Given our fragile grasp of theological truth, I have my doubts. Yet reading Madueme's essay might lead one to think that the answer is an emphatic affirmation of the truth of a full-blooded version of the Augustinian-Reformed view. Although I stand within the same theological tradition, I am more wary of claiming that we Reformed Christians have a monopoly on the truth of this particular matter.

To take just one example, Professor Madueme thinks that those, like the Greek fathers, who deny original guilt are mistaken because guilt for acts of sin implies guilt for the moral corruption that gives rise to those acts. But this does not follow. I am praiseworthy for acts of virtue. Does that imply that my nature is praiseworthy because it is in virtue of my human nature that I act virtuously? Surely not. Alternatively, he reasons that if humans are not guilty for innate corruption then we cannot be guilty for sinful acts arising from such corruption. But that does not follow either. By his own lights, humans are not innately virtuous, but sinners. However, that does not mean fallen humans are not praiseworthy for virtuous acts they perform.

The point is that moral approbation or blame attaches to *actions* an agent performs, not (or not necessarily) to the moral nature with which a person is created.

Second, the idea that there was a premodern consensus on central elements of the doctrine of original sin that has been shattered by scientific advances which have gradually been accommodated by modern theologians seems rather simplistic. Moreover, it does not do justice to the careful manner in which theologians have tried to rearticulate constructive versions of the doctrine in recent times that pay serious attention to the authoritative place of Scripture and tradition in making theological judgments.[1] Theologians are always in dialogue with the biblical texts, given traditions of interpretation with respect to these texts and a range of other sources of theological authority that bear on this, including creeds, confessions, and the work of particular theologians. Included in this dialogue is a theological engagement with other areas of knowledge, including the natural sciences. Sometimes the theologian should take a particular theological stand against what is perceived to be a "scientific" consensus, such as the widespread endorsement of some sort of metaphysical naturalism (very roughly, the idea that the physical world is all there is, so that giving an account of the physical world involves giving an account of all that exists to be explained).[2] However, sometimes we *should* listen to the scientists and look again at how we read Scripture where there is salient evidence. A notorious example of this is the Copernican revolution in cosmology, which was hindered by theological mismanagement based on particular ways of reading certain biblical texts (e.g., Ps 19:1-6).[3] But in the case of the development of human beings, where there is relevant evidence from the natural sciences, we should not be afraid to pay attention to new ways of thinking about old problems. This is not necessarily a matter of accommodating our religious views to a scientific hegemony.

---

[1]A good example in this regard is Ian A. McFarland's excellent study, *In Adam's Fall: A Meditation on the Christian Doctrine of Original Sin* (Oxford: Wiley-Blackwell, 2010).

[2]Metaphysical naturalism is, of course, not a scientific but a philosophical idea, although it is often invoked as if it were a deliverance of the natural sciences.

[3]For an accessible introduction to the biblical cosmology and how it differs from our own, see Robin A. Parry, *The Biblical Cosmos: A Pilgrim's Guide to the Weird and Wonderful World of the Bible* (Eugene, OR: Cascade Books, 2014).

Rather, it is about the reinterpretation of certain religious views in light of scientific evidence that suggests we have misunderstood the nature of certain religious claims. In the case of Copernicus, the religious leaders of the time misunderstood the biblical texts that suggest the earth is literally immovable, with the heavenly bodies in orbit around the earth. In the case of human origins, I suggest that something similar is true, the relevant changes having been made.

RESPONSE TO GREEN

The essay by Joel Green is, in some respects, one step away from my own views. He provides a clear and plausible case for a Wesleyan-Arminian doctrine of original sin, which he regards as a kind of modified (perhaps *moderate*) Augustinianism. However, there are important areas of convergence between our two positions. Let me mention several of the most salient.

To begin with, in setting forth the conceptual content of the Wesleyan doctrine, Green writes, "Wesley's doctrine of original sin . . . maintained emphases on the corrupt nature of humanity and the pervasiveness of sin, but he excluded the idea that the transfer of original sin included the transfer of guilt. No one will receive eternal damnation because of Adam's guilt." Not only is original guilt excluded on this Wesleyan account, sin is regarded as a disease—both of which are consistent with the moderate Reformed position I have advocated. Toward the end of his essay, Green affirms that, for Wesley, the primary significance of human sin was soteriological. That is, it made it clear that human beings were in need of salvation in Christ—the healing of the disease. This also seems right to me.

Professor Green is also concerned that we do not wed a doctrine of sin to a particular etiology—that is, a particular way of understanding the origin of sin. Was there a historic aboriginal pair from whom all humanity are descended and who introduced sin to the human family? Professor Green is clearly skeptical of such a view and closes his essay with a just-so story that provides one way of thinking about the doctrine that does not require monogenism. This too is in keeping with the way in which I have prescinded from making a judgment about this vexed theological question.

However, our views do diverge in places—for instance, Professor Green's endorsement of the Wesleyan doctrine of prevenient grace. In one footnote he cites historical theologian Roger Olson with approval:

> The free will of human beings in Arminius's theology and in classical Arminianism is more properly denoted freed will. Grace frees the will from bondage to sin and evil, and gives it ability to cooperate with saving grace by not resisting it. (Which is not the same as contributing to its work!)[4]

This is clearly not consistent with a Reformed account of the bondage of the will and, for most in the Reformed tradition (myself included), a version of theological compatibilism.[5] But further comment on this would take us too far afield, and, in any case, the general outline of the difference between Wesleyan and Reformed views on this matter is well known.

This brings me to a second area of disagreement. In the middle section of his essay, Professor Green spends some time thinking about the biblical foundation of the doctrine of original sin. He maintains that there is little biblical foundation for the idea. The fall narrative is not axiomatic for later discussion of sin in the Old Testament or intertestamental works. Nor is it the point of departure for Paul's account of sin (or James's). He makes the fairly common claim that the Augustinian translation of Romans 5:12 is a mistake (a point also discussed, in a rather different fashion, by Andrew Louth in his constructive contribution to this volume). According to Professor Green, the phrase, ἐφ᾽ ᾧ πάντες ἥμαρτον (*eph' hō pantes hēmarton*) does not imply that Adam is the one "in whom" all have sinned (per the Augustinian misreading of this phrase). Rather, it should be rendered something like "since everyone has sinned," which, in the context of the whole verse, Green translates, "Just as through one human being sin came into the world, and death came through sin, so death has come to everyone, since everyone has sinned." Set in the broader context of Pauline theology, Professor Green maintains that Paul's position is much milder than traditional

---

[4]Roger E. Olson, *Armininan Theology: Myths and Realities* (Downers Grove, IL: InterVarsity Press, 2006), 142.

[5]Theological compatibilism is (very roughly) the idea that God determines all that comes to pass and that this is consistent or compatible with human freedom. Elsewhere I have argued that it may be possible to be Reformed and libertarian with respect to human free will. See, e.g., Oliver D. Crisp, *Deviant Calvinism: Broadening Reformed Theology* (Minneapolis: Fortress Press, 2014).

Augustinians have thought. As a consequence of Adam's primal act, "sin as a hegemonic force was let loose in the world," so that "Adam's disobedience set in motion a chain of consequences, one sin leading to the next, not because sin is basic to the human condition but because Adam set the pattern for all humanity." In this connection he (in my view, rightly) points out that Paul's concerns in this regard may not match our own. We should be wary of anachronism—that is, reading into Paul a doctrine of original sin that is a later doctrinal development postdating Augustine.

Although I am sympathetic with much of what Professor Green says here, I would register several caveats. First, we should be careful not to conflate the frequency with which a concept is mentioned with its importance in a particular tradition. The term *Trinity* appears nowhere in Scripture, nor does it contain a clear, unambiguous statement of the doctrine of the Trinity. But I cannot imagine any serious theologian claiming that for this reason we can excise the doctrine of the Trinity from the Christian faith because it is clearly stated only after the New Testament had been completed for centuries. It seems to me that something similar can be said with respect to sin and original sin in Scripture. Even if original sin is not mentioned in the text of Scripture, and the doctrine is nowhere clearly stated, this does not mean it is a doctrine alien to the right understanding of the text.

Second, even if we concede that Professor Green and others are right about how to translate Romans 5:12, so that Augustine's rendering of the verse is mistaken, this does not necessarily defeat Augustine's claim (famously repeated in the *New England Primer*) that "In Adam's Fall, We sinned all." For Romans 5:19, which bookends the Adam Christology of this section of the epistle, tells us "For just as by the one man's disobedience the many *were made sinners*, so by the one man's obedience the many will be made righteous." The relevant phrase here is ἁμαρτωλοὶ κατεστάθησαν οἱ πολλοί (*hamartōloi katestathēsan hoi polloi*)—that is, "the many were constituted [made] sinners." The sin of the one (Adam) constitutes the many sinners, just as the righteousness of the one (Christ) will constitute the many righteous. If that is right, then this verse seems to be much closer to a more Augustinian reading of Paul's Adam Christology than Green's reading suggests. For the typology is such that something Adam does *constitutes* the many sinners, and something Christ does *constitutes* the many righteous in the sight of God. Although this is not the same as saying all sinned *in* Adam, it is significantly stronger than saying we have all sinned *like* Adam.[6]

What is more, by his own admission, Green is providing his readers with a particular way of thinking about original sin—namely, an account consistent with the Wesleyan-Arminian tradition of theology. Naturally, the way he understands the biblical basis for this doctrine, and its development in the history of theology, reflects the starting assumptions of Wesleyan-Arminianism. That does not mean he is wrong, of course. It just means that his position is not the *only* or even the only *plausible* way of thinking about the doctrine of sin consistent with Scripture and tradition. Hermeneutical and theological decisions have to be made in setting forth constructive theological positions, and this is as true for the biblical scholar as it is for the systematic theologian—as I am sure Professor Green (himself no mean theologian) would agree.

RESPONSE TO LOUTH

Professor Andrew Louth has written an essay that provides us with a clear and concise version of an Orthodox understanding of human sin—the *ancestral sin*, as it is usually called in Orthodox theology—as well as its impact on the whole of creation. It is arguably yet one more step removed from my own position, theologically speaking. For this reason, I consider it here as the third of my four interlocutors. What Professor Louth has provided his readers in his essay is an excellent treatment of the doctrine that is a fine companion to his recent introduction to Orthodox theology.[7]

He frames his concern, as one might expect, in terms of the conceptual cleavage between the Eastern, Greek-speaking churches and Western, Latin-influenced churches. But this, he thinks, belies a deeper difference. This is a difference of theological starting point. The Western churches begin with the fall and move from there to consider the doctrine of salvation via an understanding of the corruption and guilt of humanity

---

[6]Another New Testament passage relevant in this connection is Hebrews 7:10, which, in arguing for the superiority of Melchizedek's priesthood over Levi, says that Levi "was still in the loins of his ancestor when Melchizedek met him." This raises some interesting metaphysical questions, although space prohibits the full explication of this point here.

[7]Andrew Louth, *Introducing Eastern Orthodox Theology* (Downers Grove, IL: IVP Academic, 2013).

complicit in Adam's primal sin. By contrast, the Eastern churches begin with human beings made in God's image and move from there to an understanding of human life in communion with God through *theosis* that is interrupted by the cosmic implications of the fall. Although this Orthodox alternative does deal with sin (though not *original* sin, strictly speaking), it is more about participating in the divine life through Christ. As Louth puts it at one point, in Eastern Orthodox thought, "the lesser theological arc (as we might call it) of fall-redemption is subordinate to the greater theological arc of creation-deification."

Although I have not spelled this out in my contribution to this volume, I am very sympathetic to Louth's concerns here. But I am bound to say that important representatives of the Reformed tradition have gone before him in this regard. I think, for example, of the twentieth-century Scottish theologian Thomas F. Torrance, whose work echoes the Athanasian idea that God "became human, so that the human might become God." Some of my own recent work has been an attempt to do just what Louth suggests, providing a Reformed way of thinking about humanity in terms of the divine image and our need for *theosis* that echoes something of Torrance in this regard.[8]

Louth is also right, I think, to point to the patristic notion that salvation is not so much about release from Adam's guilt as it is the defeat of death. But here too there are resources in Western theology that echo at least some of these sentiments, as I have tried to point out in my own essay. Finally, I think Louth is right when he puts his finger on the cosmic significance of the primal sin, along with the way in which (in an Orthodox way of thinking) our sin is part of a web of accumulated sin that includes the sinful activity of our forebears as well. We are caught in this web and cannot extricate ourselves without divine grace.

However, I am also bound to register what for me is an important difficulty with Louth's presentation. In the context of expounding the doctrine of ancestral sin in terms of a web of human sinfulness going all the way back to our first parents, he raises the issue of whether this is *sufficient* as an account of sin. As he puts it, for defenders of original sin, like myself, the

---

[8]See Oliver D. Crisp, *The Word Enfleshed: Exploring the Person and Work of Christ* (Grand Rapids, MI: Baker Academic, 2016).

ancestral sin view "seems to leave open the possibility (even if totally exceptional) of someone living a blameless life." And this, of course, is the fundamental worry Augustine had with Pelagius's doctrine. The problem is, Louth
never really addresses this objection to his position head on. He never explains how the Orthodox doctrine of ancestral sin can avoid the traditional
Augustinian objection that it leaves conceptual room for the existence of
someone that is, for all practical purposes, without sin. This, it seems to me,
is a serious lacuna in his presentation.

Those sympathetic to a moderate Reformed doctrine of original sin will
not want to embrace the notion of original guilt. Yet we surely do need to say
something about the moral corruption of human nature—that is, we need to
affirm something more than ancestral sin: we need to affirm something like
original sin. I am not suggesting that Louth's presentation, or the Orthodox
view more generally, is, or implies, Pelagius's doctrine. But I am suggesting
that the Orthodox view Louth puts forward appears to be insufficient as it
stands, and it needs to address the concerns raised by those Christians in the
Augustinian tradition, for whom "the possibility (even if totally exceptional)
of someone living a blameless life" is a real theological worry when it comes
to giving a satisfactory account of theological anthropology.

RESPONSE TO WILEY

I have benefited from reading Tatha Wiley's book on the development of the
doctrine of original sin.[9] I learned from her essay in this volume as well.
However, the position she develops in her contribution is the furthest removed from my own position, which is why I consider her contribution last.
Wiley seeks to reconceive the doctrine of original sin in light of evolutionary
developments, drawing on the work of the twentieth-century Jesuit theologian Bernard Lonergan. His transcendental method permeates her essay. In
her way of thinking, the story of the human fall in the primeval prologue of
Genesis 1–3 and the evolutionary understanding of human development are
not competitors seeking to explain the same data via incompatible narratives.
Rather, these "must be truths on completely different planes." The Genesis
narrative is merely symbolic; the scientific narrative is realistic. Like Lonergan,

---

[9]Tatha Wiley, *Original Sin: Origins, Developments, Contemporary Meanings* (Mahwah, NJ: Paulist
Press, 2002).

Wiley regards sin as fundamentally a failure of *authenticity*. What she wishes to see is "a further development of the doctrine" beyond modern attempts to shore up the Genesis story in the teeth of scientific change. She writes,

> As it once transitioned from a largely metaphorical, symbolic apprehension to one more grounded in theory, so now the doctrine needs to transition through a further differentiation to be based in the verifiable categories of interiority, in which we find "sustained unauthenticity"—the human inability to sustain authenticity—to be the core meaning of our "root sin." (124)

Let me make two comments on Wiley's presentation. First, although I agree that contemporary theologians need to take seriously the challenge to the doctrine of original sin posed by scientific developments, it is not at all clear to me that in order to do this contemporary divines must be quite as revisionist as Wiley suggests. My own position is that there is indeed good reason for careful reflection on what is essential to the doctrine of original sin, as I hope was made plain in my own constructive essay. But the sort of mild modification I have in mind (if it is a modification at all) is rather different from the wholesale reconstruction of the doctrine, which, it seems to me, is what Wiley recommends. My own view stands within a confessional tradition, whereas, in important respects, Wiley's view moves beyond confessionalism, pressing in a theologically constructive direction instead. In theology, significant revision to the tradition requires a correspondingly significant argument. Compare the adjustments to revising a naive view of the biblical cosmology if one is a Copernican, as almost all modern people are today. Such changes seem intuitive to us today, but we can also give good reasons for them—reasons that are compelling. The point I am making here is that I am not clear from Wiley's presentation what *compelling* reasons there are for the kind of doctrinal reconstruction she advocates. She would need to say more than she has here in order for me to see the need for the fairly comprehensive changes she suggests.

Second, and more briefly, given that much of the reasoning Wiley deploys depends on concepts to be found in the transcendental Thomism of Lonergan, those (like myself) unsympathetic to the sort of Thomism Lonergan develops will find little reason to follow her (and his) lead. As a result, I find my own position rather out of step with important aspects of Wiley's account.

8

A Wesleyan Response

JOEL B. GREEN

First, let me say a word of appreciation to my conversation partners in this volume. I have learned from each of them. I am grateful for Andrew Louth's careful and reflective parsing of the Orthodox approach to original sin, together with the way his essay lays bare something of the deep roots of his ecclesial and theological tradition; for Hans Madueme's ardent defense of an Augustinian-Reformed view—which, as he notes, has often been taken as *the* doctrine of original sin; for Tatha Wiley's grasp of diverse ways the idea of original sin has been and continues to be represented, her awareness that our theological work cannot neglect contemporary science, and her foray into reconceiving the doctrine accordingly; and for the exemplary irenicism and clarity with which Oliver Crisp lays out a moderate Reformed understanding. John Wesley wrote regarding the doctrine of justification that he did not differ from Mr. Calvin "a hair's breadth."[1] This could not quite be said of Crisp's Calvinism and a Wesleyan account of original sin, but it remains nonetheless that his proposal opens many avenues for Wesleyan-Reformed conversation on this matter. Of course, as I noted in my original essay, a Wesleyan theology of original sin has as one of its primary influences the views of the early church, including its Eastern theologians, so it is not surprising that the hearts of many Wesleyans would be warmed while reading Louth's reflections.

---

[1]John Wesley, "Letter to John Newton, 14 May 1765," in *The Letters of John Wesley*, ed. John Telford (London: Epworth, 1931), 4:298. See the comparison of Wesley and Calvin on this and related matters in Don Thorsen, *Calvin vs. Wesley: Bringing Belief in Line with Practice* (Nashville: Abingdon, 2013).

Second, by way of interaction with these conversation partners, I want to bypass the option of engaging each one serially and thereby indicating points of agreement and disagreement. Instead, I will identify three overarching concerns raised in my reading of their contributions. The first two of these have to do with questions of theological method, particularly what counts as primary sources for theological reflection: What is the role of Scripture in theology? and How ought theology to account for the natural sciences? The third is less pressing but nonetheless important, centering on how we characterize the church's understanding of the doctrine of original sin.

SCRIPTURE AND THEOLOGY

I am puzzled that some of my conversation partners have little apparent need for the witness of Scripture or seem to have little interest in or appreciation of biblical studies—as though the formulation of Christian doctrine might proceed apart from engagement with the Bible, or as though the meaning of certain phrases would be self-evident, apart from the hard work of theological exegesis. On this latter point, my concern is exacerbated since Romans 5–7, pivotal in much of the discussion historically and today, has been the focus of so much interpretive work. As I raise this concern, I recognize that the Eastern tradition differs in significant ways from the Western regarding what constitutes academic study of the Bible—the Eastern tradition emphasizes analogical interpretation and the privilege it accords to patristic exegesis, while the Western tradition holds commitments to various forms of historical analysis. I also recognize decades of troubled relations between biblical studies and systematic theology. In the modern era, biblical scholars increasingly identified themselves as historians, with the result that they increasingly participated in a project committed to moving forward (in Ernst Breisach's words) "without any practical interest, be it lessons, devotion, entertainment, or propaganda."[2] Biblical studies has not been particularly kind to the theological enterprise, owing to its emphasis on the diversity of perspectives in the Christian Bible (With so many voices speaking, how do we hear the voice of God in Scripture?) and because

---

[2]Ernst Breisach, *Historiography: Ancient, Medieval, and Modern*, 2nd ed. (Chicago: University of Chicago Press, 1994), 323.

modern biblical studies has tended to portray "the strange world of the Bible" as profoundly *other* in comparison with contemporary life. N. T. Wright rightly observed that "many systematic theologians . . . have become impatient with waiting for the mountain of historical footnotes to give birth to the mouse of theological insight."[3] Recognition of these matters, however, cannot dislodge the central question of how the witness of Scripture might contribute to formulations of the doctrine of original sin.

By way of example, we can focus for a moment on Paul's letter to the Romans. Paul actually provides three accounts of sin in Romans 1–7.[4] In the first (1:18–5:11), he narrates the story of the human family that chose creation over the Creator and, consequently, was given over to its own desires and distortions (1:18–32). Here, the prototypical sin is idolatry: "They exchanged the glory of the immortal God for images that look like mortal humans: birds, animals, and reptiles" (1:23)[5]—with idolatry heading a lengthy list of sinful behaviors. Human agency leads to divine response, with human choices mirrored by God, who hands humanity over to their cravings (1:24, 26, 28). In the end, in a clever play on words, "since they didn't think it was worthwhile to acknowledge God," God delivered them over to ways of thinking that could not distinguish what is worthwhile (1:28).[6] It is not hard to hear in the background reminiscences of the Adam story of Genesis 2–3. As James D. G. Dunn has it, 1:18-32 reflects the life of Adam, "who perverted his knowledge of God and sought to escape the status of creature," thus setting the pattern for the idolatry that would characterize Israel and, indeed, all humanity.[7] Given this identification of the basic sin as idolatry, Romans 1 may also remind us of what would have been Exhibit A for Israel's

---

[3]N. T. Wright, "The Letter to the Galatians: Exegesis and Theology," in *Between Two Horizons: Spanning New Testament Studies and Systematic Theology*, ed. Joel B. Green and Max Turner (Grand Rapids, MI: Eerdmans, 2000), 206.

[4]Cf. Susan Grove Eastman, *Paul and the Person: Reframing Paul's Anthropology* (Grand Rapids, MI: Eerdmans, 2017), 109-25; and Simon Gathercole, "Sin in God's Economy: Agencies in Romans 1 and 7," in *Divine and Human Agency in Paul and His Cultural Environment*, ed. John M. G. Barclay and Simon J. Gathercole (London: T&T Clark, 2007), 158-72.

[5]Unless otherwise noted, translations of biblical texts follow the Common English Bible.

[6]That is, their failure to acknowledge God (οὐκ ἐδοκίμασαν τὸν θεόν, *ouk edokimasan ton theon*) is mirrored in their consequently unfit mind (ἀδόκιμον νοῦν, *adokimon noun*).

[7]James D. G. Dunn, *Romans 1–8*, Word Biblical Commentary 38A (Dallas: Word, 1988), 53. Note the repetition of γνωστός (known) in Genesis 2:9 and Romans 1:19, and the use of the verbal form γινώσκω (I know) in Genesis 2:17; 3:5, 7, 22 and Romans 1:21.

sinful inclinations—namely, the story of the golden calf (Ex 32). Throughout this section of the letter, we find repeated references to sin as the outworking of human agency: they sin (2:12; 3:23), they take counsel with each other to do evil things (3:8), and they practice sinful behavior (1:32; 2:1-3).

The second account identifies sin—or, better, Sin (a malevolent, enslaving power)—as an agent influencing or causing humans to engage in sinful actions (5:12–7:6—about which I had more to say in my earlier essay). On the one hand, through Adam and from Adam, Sin entered the world and ruled in death (5:12-21). On the other hand, death came to everyone because everyone sinned. That is, Sin entered the world because of Adam *and* Adam's disobedience had a ripple effect on the human family. One of the pressing questions for a doctrine of original sin is how best to explain this ripple effect, and this might direct one to analogies with chaos theory (with the human family understood as a system thrown off kilter through the action of its early ancestors) or with emergence theory (with s/Sin understood as an emergent entity, arising from human behavior while also holding human beings captive).[8]

As an aside, I should respond to Louth's remark regarding Romans 5:12. For him, claims that Augustine misconstrued this Pauline text are wide of the mark since Augustine's Latin text represents a perfectly acceptable translation of Paul's Greek. It is hard to know what to make of this comment since I am confident that Louth is not unaware of how translators do their work nor of basic semantic theory distinguishing *possible* from *actual* senses of a text. To give a single example, during the 2018 NBA finals, a commercial aired that featured IBM supercomputer, Watson, as a basketball analyst. Watson humorously refers to a three-point shot as "nail[ing] a jumper from a densely populated urban area." A human commentator corrects the computer's idiom: that shot was taken from "way downtown." In a rather wooden way, Watson's terminology was correct, I suppose, but it did not work very well in that discourse situation. In the same way, we recognize that translation from Paul's Greek to Latin or English is not a matter of substituting this word for that one, nor of determining simply what is possible; accordingly, when commentators refer to Augustine's text as a mistranslation of

---

[8]On the latter, see Matthew Croasmun, *The Emergence of Sin: The Cosmic Tyrant in Romans* (Oxford: Oxford University Press, 2017).

Paul's Greek, they are not saying that Paul's Greek could not be read in another way but rather that Paul's discourse is represented best with these words, not those.[9] Accordingly, it makes a lot of difference to our reading of Paul that his phrase ἐφ᾽ ᾧ (*eph' hō*) is best translated as a marker of causation, "since everyone has sinned," and not, with Ambrosiaster and Augustine, as a reference to humanity's having sinned *in quo*, "in whom"—that is, in Adam.[10] The latter recruits Paul as an early Augustinian in a way that would be surprising to those who read Paul's words in the church's first centuries— that is, to those who did not find there a foundation for the view of original sin that would surface among Augustine and his kin.

Paul's third account of human sinfulness (7:7-25) comprises the apostle's response to the question, "So what are we going to say? That the Law is sin?" His immediate answer: "Absolutely not!" (7:7). Here we find points of contact with Paul's account in Romans 1 as well as a key development in his perspective on Sin, grounded in what he has argued in Romans 5–6. Thus, the two actors in Romans 1 (humanity and God) are replaced by Sin and the law, with Paul's account turning on the ruse Sin plays on humans. Sharply put, Sin affects the way humans perceive the law (i.e., not by rejecting the law but by distorting human understanding of the law) and the way humans perceive their own behaviors (i.e., what humans think is good turns out to be sinful), so that Sin provokes the very craving the law prohibits.[11]

For Paul, humans are not victimized by Sin's power and prowess. This is clear enough in Romans 1:18-32, where God's handing humanity over is in each case a response to the prior sinful exercise of human agency. In Romans 5, too, humans are portrayed with agency: as sinners, as weak, and as God's adversaries (vv. 6, 8, 10). Moreover, Paul's portrait of humanity concerns the entire human family—interconnected, interdependent, across time and space, with the sin of our earliest ancestors, we might say, spreading across all of humanity, like ripples radiating outward from a pebble tossed into a pond. Paul thus underscores the entire human family's solidarity in sin and interprets human sinfulness as a sign of human fragility and

---

[9]Cf. Umberto Eco's account in *Experiences in Translation*, Toronto Italian Studies (Toronto: University of Toronto Press, 2001).

[10]See the discussion in my essay, pp. 69-71.

[11]Cf. Gathercole, "Sin in God's Economy."

culpability, the result of which is that, without exception, all humanity stands in need of Christ's work.

Expanding on my earlier essay, I have thus sketched a few remarks on Paul's understanding of sin and sinfulness as this is recounted in Romans 1–7. More could be said about Paul, about the other texts I discussed earlier (Genesis 3 and the letter of James), and other biblical materials as well. But I hope I have said enough to warrant and illustrate the concern I have raised in this section of my response, in which I press some of my conversation partners in this volume to be more forthcoming in their work with Scripture and engagement with biblical studies. Although it is true we do not move naively from biblical text to ecclesial doctrine—as though no other factors were at work in our theological reflection, or as if we were not open to other sources of God's speech—Christian theologians have long insisted that, among theology's sources, Scripture occupies pride of place and serves an authoritative role.

There is no single way to weave scriptural perspectives into a doctrinal tapestry. However, we can say that, read against the backdrop of his Jewish milieu and in relation to his own argument in Romans, Paul simply is not concerned to respond or contribute to many of the traditional interests of the doctrine of original sin. Paul does not affirm that the entire human family is implicated in Adam's sin, affirming instead, with other biblical and extrabiblical Jewish texts, human choice and responsibility. This means that we cannot claim that a full-blown doctrine of original sin is waiting to be read off of the pages of Scripture, even if we can say that some aspects of the doctrine have developed from scriptural warrants. This is the case regarding theological claims that the human heart leans toward sin and that sin pervades the human family. Sin's etiology is less clear in Scripture, and this lack of clarity also ought to exercise constraint on our accounts of original sin.

SCIENCE AND THEOLOGY

If it is a truism that theology is a world-encompassing discipline, then it follows that theology potentially consults with all fields of inquiry in its work. I found it puzzling, then, that some of my conversation partners either had little or nothing to say about science, took a neutral position vis-à-vis scientific discovery, or communicated hostility toward science. If theology is critical and constructive inquiry into the church's faith, witness, and practices, then it is hard to understand how it would not be influenced by the natural sciences.

Before saying more about the importance of science, let me lodge two caveats. First, I am making no claim concerning *how* science must influence the theological task. Michael Fuller has outlined a continuum of five potential responses, illustrating those responses historically with regard to the church's initial reception of Darwin and prospectively with regard to breakthroughs in artificial intelligence. These responses include (1 and 2) rejecting either religion or science, and (3) ignoring scientific discovery. In my view, none of these first three responses is appropriate to the theological enterprise. A more positive role for science would be granted by (4) a "soft" use of science, according to which scientific development is analyzed for how it might cast light on traditional theological ideas, and (5) a "hard" use of science, which "involves studying the findings of science and, if they are felt to be irrefutable, re-moulding [*sic*] traditional theological doctrines in the light of them." Fuller continues,

> This re-moulding may be done purely under the influence of the scientific innovation in question, but it is more likely that it will be done through a critical re-examination of the theological material in question as a result of that influence, or perhaps through the re-discovery [*sic*] of alternative articulations of doctrine from past centuries.[12]

Using Fuller's typology, not least in a discussion of original sin, I would have anticipated more from some of my conversation partners regarding these latter two options.

As a second caveat, I want to acknowledge the reductive naturalism of the so-called hard sciences today. In this regard, theologians and natural scientists are often separated by distinctive habits of mind—the one concerned with observable, repeatable chains of natural cause and effect, the other more open to the Other and to mystery, with a greater focus on meaning, including transcendent significance. Accordingly, I tend to think of the contrast between theology and science in narrative terms. Working with the same data points (what narratologists call a story's elements), scientists and theologians

---

[12]Michael Fuller, "A Typology for the Theological Reception of Scientific Innovation," *Science & Christian Belief* 12 (2000): 119-20.

choreograph those data in different ways, with the result that they explain their significance within different plot lines (although neither should simply ignore those data).[13] In short, even if science refers to the disciplined, systematic examination of the cosmos by means of empirical observation, and even if science locates God outside its explanatory purview, this does not negate the possibility that science tells us something about God and God's ways. And, in the twenty-first-century West, failure to account for the findings of science seems fatal to the theological enterprise. This is true not only because ours is a culture increasingly aware of such findings but also because, inevitably, science is and must be integral to theological reflection.

The beginnings of the natural sciences in the 1600s drew inspiration from the hoary notion of God's two books, the Bible and the natural world. For example, the father of modern neuroscience, Thomas Willis, identified his research as an examination of "the Pandects of Nature, as into another Table of the Divine Word, and the greater Bible: For indeed, in either Volume there is no . . . Page certainly which shews not the Author, and his Power, Goodness, Trust, and Wisdom."[14] If God made the world, then the world displays God's character.

For many, this perspective on the natural order is rooted in Paul's words, "This is because what is known about God should be plain to them because God made it plain to them. Ever since the creation of the world, God's invisible qualities—God's eternal power and divine nature—have been clearly seen, because they are understood through the things God has made" (Rom 1:19-20), or in words from the Psalter, "Heaven is declaring God's glory; the sky is proclaiming his handiwork" (Ps 19:1). Jesus wonders, Do not flowering plants and wild birds provide insight into God's goodness (Mt 6:25-34)? In short, even if God's self-disclosure reaches ultimate expression in Jesus Christ ("the light of God's glory and the imprint of God's being" [Heb 1:3]), God has nonetheless spoken through all that he has created. It follows that we who serve him must practice vigilance concerning how our understanding of God may be sharpened, even corrected, through ongoing exploration of these means by which he makes himself known to us.

---

[13]For this distinction, see, e.g., Seymour Chatman, *Story and Discourse: Narrative Structure in Fiction and Film* (Ithaca, NY: Cornell University Press, 1978).
[14]Thomas Willis, *The Anatomy of the Brain and Nerves* (1681; repr., Birmingham: McGill-Queens University Press, 1978), 51-52.

How do these reflections bear on our thinking about original sin? To put the matter pointedly, evolutionary biology has undermined belief that human history began with a single couple and that our history can be separated by "the fall" into two eras: Paradise and Paradise Lost. Even if some imagine that they can maintain these elements of the traditional doctrine of original sin, it is increasingly clear that others are incapable of such cognitive gymnastics;[15] still others have begun constructing accounts of original sin that prioritize evolutionary biology over Augustinian formulations.[16]

True, some, perhaps many, of Paul's readers today are troubled by the influence of evolutionary biology because of the theological weight Paul has placed on Adam. What are we to make of his claims regarding Adam if, as evolutionary biology has it, the human family cannot be traced back to a single man or first couple, and that death in this world preceded the appearance of humans by millions of years. Although I have no reason to doubt that Paul himself thought of Adam as a historical person, this does not require the further step of reasoning that his argument stands or falls on the historical existence of a first human, Adam (or on a historical fall). Let me sketch three reasons for this.

First, as I demonstrated in my earlier essay, we have no scriptural basis for speaking in terms of "the fall of humanity," at least in the traditional sense. That is, a historical fall might be a desideratum for some later theological constructions, but scriptural reflection on sin, which assumes the universality of sin without documenting its origins, has no such need. Accordingly, this is not a case of science against Scripture.

Second, this would hardly be the first or only case of biblical writers' drawing on prevailing but erroneous scientific views to speak truly of God and God's engagement with the world. Let me mention two examples. In Luke 11:34-36, we find these words from Jesus:

> Your eye is the lamp of your body. When your eye is healthy, your whole body is full of light. But when your eye is bad, your whole body is full of darkness.

---

[15]Cf., e.g., David Kinnaman with Aly Hawkins, *You Lost Me: Why Young Christians Are Leaving Church, and Rethinking Faith* (Grand Rapids, MI: Baker, 2011), 131-48.

[16]E.g., Patricia Williams, *Doing Without Adam and Eve: Sociobiology and Origin Sin*, Theology and the Sciences (Minneapolis: Fortress, 2001); and Daryl P. Domning and Monika K. Hellwig, *Original Selfishness: Original Sin and Evil in the Light of Evolution* (Aldershot, UK: Ashgate, 2006).

Therefore, see to it that the light in you isn't darkness. If your whole body is full of light—with no part darkened—then it will be as full of light as when a lamp shines brightly on you.

Obviously, Jesus uses darkness/light as metaphors of ethical life, but how? To understand his point, we need some background in ancient ophthalmology.[17] Two views were popular. Plato and Galen regarded the eyes as channels for the release of the body's own light; Jesus, too, assumes this view, which is called extramission. Intromission, Aristotle's preferred view, holds that eyes detect light from outside the body and serve as the doorway for visual perception. In extramission, the eye is like a flashlight. For Jesus, a good eye radiates good light whereas a bad eye radiates bad light (or no light at all). The critical question, then, is whether the eyes are sick or healthy, for this tells us whether a person is full of darkness or full of light. As Luke tells the story, Jesus uses a once-popular eye science to characterize faithful life. We can learn from his message even though we reject the science on which it is based.

This example from the Gospels underscores how biblical texts—and not only biblical interpreters—are implicated in scientific understanding, a point equally made in 1 Corinthians 15. In his efforts to identify the nature of the resurrection body, Paul thinks in terms of five elements: earth, fire, wind, water (all of this world), and a fifth, *quintessence*, associated with the stars and other astral bodies. Using an outdated periodic table, the apostle thus contrasts a body constructed from the stuff of the earth, a dusty body well suited to earthly life, with a body made of heavenly stuff and thus well suited to heavenly life (15:47-49).[18]

Third, thinking more narrowly of Paul's argument in Romans 1–7, we should not overlook the point that the apostle's thesis has less to do with Adam and more to do with Christ. He wants to show that Christ is the savior of all humanity, Jew and Gentile, so he needs to demonstrate that all stand on level ground with respect to their need for salvation. Paul does not require belief in the historicity of a first parent named Adam, nor the view that Adam's sin defines what is essential to the human condition. What

---

[17]See David C. Lindberg, *Theories of Vision from al-Kindi to Kepler* (Chicago: University of Chicago Press, 1976), 1-17.

[18]See Alan G. Padgett, "The Body in Resurrection: Science and Scripture on the 'Spiritual Body' (1 Cor 15:35-58)," *Word & World* 22 (2002): 155-63.

Paul's argument requires is this affirmation of human solidarity, Jew and Gentile, in sin—and, therefore, in death. The first part of this affirmation is in place already, having been set out in Romans 1–3. His appeal to Adam's sin in Romans 5 thus plays an adjunctive role to that earlier material. Accordingly, Paul can assume in Romans 5 the universality of sin as a warrant for his further affirmation that all humanity, implicated in death, stands in need of "eternal life through Jesus Christ our Lord" (5:21).

As Scripture and science are inseparably related, so are theology and science. Invariably, we wear our assumptions about the cosmos when we come to Scripture and to theological reflection. Indeed, interpreters have always read the Bible from within their own scientific understandings. Additionally, ancient scientific views are fully integrated into the Bible itself, as the biblical writers drew on scientific views present in their times to speak of God and God's engagement with the world. It seems obvious, then, that the question is not *whether* science will have influence but rather *which* science and *whose* science. And here is a corollary: Will we allow select, perhaps long-held scientific perspectives on the world to parade as timeless truths, or will we continue to explore the cosmos for what it tells us about God and God's ways?

IS THERE A DOCTRINE OF ORIGINAL SIN?

Finally, I want to register a concern about how the doctrine of original sin is represented in our discussions. Even a brief survey of the early church demonstrates a general lack of interest in sin's etiology, that Genesis 2–3 was read in ways that did not provide a warrant for later notions of the fall of humanity, and that humans were regarded as both free and responsible for the exercise of their freedom. The ecumenical councils do not weigh in on the question of original sin, and the global church has never had a singular understanding of the doctrine.[19] Furthermore, Protestantism is more variegated than the Reformed tradition. Although the Augustinian doctrine of original sin has had enormous influence, it remains the case that some Protestant movements, including contemporary evangelical ones, do not fly the Augustinian banner. (I am thinking of my own Wesleyan tradition, for example, but some

---

[19]In addition to her essay in this volume, see Tatha Wiley, *Original Sin: Origins, Developments, Contemporary Meanings* (New York: Paulist Press, 2002).

Anabaptists also come immediately to mind.[20]) Accordingly, I would be grateful if, in the ongoing conversation regarding original sin, references to what evangelicals hold to be true, to the Protestant view, and the like, disappeared, since the plurality of positions resists such reductionism. If what we have said is true of the ecumenical creeds and the church's historical positions, it is also true that Scripture itself provides us with more latitude for reflection and constructive thought than the traditional doctrine might have suggested.

A WESLEYAN WAY FORWARD

I am grateful that I was reared in a Wesleyan-Methodist world that emphasized the authority of Scripture *and* welcomed scientific discovery. I grant that this is not true of all Wesleyans, or of all Methodists, but it is true of those who have drunk deeply from the Wesleyan well. As a result, although Wesley could neither have anticipated the findings of evolutionary biology nor predicted the directions biblical studies might take, he nonetheless prefigured ways of learning from science, drawing on the wisdom of the early church, and of according privilege to Scripture. And the particulars of a Wesleyan view of original sin continue to convince.

For Wesley, original sin must be located within the arc of a soteriological journey that runs from creation to new creation, that features the empowering grace of God, and that leads to human beings perfected in love. He found a way to navigate among the central Protestant affirmations of original sin and of salvation by faith alone through his emphasis on prevenient grace. Even if all are dead in sin, and so unable to respond to God, no one is bereft of God's grace. Working in every human life, prevenient grace generates "the first wish to please God, the first dawn of light concerning his will, and the first slight transient conviction of having sinned against him."[21] The work the doctrine of original sin performs is soteriological, then, so the ubiquity and power of sin are fundamental—even if, in the end, we affirm that prevenient grace reestablishes a small measure of freedom in human beings, enabling them to respond to God's initiative.

---

[20]Cf. John E. Toews, *The Story of Original Sin* (Eugene, OR: Pickwick, 2013); Toews draws on such contemporary theologians as the "baptist" James McClendon and the Mennonite Thomas Finger.
[21]John Wesley, "On Working Out Our Own Salvation," §2.1, in *The Works of John Wesley*, vol. 3, *Sermons III (71–114)*, ed. Albert C. Outler (Nashville: Abingdon, 1986), 203.

9

An Eastern Orthodox Response

ANDREW LOUTH

Let me begin with my first impressions after reading the other four contributions. First of all, I was struck that there seemed no truly liberal Christian contribution—that is, no contribution from the position of most of those who taught me theology in the 1960s when I studied at Cambridge under such teachers as Maurice Wiles, Stephen Sykes, and Geoffrey Lampe. What then seemed the prevailing trend in theology (one that I rebelled against) now seems to have no presence at all. I do not think this is because of any bias in the editors who chose the contributors; it seems to me to represent a fairly general shift in attitude among Western Christians over the last half century. A "liberal" take on the fall and original sin would have been to regard these doctrines as dead weight from the past and worthy of little or no attention within a modern intellectual worldview (the ground for this had been well prepared by such learned, though inconsequential, tomes as N. P. Williams's *The Ideas of the Fall and of Original Sin* [1927], not mentioned, I think, by any of the contributors to our volume). Instead, all the four articles take the doctrines of the fall and original sin as a significant theme in the Christian theological tradition. The way the four essayists from the Western tradition engage with these doctrines is certainly different, and some of them certainly suggest that there are other Christians who do not take these doctrines seriously (most sharply Madueme), but in fact they all treat these doctrines as part of the inherited theological tradition. A significant advantage of engaging with an inherited theological tradition, as in all the approaches found in this volume, is that one finds oneself receiving, and in some sense accepting, ideas and concepts from the tradition of theological reflection within the church that are freighted with considerations by thinkers, preachers, and men and women of prayer who had significantly different preconceptions from our own, belonging as they do to the early twenty-first century. It seems to me that this gives a certain grit to present-day reflection—an engagement with ideas that do not really belong to our own limited cultural context—that can act as a stimulant to searching thought. There seems to me to be plenty of evidence of this in the four other views (it is not my business to respond to my own contribution, although I hope that something like this is true of my contribution too).

The fall and original sin are parts of the historical theological tradition that must be engaged—and from a specific place in the (now sadly divided) tradition of Christian reflection. Each essay makes clear in what tradition the author stands—Oliver Crisp is "moderate Reformed," Joel Green is Wesleyan Methodist, Hans Madueme is Augustinian-Reformed, and my contribution reflects an Orthodox approach. Tatha Wiley does not make explicit in her title that her approach is (Roman) Catholic, but no one could read more than a few pages before realizing that such is her stance within the tradition (the position of the "church" is tracked by reference to Pope Pius IX and the Second Vatican Council, and her theological lodestar is the Canadian Jesuit of the last century, Bernard Lonergan). In all cases, *tradition* is understood in a more or less clearly identifiable way. Furthermore, other points of commonality exist among the four essays from Western traditions.

All essays, in different ways, acknowledge that there are limits to theological understanding. Crisp, from a "moderate Reformed" perspective (offered, explicitly, as a "basis for ecumenical rapprochement with other strands of the Christian tradition"), underlines at one point that the position he is putting forward "prescinds from any judgment" about monogenism (that all human beings are descendants of Adam and Eve). Madueme says at one point that "we should not apologize here for invoking mystery, for some things are beyond our ken (Deut 29:29)." And Wiley asserts that "no matter the conceptual formulations, they are not the mystery itself." I could not find anything explicit about the limits of theological understanding in Green's essay, but Wesley's sense of the limited remit of theology pervades what he has to say. What is often called the apophatic dimension of theology is then generally acknowledged in the contributions, though with a certain reluctance. Except for Wiley, it is an acknowledgment of the limits of theology, not the recognition that such an apophatic dimension is integral to any attempt to discern the mystery of God and of Christ. There is nothing (save in Wiley) to match Vladimir Lossky's assertion that "the apophatic way of Eastern theology is the repentance of the human person before the face of the living God."[1]

A further point of commonality, which is hardly surprising, is that all the essayists find it necessary to engage with Darwin's theory of evolution; what is striking is the variety of ways in which this engagement takes place. Madueme seeks to draw a firm line between biblical teaching and the deliverances of modern science—a line that separates the scientific and the historical from the revelatory and the dogmatic—but in this he seems to be alone. Crisp, however, is not as far from Madueme on this as one (or he?) might expect; his moderate Reformed position is compatible with the theory of evolution but does not require it: "The moderate Reformed account is not committed to some doctrine of evolutionary history; it is also consistent with the idea that God specially created the world out of nothing and fashioned human beings from dust and ribs." There seem to be echoes here of a presumed opposition between evolution and creationism that, to my mind, schooled on the other side of the Atlantic, seems forced.

Green is much clearer that Christian theology needs to heed the discoveries of modern science, and he helpfully reminds us that, in Wesley's eighteenth century, these discoveries were not initially perceived as alien to the faith (being, in fact, often made by clergymen). Wesley, Green argues, would have listened to what the sciences had discovered (and gives some examples of the way in which indeed he did), placing side by side God's revelation—in the book of Scripture and in the book of nature.

Wiley goes much further and sees that the changes in modern ways of understanding the world and our place in it demand that the church and theologians fundamentally "recast" traditional doctrines (taking the term from Bernard Lonergan and emphasizing, "*recast*, not simply rewritten"). In

---

[1] Vladimir Lossky, *The Mystical Theology of the Eastern Church* (London: James Clarke, 1957), 238.

the limited space allowed her, Wiley proposes a radical program for theology and makes a valiant attempt to indicate what this might mean.

All accept that the account in Genesis (chapters 2 and 3) of the creation of humans and the primal sin of human forebears is the source of the traditional doctrines of the fall and original sin. All, except Madueme, are concerned to revisit the Genesis account and derive from it a different story than the one presupposed by traditional Western doctrine. For all of them, it is Augustine's interpretation of this account that has proved fundamental to Christian doctrine (in the West). Green and Wiley insist most clearly on reconceiving the meaning of the Genesis account, while Madueme argues, with forthright clarity, that an Augustinian account is the only theologically viable interpretation. Green provides the most elaborate account of how we need to reconceive Genesis 3, pointing out that the "traditional" interpretation is not found in Christian theology until the late fourth century with Ambrosiaster, who influenced Augustine. We are taken on a tour through several Second Temple Jewish texts, from which Green draws the conclusion that the older understanding of Genesis 3 held that Adam's disobedience resulted in mortality, rather than the taint of original sin, and that human beings were seen as remaining responsible for their own actions. Green's tour then continues—perhaps surprisingly—through a discussion of the epistle of James before coming to the apostle Paul. Approached in this way, Paul's ideas seem to be quite at home in this world of Second Temple Judaism rather than marking a fundamentally new departure. Crisp might well concur with Green's treatment (that is for him to say), but his approach is determined by an attempt to define an acceptable and believable doctrine of original sin, and his contribution remains (as Crisp himself says) at a philosophical-theological level rather than engaging directly in biblical and exegetical concerns.

Wiley is perhaps the most radical, arguing that the Bible remains largely at the level of symbolic apprehension, which stands in marked contrast to a "scientific apprehension," something that now needs to be radically recast. If I take issue with any essay at a fundamental level, it is here. The conviction that theology has to be concerned with scientific apprehension (something that Wiley, rightly I think, regards as having been the way of scholastic theology, although with scientific presuppositions that are no longer ours) rather than "symbolic apprehension"—a contrast expressed a little earlier in terms of a movement from "metaphor" to "more technical terms"—seems to me profoundly wrong, misconceiving the nature of theological understanding. This shift certainly took place in Western theology and is fundamental to the enterprise of scholasticism; for Wiley this shift needs to be thought through again so as to take account of the change in "scientific" understanding between the Middle Ages and our own times, influenced not just by the rise of the scientific project of the early modern period but by more recent developments in the modern scientific worldview, such as the theory of evolution and, I daresay, Einstein's theories of special and general relativity as well as quantum mechanics. Wiley seems unaffected by the doubts of such as Hans-Georg Gadamer about how much the enterprise of modern science has fundamentally affected human understanding. (It is curious that Lonergan himself had studied Gadamer and followed him fairly closely, at least episodically, in *Method in Theology* but remained with a notion of "scientific" understanding, admittedly somewhat more refined than earlier notions of scientific method.) But although the scientific approach seems demonstrably proven by its success (measured, however, in its own terms), this success is achieved by a narrowness of perception, a concentration on what can be quantified, that prescinds from much of what has good claim to count as human understanding and furthermore deals with such a skeletal view of the world as to render it fundamentally alien to human indwelling (and indeed to any sense of God's presence and providence). In his book *Elements of Faith*, the modern Greek philosopher Christos Yannaras has this to say about the "apophatic attitude":

> The apophatic attitude leads Christian theology to use the language of poetry and images for the interpretation of dogmas much more than the language of conventional logic and schematic concepts. The conventional logic of everyday understanding can very easily give man a false sense of a sure knowledge which, being won by the intellect, is already exhausted by it, completely possessed by it. While poetry, with the symbolisms and images which it uses, always exhibits a sense from within the words and beyond the words, a concept which corresponds more to common experiences of life and less to cerebral conceptions.[2]

---

[2]Christos Yannaras, *Elements of Faith: An Introduction to Orthodox Theology* (Edinburgh: T&T Clark, 1991), 17.

Would that were so! Alas, Orthodox theology, like much other theology, is too enamored with logic and concepts and too closed to poetry. To return to Wiley, despite my fundamental reservations about what she thinks theology should be about, in her attempt to distill from Lonergan's "transcendental method" a "recast" understanding of the fall and original sin, there is more real thought than found elsewhere in this volume . . . and surprises!

As I read her, Wiley approaches original sin through the notion of a "root sin"—the root, I take it, from which all sin stems, which she identifies with privilege, citing in support Galatians 3:28 (thought by scholars, she says, to be a "fragment of a baptismal liturgy," a perception cued, I imagine, by the previous verse: "As many of you as were baptized into Christ have clothed yourselves with Christ"). Root sin is what we have been delivered from by baptism in Christ, and it is not some merely individual fault but rather a sense, deeply rooted in all societies, that our societal belonging is expressed in relationships based on privilege. Reading this thought (to me, novel though immensely attractive), I found my mind turning toward the slave girl Blandina, the heroine, as it were, of the account of the martyrdom of the Christians of Lyon and Vienne in AD 177, as reported in the letter to the friends and relations of these Christians back in Asia Minor—written, very likely, by St. Irenaeus and preserved in Eusebius's *Church History* (*EH* V. 1). Blandina is consistently described as γενναῖος, εὐγενής (*gennaios, eugenēs*, noble, well-born); as she is hung on a post and exposed to the wild beasts in the arena, she seems to "hang there in the form of a cross," so that the fellow Christians, in their suffering, behold "in the person of their sister him who was crucified for them." The divisions of late Roman society, embodying privilege, are done away in this slave girl—"no longer slave or free, . . . no longer male and female"—dying for Christ, dying in union with Christ.

This is, I think, more at the level of symbolic apprehension; scientific apprehension is disclosed for Wiley through Lonergan's transcendental method, in which sin is seen as a "radical dimension of lovelessness" and root sin, original sin, seen as "sustained inauthenticity"; Wiley finds "authentic being" in self-transcendence. I do not think one needs to go to Lonergan to find such an analysis of what it is to be human, what fundamentally frustrates that status, and what is required to overcome that frustration. The heroic virtue of sanctity itself is not an achievement (as the word *virtue* might suggest) but a gift. The same holds true for the capacity to receive it: the gift of being loved by Christ and responding to that love. Wiley cites Walter Wink, who remarks that "the gospel is not a message of personal salvation from the world, but a message of a world transfigured right down to its basic structures" (by which I think she means societal structures, although it would presumably not exclude cosmic structures).

Madueme's account, both of Genesis 3 and original sin, stands in sharp contrast to these approaches. He presents us with a robust defense of the Augustinian-Reformed view, original guilt and all. He takes Paul to read Genesis 3 as real history, dismissing the view that the first eleven chapters of Genesis are a kind of symbolic history and that real biblical history begins only with the story of Abraham in chapter 12. For Madueme the fall, although utterly real, is not to be regarded solely in a negative light; in reality, as he puts it, the fall is the midwife of the gospel and presupposes the original goodness of creation, a "truth brimming with hope." One aspect of what Madueme regards as the traditional Augustinian-Reformed view is that the fall is taken to be cosmic. I confess I found myself skeptical about this. It seems to me that Augustine prescinds from the notion of a cosmic fall, his sense of the coherence between the human and the cosmic having been, in some way, obscured. This sense of the coherence between the human and the cosmic was part of the Platonic legacy in the Greek patristic tradition. Augustine's failure to grasp this can be seen in a context somewhat removed from the question of the fall and original sin—namely, in his conception of time. For the Platonic tradition time was cosmic: time was a moving image of eternity, manifest in the cyclical movement of the heavenly spheres. When Augustine comes to consider the nature of time in *Confessions*, time for him has ceased to be understood as cosmic but is rather something interior: a distension, stretching, of the soul, *distentio animi* (*Conf.* 11.26.33). Having lost his sense of the cosmic, or had it obscured, Augustine has to find the meaning of original sin within: it becomes something belonging to the soul, passed from soul to soul (although Augustine was at a loss for how this could take place; traducianism would have provided a straightforward account, but it seemed bound up with a materialist notion of the soul, which he had abandoned, and creationism offered no explanation). This intuition was very deep and early in Augustine. It may be that the Pelagian controversy forced on him clarifications that perhaps turned out to be obfuscations, but his sense that sin can be traced back to the very beginning of each individual's existence can be found long before he encountered Pelagius. Right at the beginning of the *Confessions* he displays his irritation—not unusual in celibate males in my experience—at the noisy jealousy of babies at the breast (cf. *Conf.* 1.7.11): evidence for him of original sin, even in the tiniest infant. I welcome Madueme's endorsement of the cosmic dimension of sin, but I am not sure how native it is to the Latin Augustinian tradition. There is something refreshing, even exhilarating, about Madueme's robust defense of his tradition, and he makes many good points against modifications of that tradition in the interests of accommodating modernity. There is, indeed, a danger of falling into Manichaeism if one attempts to assimilate the physicalist or biological reductionism so frequently taken for granted in intellectual circles nowadays. Some of his strategies in defense of the Augustinian-Reformed tradition— the parallelism he draws between original guilt and imputed righteousness— appear to rebound on the protagonist: such a parallelism seems more to damage the notion of imputed righteousness than to justify original guilt.

I found myself both full of admiration for the way in which wrestling with the Western doctrine of the fall and original sin seemed a fruitful struggle, yielding all sorts of insights, that would probably have been passed over if not stimulated by such engagement, but also wondering if indeed it was a notion of original sin that emerged from these attempts to defend and "recast." Crisp presents us with a doctrine of what one might call "original sin lite," while Madueme affirms a doctrine recognizable as original sin. Crisp's doctrine may be believable, but is it the doctrine of original sin? Madueme's doctrine is clearly recognizable as original sin, but can he maintain it in the context of whatever a "modern worldview" means? It provides a good platform from which to criticize the fashionable views of modernity, but will it do to reject it altogether (and it is not clear that Madueme does)? Green demonstrates some of the resources of the Wesleyan tradition, and for that we can be grateful. Wiley's attempt to recast traditional views of original sin may work well enough, but perhaps by venturing into rather more severe intellectual territory than all can endure. Whether I have done any better is for others to decide.

10

A Reconceived Response

TATHA WILEY

It is a privilege to participate in this exchange of views on our understandings of the Christian doctrine of original sin, and I thank the volume editors and my colleague contributors for this chance to wrestle with the many intertwined aspects of this inherited doctrine and the mystery they attempt to articulate.

Reading my colleagues' chapters has surfaced for me five underlying issues or questions that I think we need to address if we are to propound a viable and credible concept of original sin today. My comments are not for critiquing others but for raising questions for consideration, elaborating the point of view I have espoused in my own chapter, and urging that we recognize the problematic character of some key traditional elements in our conception of the doctrine.[1]

TWO THEORIES, NOT ONE

The inherited doctrine of original sin is actually a conglomeration of two different theories. Each has a different view of what that first sin was, the purpose of taking the first sin away, and what we are left with after sin. We might think of one as Augustine's theory, the other Anselm's.

Augustine put the finishing touches on the emergent doctrine of original sin during his debate with Pelagius. For him, concupiscence (that is, disordered desire) is a result of original sin and leads to sin but is not itself sin. Nor is concupiscence just sexual desire, although this is often a misreading

---

[1]Here I am drawing on and developing insights explored in my *Original Sin: Origins, Developments, Contemporary Meanings* (Mahwah, NJ: Paulist Press, 2002).

of Augustine. The real source of original sin is Adam's sin of disobedience, but how can the sin of one man nonetheless be universal? The means of transmitting this sin to all humankind, Augustine said, is sexual intercourse. As he did so, he indicated what he thought motivated sex: lust. He claimed that lust is an evil, even in marriage, so concupiscence figures in the transmission of original sin.[2]

In Augustine's reading of Genesis, Adam lost the ability to do the good on his own. So Augustine also developed the notion of cooperative grace as God's assistance to human freedom, enabling us to resist sin and choose the good.

The councils of Carthage (418) and Orange (529) accepted Augustine's authority on this matter. Yet original sin would not be accepted as a defined dogma of the Catholic Church until the Council of Trent in 1545. The intent at Trent was to counter Martin Luther's notion of justification by faith alone with an ecclesial solution to original sin—namely, baptism. Luther had called original sin "the deep root sin which I possess,"[3] or more powerfully, our radical self-centeredness. There is no solution to it as such, because concupiscence never goes away.

Augustine thought and wrote in the descriptive language of ordinary discourse, and he employed only a few metaphysical terms. Luther followed Augustine's and also Peter Lombard's treatment of the doctrine, which he preferred to that of Thomas Aquinas. Peter had identified original sin with concupiscence too.

Conversely, to explain or understand original sin, Anselm in the twelfth century had appropriated the metaphysical language of his fellow scholastics. His theory of original sin turned Augustine on his head. Using the medieval distinction between *natural* and *supernatural*, he conceived of original sin not primarily as a moral problem, as had Augustine, but also as an ontological problem that, without the redemption of Christ, would keep humankind from its eternal destiny with God. Original sin was not Augustine's propensity toward evil—a something—but instead a loss of the

---

[2]Remarkably, Augustine is talking about *marital* sex, where two people presumably love one another. In Augustine's world of the fifth century CE, there were many reasons for marriage, yet caring for one another was certainly among them.

[3]Martin Luther, *Lectures on Romans*, in *Luther's Works*, ed. Hilton C. Oswald (St. Louis, MO: Concordia, 1972), esp. 25:299-307.

supernatural gift of original justice. It was a privation. Because the supernatural gift of original justice is no longer a constitutive element in our nature, Adam could no longer choose and do the good simply because it is good—what this gift enabled him to do prior to sin. After original sin, he was "left to nature" and, without the help of God's grace, could choose only evil.

What was central for Augustine was the fall, but for Anselm it was the supernatural destiny of human beings with God. That is what redemption restores. He defined sin by way of medieval values. One should give honor to God. Accordingly, sin is disobedience.

Thomas Aquinas achieved the synthesis that held the two different theories of original sin together. Using Aristotelian categories, he called Anselm's negative idea of original sin the formal cause of original sin (original justice). He called Augustine's concupiscence, or inclination toward evil, the material cause. The agential cause is in the free and voluntary opposition to God that lies in human hearts, and he identified the method of transmission (i.e., sexual intercourse) as the instrumental cause.

ONE NATURE, TWO PERSPECTIVES

Since the Council of Trent (1545–1563), Catholics and Protestants have typically been distinguished by their views of being human or of human nature. Such a view is called a theological anthropology. We act sometimes as if these theological anthropologies are cast in stone, but they are choices of ideas that seem "reasonable" or "fitting." Protestants have been known for their view that human nature, after Adam's sin, is depraved or corrupt. Catholics have been taught that their nature was wounded by original sin. The Protestant reaction at the time was that Catholics were close to Pelagianism—a favorite slur—and, alternatively, Catholics thought that Protestants teetered dangerously close to seeing sin as inevitable.

One's theological anthropology corresponds to the way one understands the purpose of human being and human life. For example, if our purpose is to get through life "to the other side," if our goal is heaven, then it does not matter what we do, because we are not expected to do *anything*. But what if we are primarily to be co-creators with God in the upbuilding of the reign of God in the universe? Then much is expected of us! We first have to have a nature that includes the *possibility* of being a co-creator. Theologically, to articulate our anthropological insights in contemporary language, we would also have to understand how scientists think, because we live in a scientific world. We would have to give up naive premodern theological notions, because our contemporaries deserve better.

In the sixteenth-century conflict over whether there is a distinction—and what that would be—between the terms *image of God* and *likeness* (to God), we see this question of native human capability debated. Catholics took the position, using their distinction of natural and supernatural, that the image of God belonged to human nature and remained after sin. Martin Luther had already rejected the category of the supernatural, saying that it appeared as if Adam had lost something inessential to nature. John Calvin broke with Luther on this, saying that even with the corruption of their nature, human beings still retained the image of God after sin.

Transposing these concerns and insights into a contemporary framework, Bernard Lonergan, SJ, speaks of original sin as our inability to sustain authenticity. For various reasons, interferences with our conscious operations (e.g., through bias) skew our understanding and, over time, we become inauthentic. Further, we have been born into a world that has been deeply distorted by biases, such as racism and sexism. What does this mean? In an ideal world, we would be totally attentive to the needs and problems around us, insightful in addressing them, reasonable in weeding out biases and other factors that get in the way, and responsible in considering alternatives and making choices. In reality, however, although we might fulfill these imperatives once in a while, more often human beings are more or less inattentive, closed-minded, irrational, and irresponsible. This gives rise to a world marked by what Lonergan describes as the "social surd."

Thus, we can describe the conditions of human being, agency, and authenticity, and even of historical progress and decline, without ever referring to a garden.

METAPHYSICS AND THE PERSON

We routinely use metaphysical terms without thinking anything about them. *Reason* and *will* are good examples. We think we know what *reason* means, but we often confuse the products of reason with reason itself (to use a grade

school example: addition and subtraction). *Reason* is an abstract word. If we
talked about understanding, insight, and formulating instead, we would be
using empirical words that directly reflect our consciousness. They would no
longer be abstract. Or, we think we know what we mean by *will*. But if we
raised the question, Where is our will? we could not "find" it, because it is
an abstract word covering the concrete experience of choosing, deciding,
and acting responsibly. These latter words are empirical and concrete. They
can be verified. Am I being responsible? Yes or no? What alternatives am I
choosing from? What decision have I made? I can confirm each one because
each is a reality to me directly in my consciousness. This is a shift we need
to make more fully with the language of original sin.

Medieval theology was metaphysical. As such, its terms for religious
experience were abstract. What we need are empirical and concrete terms
and relations for religious experience.

As the case of original sin makes clear, we need a new anthropology, one
that more brightly illumines the gifts and challenges of being human as well
as the distortions we are prone to. Karl Marx understood knowledge to be
socially and historically situated. Ideas are always shaped by interests. There
is no transcendent perspective from which we can unassailably grasp *the
truth*. What we see is *someone's* truth or good. We are oblivious to how our
self-interest or group interests skew our understanding of what is true
or just.

For example, in our account of being human, we especially need to de-
finitively replace the gender dualism that, although predating Aristotle,
became inculcated with him. Men and women were easily distinguished by
the presence or absence of capacities required for being properly human. For
Aristotle, in brief, men have all of them and women do not.

The story gets more complicated when one adds class into the anthropological mixture. Slavery is a good example of class dynamics. Take slavery in
the seventeenth- and eighteenth-century American South. Slavery was an
economic resource and a vital element in the building of wealth. But in
descriptions of plantation slavery, it was portrayed as "taking care of slaves,"
"giving them a place to live," and so on. Masters did not talk about the slave
markets, where slaves were chained, paraded naked, branded, beaten, and
sold apart from their families. Masters were scared to death of slave revolts

and possible massacres. They latched on to biblical warrants for slavery. In the New Testament, for example, 1 Peter says,

> Slaves, accept the authority of your masters with deference, not only those who are kind and gentle but also those who are harsh. For it is a credit to you if, being aware of God, you endure pain while suffering unjustly. If you endure when you are beaten for doing wrong, what credit is that? But if you endure when you do right and suffer for it, you have God's approval. For this you have been called, because Christ also suffered for you, leaving you an example, so that you should follow in his steps. (1 Pet 2:18-21)

This is an ideology of sin. The narrator occupies a transcendent vantage point, speaking as if from God. It hints that obedience to the master—whether kind or harsh—is necessary to be right before God. Then, in a convoluted bit of reasoning, the author tries to justify suffering, seeming to come out with a justification of unjust suffering. This is one of several "household code texts" in the New Testament. Slaves are implored to obey their masters "as done for the Lord" (Col 3:22-25).

GARDEN AND HISTORICITY

Genesis 2–3 is an ancient creation story, followed by the story of the expulsion from the garden. The expulsion story gives hints of once being an etiology—or perhaps several. At least three questions are "answered": Why do we hate snakes? Why are women subject to men? Why do women have such pain in childbirth?

There are parallels to this story in the ancient world—a predominant theme among them is that woman is the originator of evil.

The use of the story in the Christian tradition has had a disastrous effect on women. It first put women's subjection to their husbands—male privilege—in God's mouth as the punishment for her sin. John Chrysostom was quite succinct: "The woman taught once, and ruined all."[4] Augustine thought that women would have been subject to men even without sin.

Woman is portrayed as being "created second and sinning first," to paraphrase 1 Timothy. The Hebrew Bible scholar Phyllis Trible examines the

---

[4]Homily 9 on 1 Timothy.

creation story.[5] She says that in the Hebrew, Yahweh-God first creates an "earthling," not an "Adam." It denotes genderless earth creature, not the proper name for a man. Words indicating sexual differentiation are not used until there is creation of *two* human beings.

The early church fit right into the patriarchy of the day. After a short period in the first century, with the active involvement of women in the Pauline churches and baptism as a real principle of equality, male privilege was firmly restored by the early patristic period.

Rosemary Radford Ruether identifies the gender dimension of patriarchy as the "original sin of sexism." Patriarchy is a historical system of victimization of women. It has embedded within it a gender dualism. In the church there has often been a denial that women possess the image of God fully as persons. The New Testament has several texts that govern the behavior of women. They are similar to this one: "Wives, be subject to your husbands as you are to the Lord. For the husband is head of the wife just as Christ is head of the church, the body of which he is the Savior. Just as the church is subject to Christ, so also wives ought to be, in everything, to their husbands" (Eph 5:22-24).

It has been difficult in a Christian theology of sin to get away from the idea—between Genesis 3 and the medieval love of order—that sin is like disobedience, an idea that works for actual sin but not for social or systemic or original sin.

But obedience aside, it has been even harder for some Christians to give up thinking of Genesis 2–3 as a historical narrative (i.e., one that tells us what *really* happened). It was not, is not, and never will be a historical account. We cannot inherit from two characters in a story.

A historical Adam has been more important to the Catholic doctrine of original sin than to the Protestant one. No one at the time of Luther in the sixteenth century questioned the story's historicity, yet it is the case that a historical Adam is less important to the Protestant side. One reason is the way in which Protestant traditions perceived the "problem" that original sin causes and justification resolves. For the Catholics, it was the combination moral-ontological problem, so they approved the way that Thomas brought together Augustine's and Anselm's distinct theories into one account. For

---

[5] See her essay "A Love Story Gone Awry," in *God and the Rhetoric of Sexuality* (Philadelphia: Fortress Press, 1978), 72-143.

Protestants (e.g., for Luther) it was an existential-religious problem. The contemporary theologian Karl Barth expressed the existential dimension succinctly: "The person is sin." Nothing escapes corruption. By a religious problem, Luther meant the problem of *unbelief* by which humankind is in conflict with God. To return to the original question, that of the significance of a historical Adam, for Catholics it gradually presented more of a problem. Eventually, Catholics were put in a position of defending the historicity of Adam and Eve in order to preserve the legitimacy of the claim of the historical reliability of the Bible itself.

DEVELOPMENT AND EXCLUSIVITY

There is no further development of the story in Genesis 2–3 in the later Jewish tradition. The story functions simply to initiate the dramatic narrative of sin and redemption within the Bible, but it is not an important story for the Jewish tradition. The story of Adam and Eve does not show up anywhere later in the Hebrew Bible. It appears in only a few noncanonical writings. There the primary issue is the origin of death, not sin. For early Christians and during the patristic period, Genesis helped to answer more of a Christological question than a question about sin: Why is Christ's forgiveness necessary for everyone? For later Christians, indeed for Christians of all times, it has also dramatized an existential question: Why are we not good?

We should be clear: there are no historical facts here. This is a dramatic narrative from beginning to end. The characters are few: God, a woman, a man, a talking snake. There are a few dramatics acts, such as the naming of the animals, eating of the fruit, the encounter with God, the subjection of the wife to her husband, and their expulsion from the garden. Remarkably, for a few thousand years, Christians glossed over the story's oddities—such as dialogue with the snake—and took it for a reliable historical account of human origins.

Further, Christians have become familiar with the Adam and Eve story as a "fall" story. But this description is not part of the story itself. It is an *interpretation* of the story.

There were no significant difficulties with the Genesis 2–3 narrative until the modern period and the work of Charles Darwin. Once terms like *natural selection* and *evolution* became routine, then the story in Genesis became oddly dissonant. Everything was wrong with it. It did not fit into our understanding of the age of the universe; the first people were too so-phisticated to be the first; the God of the second creation story does not have the divine characteristic of omniscience; God's search for a suitable companion fails and has to be renewed. Nowhere in the creation stories do we find the more modern question: How did it happen?

There was a time when theologians felt superior to scientists. Theirs was the "queen of the sciences." Ludwig Ott, author of *Fundamentals of Catholic Dogma* (1955), obviously thought this way, although he was already a little late to do so. He presumed that the church's control over biblical interpretation—and the doctrines derived from it—was absolute. He could say, "Since Adam's sin is the basis of the dogma of Original Sin and Redemption the historical accuracy of the (Genesis) account as it regards the essential facts may not be impugned."[6]

Moreover, and finally, the inherited doctrine is an exclusivist one. The Jewish tradition does not have a faith claim equivalent to original sin. Neither does any other religious tradition. It is unique to Christianity. The roots of the doctrine of original sin are in a Christological proclamation, "Jesus saves," rather than in a question about sin. It was an ecclesial statement too. It announced that original sin was a problem for everyone. No one escapes it. The solution to it—the only solution—is the church's baptism. So other religions have no salvific power, and salvation becomes the exclusive prerogative of the church.

If we really do believe that the Christian doctrine of original sin points to key aspects of being human, of human capacity and incapacity, and of our relationship with God, then to understand it responsibly and present it credibly, we must face these challenges head on. We cannot continue to leave unresolved the tensions and oppositions in traditional theories. We cannot continue to rely on a historical reading of a symbolic nar-rative. We cannot continue to rely on a theological anthropology that is skewed by gender bias and other dualisms. We cannot continue to rely on a metaphysical framework rather than an empirical one that speaks from and to people's actual experience. And we cannot pretend that the perva-sively evolutionary framework in which we now live does not demand from us a fundamentally new anthropology and biblical theology.

---

[6]Ludwig Ott, *Fundamentals of Catholic Dogma*, trans. Patrick Lynch, 5th ed. (St. Louis, MO: B. Herder Book Company, 1962), 106.

List of Contributors

Oliver Crisp is professor of analytic theology at the University of St. Andrews.

Joel Green is professor of New Testament interpretation and associate dean for the Center for Advanced Theological Studies at Fuller Theological Seminary.

Andrew Louth is professor emeritus of patristic and Byzantine studies in the Department of Theology and Religion at Durham University.

Hans Madueme is associate professor of theological studies at Covenant College.

Chad Meister is professor of philosophy and theology at Bethel University (Indiana).

J. B. Stump is vice president at BioLogos.

Tatha Wiley taught theology and New Testament at University of St. Thomas and the College of St. Catherine.

General Index

Scripture Index

FROM IVP ACADEMIC

Baptism: Three Views, EDITED BY DAVID F. WRIGHT

Biblical Hermeneutics: Five Views,
EDITED BY STANLEY E. PORTER AND BETH M. STOVELL

Christian Spirituality: Five Views of Sanctification,
EDITED BY DONALD L. ALEXANDER

Church, State and Public Justice: Five Views,
EDITED BY P. C. KEMENY

Divine Foreknowledge: Four Views,
EDITED BY JAMES K. BEILBY AND PAUL R. EDDY

Divine Impassibility: Four Views of God's Emotions and Suffering,
EDITED BY ROBERT J. MATZ AND A. CHADWICK THORNHILL

Divorce and Remarriage: Four Christian Views,
EDITED BY H. WAYNE HOUSE

Evangelical Theological Method: Five Views,
EDITED BY STANLEY E. PORTER AND STEVEN M. STUDEBAKER

Faith and Reason: Three Views, EDITED BY STEVE WILKENS

God and Morality: Four Views, EDITED BY R. KEITH LOFTIN

God and the Problem of Evil: Five Views,
EDITED BY CHAD MEISTER AND JAMES K. DEW JR.

God and Time: Four Views, EDITED BY GREGORY E. GANSSLE

The Historical Jesus: Five Views,
EDITED BY JAMES K. BEILBY AND PAUL RHODES EDDY

Justification: Five Views,
EDITED BY JAMES K. BEILBY AND PAUL RHODES EDDY

The Lord's Supper: Five Views, EDITED BY GORDON T. SMITH

The Meaning of the Millennium: Four Views,
EDITED BY ROBERT G. CLOUSE

The Nature of the Atonement: Four Views,
EDITED BY JAMES BEILBY AND PAUL R. EDDY

Predestination and Free Will:
Four Views of Divine Sovereignty and Human Freedom,
EDITED BY DAVID BASINGER AND RANDALL BASINGER

Psychology and Christianity: Five Views,
EDITED BY ERIC L. JOHNSON

Two Views of Hell: A Biblical and Theological Dialogue,
BY EDWARD WILLIAM FUDGE AND ROBERT A. PETERSON

What About Those Who Have Never Heard? Three Views
on the Destiny of the Unevangelized, EDITED BY JOHN SANDERS

Women in Ministry: Four Views,
EDITED BY BONNIDELL CLOUSE AND ROBERT G. CLOUSE

Finding the Textbook You Need

The IVP Academic Textbook Selector
is an online tool for instantly finding the IVP books
suitable for over 250 courses across 24 disciplines.

---

ivpacademic.com
